David Rosengarten Entertains

David Rosengarten Entertains

Fabulous Parties for Food Lovers

David Rosengarten

Photographs by Quentin Bacon

WILEY

John Wiley & Sons, Inc.

Published by John Wiley & Sons, Inc., Hoboken, New Jersey
Published simultaneously in Canada

For general information on our other products and services or to obtain technical support, please contact our Customer Care Department within the United States at (800)-762-2974, outside the United States at (317) 572-3993 or fax (317) 572-4002.

Wiley also publishes its books in a variety of electronic formats. Some content that appears in print may not be available in electronic books. For more information about Wiley products, visit our web site at www.wiley.com

Design by Howard Klein

Library of Congress Cataloging-in-Publication Data:

Rosengarten, David.
  David Rosengarten entertains : fabulous parties for food lovers / David Rosengarten.
    p. cm.
  Includes index.
  ISBN 0-471-46198-9 (cloth)
  1. Cookery. 2. Entertaining. I. Title.
  TX714.R6728 2004
  642'.4—dc22

                                                    2004008488

Printed in the United States of America

10 9 8 7 6 5 4 3 2 1

Contents

Acknowledgments

David Rosengarten Entertains could have never come about…without a host of people entertaining David Rosengarten.

First and foremost is the manager of my office, T.J. Robinson, who, as usual, contributed a little bit of everything—conceptualization, recipe development, recipe testing, and a watchful eye on the day-to-day logistics that the writing of a cookbook entails. T.J. makes everything run like clockwork.

Another cohort in my company—Nancy Loseke, Research Director of The Rosengarten Report—made several huge contributions. She is one of the best proofreader/copy editors I know, and she worked long hours to make sure the editorial flow of the book was silky-smooth. Additionally, her research and suggestions concerning the environments of the 16 parties in the book were absolutely invaluable; *David Rosengarten Entertains* would have been vastly diminished without her help. Other crucial help in this latter regard was supplied by Patti Fine, an intrepid event planner, who is a font of entertaining ideas; Peggy Bellar, a Louisiana native who knew a delicious thing or two about throwing a Cajun party; by Steve Raichlen, grill-master and cookbook author, who had wonderful inspirations for the book's grill parties in general; by Prasad Chirnomula, the great Connecticut restaurateur, who gave me lots of ideas for the Indian party; and Bobbi Pincus, a sensational collector of antique cookbooks, who passed on to me some terrific notions concerning the South American Steak Party.

Back on the recipe testing/recipe development front, my largest collaboration was with a starring member of my IT'S ALL AMERICAN FOOD team, David Whiteman, chef and wine expert extraordinaire. Wendy Taylor, who also worked on the last book, made valuable kitchen contributions to this one as well. And CIA graduate Jessi Tannenbaum stepped in to help us round out the Texas BBQ party, which she did with great skill.

Another debt of gratitude goes to Walter Pearce, Gregg Early, and the whole team at KCI Communications in McLean, Virginia, the company that owns The Rosengarten Report. My business world is an integrated one—and many of the wonderful things that KCI has done for The Rosengarten Report spilled over as benefits for *David Rosengarten Entertains* during the course of its production.

There are many people to thank at Wiley, starting with Susan Wyler, my old friend, a Wiley editor who set this process in motion, suggesting to me several years ago that I write a book about entertaining. Susan left the company before the book was complete, but Roy Finamore stepped in to do a great job of editing the final manuscript. All through this transition, Natalie Chapman, Wiley's publisher of culinary and garden books, did a wonderful job of moving the book along. Justin Schwartz, another Wiley editor, also helped a great deal, particularly in sorting out the many details of the photo shoot. And when the book finally fell into the hands of Wiley's marketing and public relations whizzes, P.J. Alexander and Gypsy Lovett, I was a happy author indeed.

Lastly, "happy" describes as well my relationship with my agents Kathy Robbins and David Halpern, of The Robbins Office. I am forever grateful for their faith in me, and for their hard work; these are people who magically make books happen.

Introduction

Throwing a fabulous dinner party is, incontestably, one of the great joys in life. And, to me, there is one grand reason that stands behind that joy: a dinner party is an opportunity for the host or hostess to show warmth, affection, and respect for each and every guest.

Sure, the delicious food and drink alone help to fuel the fun, but at the end of the night, it is love that envelops the comestibles. The guests' knowledge that the food and drink were selected and prepared specifically to please them creates the most golden of glows in the room.

Talented hosts have known this principle forever, at least instinctively, so the basic dynamic of the dinner party has never changed. However, the details have changed greatly with the decades, for the sense of what it takes to please one's guests is forever evolving. In my lifetime, I contend, dinner parties in America have had two major conceptual epochs. Now, with the advent of the 21st century, we are entering a third, which is the real subject of this book.

Dinner Party Epoch # 1 (c. 1950–1975)

The reigning principle was: respect your guests by serving What Sounds Good. Not many of us really knew food, but we knew what the most impressive party dishes were called. "Beef Wellington," that staple of 1960s dinner parties, is a great example—a tenderloin of beef coated with a layer of foie gras, wrapped in puff pastry, and baked. If you served Beef Wellington to your guests in 1962, it meant you loved them. Never mind that the foie gras was practically dog food from a can, and that the pastry was a frozen, leaden biscuit dough recruited for the fancy dinner effort. I remember a dinner party from that era in which the host was serving something he called "pâté"—actually a greasy chicken liver spread—on crackers. But he named it "pâté," and, sure enough, the Impressionable Young Thing sitting next to me said out loud "Pâté! I can't believe I'm eating pâté!" The host certainly made her feel loved and respected. He said the right name.

Dinner Party Epoch # 2 (c. 1975–2000)

The reigning principle was: respect your guests by serving What Looks Good. Time had moved on, and so had we; in the 1980s and 1990s, we'd all had a good look at the gorgeous plating that was ubiquitous in fancy restaurants. If we loved our guests, that's exactly what we wanted to do for them. The compliment went something like this: "I know that you know what big-league food looks like in a great restaurant, so I'm recreating that look for you." Many a home kitchen, in this era, became a workshop for stacking, towering, drizzling, and rim-dusting—just as you would find in trendy restaurants. What was the intrinsic quality of it all? That which was stacked, towered, drizzled, and rim-dusted—was it great food? "Not necessarily," is my answer; the host was striving to captivate the eye, above all.

Before continuing, might I point out that all of these efforts, in both Epoch #1 and Epoch #2, took trouble and time. Time, in a funny way, was built into these reigning principles: the more time it took me to layer your Beef Wellington, the more time it took me to create six purées which I then drizzled out of squeeze bottles onto your dinner plate in a pattern that would please Picasso, the more it proved I loved you.

Dinner Party Epoch # 3 (c. 21st Century)

Here's the great entertaining thrill of our new, dawning epoch: spending hours in the kitchen is no longer necessary to prove your love and respect! The reigning principle here is: respect your guests by serving What Is Good. The underlying assumption—now that we're all So Much More Sophisticated, now that we've all come through countless cookbooks, food magazines, cooking classes, TV shows, and journeys to Tuscany—is that we know intrinsic quality. The best way a host can compliment a guest today is to serve him or her a hunk of great bread ("Why, that reminds me of bread from Poîlane, on the Rue de Cherche-Midi in Paris!"), and a great bottle of young olive oil ("That's like the oil we tasted last summer in the Peloponnese!"); the compliment is in the selection of quality, and in the host's belief that the guest will know enough to appreciate quality in its most pristine, untrammeled, un-gussied-up form. The beauty of the timing of this epoch, of course, is that we all have access today to thousands of great products in America that simply did not exist before! Many city-dwellers can now find amazing grocery items just around their corners, but even those who live far away from commercial centers can call toll-free lines, or log on to websites, which will result in the next-day delivery of wonderful, high-quality foodstuffs.

All of the parties in this book are devoted to the good taste of your guests—and are facilitated by your good taste in procuring ingredients of the highest possible quality to please them.

Each chapter contains a series of sections that give you a perspective on the party. Before the recipes begin, I will tell you why I think the party in question is a great modern party and I'll give you, as cook-cum-host, an overview for preparing and serving the party. But the most important section that appears in every chapter is entitled "The Ingredient."

Herein lies the key to your Epoch #3 bash. I have been extremely specific in recommending to you the food products that will make your party a hit. Sometimes, I focus on one product only—like the beef brisket that will create a sensation at your Texas BBQ party. Sometimes the recommendations for a single party are multiple, as in the chicken tandoori party, where I tell you that fresh spices in general are the key to great taste here, and recommend an array of purveyors who can supply them. In most chapters, you will also find recommendations scattered throughout the chapter that steer you toward high-quality ingredients in general, whether they are the center of attention or not.

Must you follow these recommendations to use and enjoy this book? Absolutely not. If you have your own favored products, by all means use them. If you don't, but if you have no access to the ones I recommend, don't fret. My purpose is to sensitize you to the practice of seeking the highest-quality ingredients for your parties; once you start thinking that way, you'll find that your parties will be more gastronomically successful, *and* your labor in the kitchen will diminish. As an example: if you can't get the best garlic sausage in the country for your bollito misto—at least get the best garlic sausage in your town!

Now that you've found the best ingredients for your guests, what kind of environment do you create for an Epoch #3 party? You don't need to set out the china that has the toniest name, nor do you need the most "beautiful" china. What you want, above all, is to make your guest feel that you have selected something special for him or for her, something that makes sense for the party.

That's why I love to think of the parties in this book as quasi-theatrical events that show a great deal of thought from beginning to end in the details that make up a party.

However—and this is a big *however*—don't feel that you *must* follow the recommendations I've given. I have been almost absurdly specific in my extra-culinary recommendations, largely because I want you to read these recommendations and get a feel for the *spirit* of the party I've conceived. After the recipes in every chapter, you will see sections that discuss appropriate non-food aspects of the parties:

In "Set Dressing" I give you ideas for creating an environment that reflects the main culinary themes of the party. These ideas may range from ambitious concepts only for the totally committed (like a tent for your Tunisian couscous party), to small design touches that will make a big difference (like cocktail-table books about Japanese arts for your tempura-and-sake party).

For "Table Dressing," I suggest many thematic things (china, silverware, glasses) that tie together the food and drink at the party with the table on which the food and drink are served. This is a good section to read closely for each party, because it often gives you ideas that help you to visualize that party's recipes. The "tablescapes" also go beyond the realm of serving necessities; they also suggest decorative features for the table (like runners and centerpieces) that echo the party's themes.

I know full well that, for many a party, all the entertainment one needs is good food, good drink, and good conversation. But in my attempt to visualize these parties as theatrical events, I have dreamed up other forms of entertainment that you may wish to consider. Kids are allowed to have magicians at their birthday parties, no? Why can't adults offer their own kind of magic to their friends? Ideas span many entertainment possibilities—from zydeco dancing at your Louisiana Thanksgiving feast, to dominoes at your Cuban roast pig party, to a sitar and tabla combo at your Indian chicken tandoori dinner.

One of the most important sections of each chapter, however, is the list of sources, or "**Where to Find It**." Here I give you a wide range of purveyors (most of them online) who will be able to enhance your parties with thematic tableware, design elements, entertainment—and, of course, the signature ingredients. Simply browsing the web sites of these merchants will give you countless ideas for your celebrations.

Now, if you wish to follow my recommendations to the letter, terrific! If you take the general ideas but find your own specifics, terrific again! And if you wish to go along with none of the things I've recommended, to simply make your party space no more than your usual dining room with some really great food on the table—that's terrific, too! No matter what level of involvement you choose, you will at least, by reading the material, get a good emotional sense of how your party might feel, whether or not it's gussied up.

This same advice goes for the recipes in the book. I'll be delighted if you treat each group of recipes as a bundle—that is to say, if you make all of the Greek grill party recipes on the same night and have a Greek grill party. However, I'd love you to think of this book as a non-party cookbook, too; there are more than a hundred terrific recipes herein, and any one of them can easily be pulled out of context at any given time! If you don't feel like making the entire French cassoulet party, for example, but you do feel like a great salad for your next family dinner, by all means, jump in there and extract the recipe for Leafy Green Salad with Walnuts, Walnut Vinaigrette, and Crumbled Roquefort!

It's Tapas Time

A Raucous Spanish Night, at Your Casita

A Party for 12

The Menu

Gazpacho in a Pitcher

Sizzled Chorizos

Spanish Ham
(*Jamon Serrano)*

Tomato Bread
(*Pa amb Tomàquet)*

Catalan Roasted Vegetable Salad
(*Escalivada)*

Spanish Tortilla with Smoked Paprika

Piquillo Peppers Stuffed with Salt Cod

Steamed Manila Clams with Bacon and Fino Sherry

Shrimp with Garlic Sauce

Pine Nut Cake

Every night in Spain, there's a huge party spilling out into the streets from thousands of tapas bars across the country. The nightly consumption of tapas, or "little bites," is one of Spain's most enduring traditions. Typically, Spaniards finish work at a fairly late hour—say, 7PM, or even later. The next hour or two, or three, is taken up by a casual "tapas crawl"—a progressive tour of tapas bars with a little nibble and a little wine at each. The point of the exercise is meeting your friends, unwinding, discussing the day's events. You get to have a series of mini-parties before dinner.

Sadly, our culture doesn't provide as much time for casual socializing. We go directly to the restaurant for dinner, skipping the tapas time. But if you treat the venerable tapas tradition as a party *and* as dinner, you've got it made! Do it right, and your guests will feel as if they're standing in the street on Calle Laurel in Logroño, or in the Parte Vieja of San Sebastián, or around the Plaza Santa Ana in Madrid, or in the Triana section of Sevilla, enjoying the warm hospitality that is the hallmark of Spain.

The Plan

The idea here is to reproduce a tapas bar in your home. Simple enough—since a tapas bar is really just a big buffet with a pretty arrangement of dishes sitting on it throughout the course of the evening.

There are just a few special considerations for the host.

- Open the tapas barrage with a buffet table full of room-temperature dishes. You can arrange these, make them sparkle, just before the guests arrive. The start of a party is always taken up with greeting guests and making them comfortable; the buffet lets guests eat while you socialize.

- As the party progresses, and you find yourself able to break away more, you'll have time to go into the kitchen and prepare some hot tapas (clams, shrimp, and sizzled chorizos). These last-minute dishes are marked with an icon.

- Keep your eye on the buffet throughout the meal, and either remove empty platters or replenish them.

The Ingredient

Spain is truly a ham-obsessed country, and many observers believe that cured Spanish ham may be a finer thing than its more famous Italian cousin, prosciutto. If you're interested in this product, the timing's right—

because now you can serve real Spanish ham at your tapas party. It will be the star player.

Spanish cured ham—or jamon—differs from Italian prosciutto in several key ways. It is usually darker, purplish rather than pinkish. It is streaked with more fat, and wider bands of it. You'll notice immediately the difference in texture; Spanish ham is a little firmer, chewier, not quite as velvety as prosciutto. But then comes the flavor explosion. Good Spanish ham is the deepest-tasting ham in the world. It's sweet, porky, nutty, almost cheesy (in an aged example).

The U.S.D.A., in its infinite wisdom—and perhaps with a little help from the Italian prosciutto lobby—kept Spanish ham out of the U.S. for many years, claiming that it didn't meet U.S. health standards. The shakiness of their long-standing position became clear a few years back when they changed their minds and began allowing some Spanish ham to come into the country. At present, the only ham allowed in is Jamon Serrano, which comes from a white-coated pig. This is a great Spanish ham, but not the greatest Spanish ham. The greatest is Jamon Iberico de Bellota—ham from black-coated pigs that have been fattened in the mountains on acorns.

There is a great company based in Williamsburg, Virginia, called Tienda.com **(see Where to Find It, page 30)**. They sell a dizzying variety of real Spanish products, and they've also been pushing for legal changes concerning the importation of Spanish ham. Anticipating that the Jamon Iberico de Bellota will be available someday soon in the U.S., they're already taking orders from Americans for hams, as futures! Tienda.com does carry the only two brands of Jamon Serrano that have been allowed into the country: Navidul and Redondo Iglesias. I prefer the latter. You can order the ham in slices, which is very convenient for your tapas party. However, if you want to make a killer presentation, you can order a whole Redondo Iglesias ham as well as a stand to support it for slicing. Make that the centerpiece of your tapas buffet. You, or an assigned helper, will stand behind the ham at the party, shaving thin slices with a long, sharp knife, as the need arises. Your guests will be ecstatic.

Spain's great paprika-flavored sausage, chorizo, has a similar "regulations" story; it was not allowed into the U.S. until recently. Only one brand is allowed in now, and Tienda.com imports it. Chorizo comes in many styles. Some is even raw. Typically at a tapas bar, you'll find hard-cured chorizo cut into thin slices and served at room temperature alongside the jamon. Perfect! The brand from Spain available in the U.S. is Palacios, which is hard-cured. You have your choice of mild or hot (I prefer the hot, which is not hot by North American standards).

If you serve jamon and chorizo together—the cured meat glory of Spain—yours will be a tapas party to remember.

Beverage
Time

Anything and everything is consumed at tapas bars in Spain—draft beer is my recent favorite—but I've got a few very Spanish, very specific ideas for your tapas party.

I'll never forget seeing a line-up of glass pitchers on a tapas bar in Seville: the creamy orange liquid in the pitchers looked like a good cantaloupe smoothie! But it was much better than that—smooth, velvety gazpacho, served as a drink. It is a fabulous way to kick off your tapas party; have the pitcher, or pitchers, ready as your guests arrive, with plenty of glasses nearby. For the teetotalers, the gazpacho can flow all night; it goes very well with most tapas.

Chances are good that some of your guests might also like a drink with a little alcohol in it. Here are a few wine ideas that will raise the mirth level to new heights:

- Legend has it that the tapas tradition began at a sherry bar in Andalucia where flies annoyingly kept dropping into the glasses of sherry. One enterprising proprietor, so the story goes, started to "top" the glasses he served with slices of ham. The flies were kept out, and the convention of serving sherry with "toppers" was born. If you want to continue the tradition, make sure you serve *dry* sherry; the sweet, brown stuff you drink with Aunt Edna at the vicarage won't do. Two types of sherry fit the bill: Fino and Manzanilla. Both are clear, light yellow (like white wine), lower in alcohol than other sherries, and bone-dry. They are simply fantastic with food! Serve them the Spanish way: buy them in half-bottles, then stick lots of half-bottles (at least six for a party of 12) in a big tub of ice. The Spaniards do this so that the sherry can be poured all around, ice cold, as soon as it comes out of the ice. They don't like to have any sherry lingering in a bottle, getting warm while waiting for the next pour.

- You can use a white-wine glass—but the glass always used for sherry in Spain is a small one called a *copita*.

- There is an old tradition at Spanish parties of drinking wine from a communal type of pitcher called a *porrón*. It has a tall vertical spout, into which you pour the wine and with which you grab the pitcher, and a slanted spout with a narrow opening. A guest picks up the *porrón*, raises it high in the air, throws his head back, and spills forward an arc of wine that, if all goes well, lands in his mouth; the drinker's lips never touch the *porrón*. After a good gulp, the *porrón* is passed to the next guest. Drinking from a *porrón* becomes a kind of party game, because people do it at different levels of proficiency (supply bibs for those who care about their clothes!) and with idiosyncratic styles. It's better than karaoke!

● The Spaniards rarely put good wine in the *porrón;* the experience is more about the fun of trying to get the liquid to your mouth. What I've seen in *porrónes* more than anything else in Spain is rosé, or rosado; good ones are made in the Navarra region.

● A really good sangria is a terrific, refreshing drink—great for warm nights. The night before, fill pitchers halfway with sections of orange (skin on) and apple. Fill the pitchers two-thirds of the way with rich but simple red wine (the Spaniards always use red; white sangria is an American thing). Jug red from California works just great. Refrigerate. Just before serving a pitcher, add a handful of ice cubes, a little Grand Marnier to taste, and a splash of club soda. Mix with a long wooden spoon; leave the spoon in the pitcher and place the cold sangria on the buffet table near empty wine glasses.

● Spain makes some of the best red wines in the world, and you often see them being tippled at tapas bars. In a raucous party with 12 people, providing a great red with the focus it deserves may not be the easiest thing to do. But do consider offering bottles from such *denominaciones* as Rioja, Ribera del Duero, Somontano, Penedes, Toro, Priorat, and Montsant.

The Recipes

Gazpacho in a Pitcher

· · • · ·

Here's a great recipe that is far from the pulpy, clunky, separating gazpacho so often seen in the U.S. The smoothness comes from the inclusion of soaked bread and olive oil.

A very important factor in the gazpacho's texture is the type of blending machine you use. A food processor is good because the work bowl is so large—but it's not ideal, because the finished product will probably not be super-smooth. I transfer the almost-finished gazpacho from my food processor to my smaller but higher-powered blender, which makes the gazpacho much smoother. To get truly authentic Spanish smoothness, finish the gazpacho by passing it through a sieve.

makes eight 6-ounce drinks

> **1 pound ripe tomatoes, cored**
>
> **1 pound cucumbers**
>
> **1 ½ pounds red bell peppers**
>
> **1 ounce crustless French or Italian bread (weighed after the crust is removed)**
>
> **2 medium cloves garlic, chopped**
>
> **1 cup coarsely chopped sweet onion**
>
> **6 tablespoons good olive oil (preferably from Andalucia)**
>
> **¼ cup sherry vinegar**
>
> **2 tablespoons tomato paste**
>
> **Kosher salt and freshly ground black pepper**
>
> **A few pinches pimentón (smoked Spanish paprika), optional**

1. Place the tomatoes in a small pot of boiling water for 1 minute. Remove with a slotted spoon and peel. Cut the peeled tomatoes in quarters, and working with your fingers, remove the seeds. Place the peeled and seeded tomatoes in the work bowl of a food processor.

2. Peel the cucumbers, and cut them in half lengthwise. Scoop out the cucumber seeds with a tea-spoon. Cut the cucumbers into coarse chunks and add them to the food processor.

3. Place the peppers directly on an open flame (such as the flame on your stove top) or under a broiler. Scorch them so that they char evenly; this will require turning them every few minutes with a pair of tongs. When the peppers are completely blackened (after about 10 to 12 minutes), remove them from the flame or broiler and place them in a paper bag. Close the bag, and let the peppers rest for 20 minutes. Remove them from the bag and peel off the blackened skin with your fingers. Remove and discard the stem and seeds. Some blackened peel may remain on the flesh, which is acceptable; make sure you do not wash it away with water. Add the flesh to the food processor.

4. Soak the bread in a bowl of cold water for 1 minute, then squeeze out the water. Add the bread to the food processor along with the garlic, onion, olive oil, vinegar, and tomato paste. Process for a few minutes, until a smooth purée is achieved. Transfer to a blender, if desired, and blend further. Season with salt and pepper. Add pimentón, if desired. Refrigerate for 3 to 4 hours.

5. Pour the gazpacho through a sieve. Check the seasoning before serving. Serve from a large pitcher, pouring the gazpacho into individual glasses.

 Sizzled Chorizos

Later in the party, as you're bringing hot food out of the kitchen, bring out these thicker slices of less-cured chorizo, sizzled in a pan.

Your work starts with the choice of chorizo. Palacios (page 8) is good for slicing and serving at room temperature, but it's cured a little too much for cooking. For cooking, you want a fresher, softer sausage. Help is at hand. A number of companies in the U.S. are making Spanish-style short-cure fresh chorizo; this is exactly what you want for the sizzling version. My favorite producer is Los Galleguitos. Their chorizo is sold by internet retailer Tienda.com **(see Where to Find It, page 30)**.

serves 12

2 pounds soft–cure chorizo

Cut the chorizos into slices that are about ¼ inch thick. Cook the slices in a single layer in a heavy sauté pan over medium heat until they are browned on both sides and warmed through; this should take about 2 minutes per side. Serve immediately on a platter, or hold in a 200°F oven while you sauté more slices. Serve with toothpicks for easy pick-up.

Jamon Serrano and Chorizos

• • ● • •

If you've chosen to purchase the pre-sliced ham made by Redondo Iglesias (page 8), your job is simple: just lay it out on platters, the slices not overlapping, at room temperature. Replenish as needed. Three $1/2$ pound packages should cover your needs for a party of 12. If you'd prefer to shop locally, you can substitute $1\,1/2$ pounds of thinly sliced prosciutto from your local deli.

If you've chosen to go whole hog—that is, to purchase an entire 15-pound Redondo Iglesias ham—you'll have a lot more to do. You'll also have deeper-tasting ham.

Your first whole-ham choice concerns the bone: do you want it in or out? If you order a boneless ham, and if you have an electric meat slicer, your slicing issues are solved; simply mount the machine on the buffet table and carve off very thin slices of the ham as the need arises.

Most ham mavens, however, say that bone-in hams develop more flavor. A bone-in ham is impossible to carve with a meat slicer, of course; a long, sharp knife is required, and the dexterity to shave off thin slices. In Spain, whole hams are traditionally placed in a kind of metal brace that holds and steadies the ham as it's sliced. You can buy this contraption, called a *jamonera*, from Tienda.com **(see Where to Find It, page 30)**. You place the ham in it so that its meatiest side is standing straight up; you don't want to cut from the two wide and broad sides. Then you make a long, thin cut all along that top edge, releasing one long, thin slice of ham. Sometimes you'll find the exposed edge will give you two or more shorter slices of ham. Fear not. When you place them side by side on a platter people will adore them no matter what their length or thickness.

Chorizo is easier. After you've purchased your mild or hot Palacios chorizo (page 8), simply cut very thin slices with a very sharp knife. I like to start cutting on the bias so each slice, rather than being round with a small diameter, is oval, with much greater length across the slice. Start the party with a platter of room-temperature slices; make sure you have more chorizo at room temperature ready to be sliced as needed. A party of 12 should require no more than two packages of Palacios chorizo, each one 9.5 ounces.

Tomato Bread

· · ● · ·

(Pa amb Tomàquet)

You will see Catalan tomato bread at many restaurants and tapas bars in Barcelona—and that's a very good thing, because it is insanely delicious for such a simple preparation. Grill bread. Rub with tomato. Drizzle with oil, sprinkle with salt. That's it. Of course, you'll need really good bread. And, for maximum impact, you'll need really ripe, red tomatoes. But remember, *pa amb tomàquet* is not bread with tomatoes on it; it's more like bread painted with tomatoes. Once the painting is done, you could add a few flourishes to the canvas, as the Catalans do: slices of ham, anchovies, fine canned tuna in olive oil. Or you can eat the slices all by their blessed selves. Bring the first batch to the buffet table at the start of the party; it can stand for quite a while.

serves 12

> **36 slices of good country-style French or Italian bread,
> cut ⁵⁄₈ inch thick**
>
> **18 large, high-quality canned tomatoes, such as Muir Glen brand,
> drained very well (see Cook's Note)**
>
> **Best-quality extra-virgin olive oil (preferably Spanish), for drizzling**
>
> **Kosher salt**

1. Place the bread slices over a charcoal fire or under a heated broiler until they're dark golden brown on both sides. (Work in batches; see Cook's Note below.)

2. Cut the tomatoes in half crosswise and, using half a tomato for each slice of toast, rub the tomato into the toast (on one side only). As you rub, let the tomato collapse into a thin red layer of flesh and seeds and juice, completely covering the surface of each slice. Discard any remaining tomato pulp, or reserve for another use. Drizzle each slice with a bit of olive oil, sprinkle with a few grains of salt, and serve.

> COOK'S NOTE: *If it's late summer, and you have great fresh tomatoes, by all means use those instead of canned ones (again, half a medium tomato takes care of 1 slice of bread). Please note that I have suggested 3 slices of bread per person at the party. This may be excessive, but a host always wants to be prepared. I'd advise preparing and serving 12 slices as part of the opening buffet. When they disappear, you go into the kitchen and produce more. Replenish the platter throughout the party.*

Catalan Roasted Vegetable Salad

(Escalivada)

Here's a modern version of an old Catalan classic. The vegetables were originally cooked in wood ashes, but it's much easier for modern party-makers to follow the lead of modern Catalan restaurateurs and cook them in the oven! This recipe also accommodates the new-fangled impulse of turning the vegetables into a kind of purée; in this version, you get whole ones and chopped-up ones—a nice contrast, and a textural treat. Serve near lots of good bread.

serves 12

> **2 medium eggplants (about ¾ pound each)**
> **Extra-virgin olive oil**
> **1 green bell pepper, halved**
> **4 red bell peppers, halved**
> **2 large onions, cut into eighths, root end attached**
> **2 teaspoons kosher salt**
> **Freshly ground black pepper**
> **2 tablespoons fresh lemon juice**
> **3 cloves garlic, minced**
> **7 tablespoons extra-virgin olive oil**
> **3 tablespoons chopped curly parsley**

1. Heat the oven to 500°F.

2. Puncture the eggplants in a few spots with a toothpick. Rub the eggplants with a bit of olive oil and place on a sheet pan. Place the peppers and the onions, cut side down, on another sheet pan. Roast all the vegetables for 10 minutes. Turn the vegetables over and roast another 10 minutes, or until the eggplants are tender, but not completely collapsed. Remove the vegetables from the oven, cover the pans with foil, and allow the vegetables to steam until cool enough to handle.

3. Lower the oven temperature to 375°F.

4. Using a paring knife and your fingers, peel and seed the peppers, but do not rinse them. Cut 6 of the red pepper halves lengthwise in half again (giving you 12 large quarters) and place in a mixing bowl. Remove 24 of the largest leaves of onion, discarding the dry, outermost onion leaves, and add to the bowl of large red pepper pieces.

5. Coarsely chop the remaining onion and place in an ovenproof baking dish. Cut the 2 remaining red pepper halves and the green pepper halves into $1/4$ x $1/2$-inch pieces and place them in the baking dish with the onions. Split the eggplants lengthwise and, using the side of a knife, scrape the flesh free from the skins. Discard the skins. Coarsely chop the flesh and add it to the baking dish.

6. Whisk the salt, black pepper, lemon juice, and garlic in a small bowl. Slowly whisk in the 7 table-spoons olive oil to make a dressing. Add all but 2 tablespoons of the dressing plus 1 tablespoon of the parsley to the baking dish, tossing well to combine with the chopped vegetables. Place the baking dish in the oven for 15 minutes. Remove, and let the vegetable mixture come to room temperature.

7. When ready to serve, mound the vegetable mixture at the center of a serving plate. Toss the large red pepper and onion pieces in the mixing bowl with the remaining 2 tablespoons of dressing, and alternately arrange them in a spoked pattern around the mound. Scatter the remaining 2 table-spoons of chopped parsley over all.

Spanish Tortilla with Smoked Paprika

• • • • • •

There is no dish more widely seen on tapas bars throughout Spain, or more revered, than this wonderful potato-and-egg pie. This is not an omelet, though you do want it to be a little moist inside. It's more like a frittata. Think "potato bound by tender egg." The following version is the classic, save for one tweak: a little bit of Spain's great smoked paprika adds a wonderful complementary flavor.

serves 12

¾ cup extra-virgin olive oil

1 small onion, halved through the root end and thinly sliced

1 ½ teaspoons smoked Spanish paprika or sweet paprika, plus additional for garnish (see Cook's Note)

2 large russet potatoes (about 10 ounces each), peeled and halved lengthwise

Kosher salt, as needed

8 large eggs, as fresh as possible

½ teaspoon sugar

1. Add 3 tablespoons of the olive oil, the onion, and the paprika to an 8- or 9-inch nonstick skillet and place over medium heat. Cook gently for 4 minutes, stirring occasionally, without coloring the onion. Add the remaining oil and let it warm. Meanwhile, slice the potatoes crosswise into very thin slices, a bit less than ⅛-inch thick. Add them to the onion and oil mixture in handfuls, spreading out each addition and sprinkling them with salt as you go. Cook the potatoes over medium-low heat for about 20 minutes or until they are just tender, gently stirring them to both separate the slices and bathe them in the flavored oil. You don't want them to brown, so adjust the heat as necessary.

2. When the potatoes are just tender, remove the pan from the heat and allow potatoes to rest in the oil for 4 to 5 minutes. Drain potatoes in a colander set over a bowl. Reserve 2 tablespoons of oil, and either discard the rest or save it for another use.

3. Beat the eggs with the sugar and a pinch of salt in a large bowl. Transfer the still-warm potatoes and onion to the bowl of eggs. Combine thoroughly and let the mixture rest for 30 minutes. Wipe the skillet clean, and return the 2 tablespoons reserved oil to the skillet.

4. Place the skillet over medium-high heat until the oil is hot but not smoking. Add the egg and potato mixture, shaking and swirling the skillet for about 25 seconds. Reduce the heat to medium-low, distribute the potatoes evenly in the skillet, and cook until the bottom is light golden in color, and the top is just beginning to set, about 6 to 8 minutes. Remove the skillet from the heat and invert a large plate over the tortilla. Then, in one quick motion, turn the plate and skillet over so that the tortilla falls on the plate. Very quickly slide the tortilla into the skillet and continue to cook over medium heat until the eggs are just set in the middle but still moist, about 3 minutes more. Remove to a plate.

5. Let the tortilla come to room temperature. Sprinkle with additional paprika just before serving. To serve, either cut the tortilla into wedges, or make diagonal cross-cuts so that many bite-sized pieces are created. If you've gone the latter route, stick toothpicks into each piece.

> COOK'S NOTE: *Smoked Spanish paprika (called pimentón) is available from Tienda.com* **(see Where to Find It, page 30)**.

Piquillo Peppers Stuffed with Salt Cod

· · • · ·

The Spanish region of Navarra is supplying the international marketplace with terrifically sweet, deep-tasting red peppers called piquillos; they come packed in brine in jars or cans. In Spain, it is very common at tapas bars to see stuffed piquillo peppers—as in the recipe below, where the peppers are stuffed with another Spanish favorite, *bacalao* (salt cod). This recipe can be completed 6 to 8 hours ahead and held at room temperature. The toothpick issue is up to you: Do you remove them from the piquillos, or leave them in? Hint: toothpicks are very big at Spanish tapas bars.

serves 12

1 pound salt cod, soaked (see Cook's Notes)

⅓ cup extra-virgin olive oil

2 small onions, finely chopped

½ stalk celery, finely chopped

1 (28-ounce) can of tomatoes, chopped, liquid reserved

1 teaspoon kosher salt, plus additional as needed

¼ teaspoon sugar

½ teaspoon sweet paprika

2 sprigs thyme

8 large cloves garlic, minced

2 tablespoons all-purpose flour, plus additional for dredging

4 cups whole milk, warmed

Freshly ground black pepper

Inexpensive olive oil for frying the peppers

3 (8-ounce) jars prepared piquillo peppers (see Cook's Notes)

2 large eggs beaten with 2 tablespoons water

2 tablespoons chopped curly parsley

1. Place the soaked salt cod in a large saucepan, cover with water by 2 inches, and bring just to a simmer over medium-low heat. Remove the pot from the heat and let it cool for at least 30 minutes before draining. Discard the water. Using your fingers, finely shred the cod, removing any bones and cartilage as you work.

2. Meanwhile, make the tomato sauce: Add half of the olive oil to a medium skillet and place over medium heat. Add half of the onions and all of the celery and cook, stirring occasionally, until the onion is golden, about 10 minutes.

3. Add the tomatoes, their liquid, 1 teaspoon of salt, the sugar, paprika, and thyme, and bring to a simmer. Cook gently until most of the liquid has evaporated, about 30 minutes, stirring occasionally. Pass the mixture through a food mill to make a loose, smooth purée. Taste for seasoning, set aside.

4. Make the salt cod stuffing: Heat the remaining olive oil and onions in a large skillet over medium-low heat. Cook gently for 5 minutes; add the garlic and cook another 5 minutes, stirring occasionally. Don't let the mixture brown. Raise the heat to medium, add the shredded salt cod, and stir well to coat with the flavored oil. Continue to cook about 5 minutes more, scraping up any fish bits that stick to the pan. Stir in the flour and, using a wooden spoon, add the warm milk, 1/2 cup at a time. Wait for each addition to be nearly absorbed before stirring in the next. When the last of the milk has been absorbed and the mixture resembles loose tuna salad, turn off the heat and let it cool. Season generously with black pepper.

5. Heat the oven to 350°F.

6. Pour oil into a large, heavy skillet to a depth of 1/3 inch and heat to 365°F. Stuff each piquillo pepper with about a tablespoon of the salt cod mixture and close with a toothpick. When ready to fry the peppers, dip each one in the egg and then the dredging flour, shaking off the excess. Fry the peppers in batches until golden on both sides. Drain on paper towels.

7. Place the peppers in an ovenproof serving dish and top with tomato sauce. Bake for 15 minutes.

8. Serve at room temperature garnished with the parsley.

> COOK'S NOTES: Salt cod varies in thickness and in saltiness, so soaking directions are necessarily imprecise. The goal is to return the fish to its original, moist, hydrated state, and to draw out most of its salt. Put the salt cod in a bowl and cover completely with cold water. Let the fish soak for 24 to 36 hours, changing the water at least 4 times during this period. It's now ready to be used in any recipe calling for prepared salt cod.
>
> Piquillo peppers, unique to the Ebro River Valley in Northern Spain, are harvested in the fall, roasted over wood fires, hand-peeled, and packed in their own juices (or brine) in cans or jars. Though their sweet flavor is reminiscent of roasted red bell peppers, they carry a grace note of piquancy that is very friendly to a cargo of bacalao. Before stuffing, drain the peppers and dry them on paper towels. Carefully remove any errant seeds that might cling to the interior flesh. Tienda.com **(see Where to Find It, page 30)** sells the peppers in 8-ounce jars, each holding 8 to 12 whole peppers. Or, should you find yourself helplessly addicted, the peppers also come in 4.2-pound jars, each holding a minimum of 68 peppers.

Steamed Manila Clams with Bacon and Fino Sherry

· · • · · ·

All over shellfish-obsessed Spain, you will find hot tapas made with clams in an aromatic broth. This dish is best when cooked at the very last minute. You should place single-portion bowls of it on the buffet table, along with spoons and little forks.

serves 12

$1/2$ pound good-quality country-style bacon, thickly sliced (about $1/8$ inch), each slice cut into $1/2$-inch pieces

2 tablespoons extra-virgin olive oil, plus additional for drizzling

9 large cloves garlic, minced

1 cup Fino sherry

1 cup dry white wine

1 cup water

2 sprigs thyme

2 bay leaves

2 whole cloves

$1 1/4$ teaspoons ground coriander seed

Scant $1/8$ teaspoon cayenne

48 Manila clams, well scrubbed (see Cook's Note)

2 tablespoons finely minced cilantro, plus a few dozen whole leaves for garnish

1. Bring a medium-sized pot of water to a boil. Add the bacon and blanch it for 1 minute. Scoop it out with a small strainer, and rinse under running water until cool. Pat the bacon dry with paper towels, and transfer it to a stockpot large enough to hold all the clams. You'll need a lid for the pot.

2. Place the pot over medium heat and add the 2 tablespoons of oil. Cook the bacon, stirring occasionally, until just crisp at the edges, but still tender. Remove it with a slotted spoon and set aside. Stir the garlic into the oil, and cook until pale golden in color. Add the sherry, white wine, water, thyme, bay leaves, cloves, coriander seed, and cayenne; raise the heat to high and bring to a boil. Reduce the heat, and let the mixture simmer until reduced in volume by half. The recipe can be prepared in advance to this point.

3. Bring the liquid to a boil over high heat, add the clams, and cover the pot. Cook the clams, shaking the pot and stirring occasionally until most of the clams have opened, about 5 to 10 minutes. Add the reserved bacon and the minced cilantro; toss well to distribute. Transfer the clams to heated serving dishes and ladle the broth over the clams. Drizzle with additional olive oil and garnish each serving with the cilantro leaves. Serve immediately with good bread to sop up the broth.

COOK'S NOTE: Manila clams are from the Pacific and are quite tender after steaming. The East Coast clams tend to get rubbery when steamed. New Zealand cockles are a good substitute if you can't find Manila clams.

Shrimp with Garlic Sauce

· · • · ·

One of my favorite hot tapas—and one that's extremely easy to make—is shrimp with garlic sauce. Serve with lots of bread for dunking.

serves 12

> 24 large cloves garlic, thinly sliced
> 1 ½ cups extra-virgin olive oil, preferably Spanish
> 2 pounds medium shrimp, peeled and deveined, with their tails
> 1 tablespoon kosher salt
> 1 teaspoon sweet paprika
> ¼ teaspoon cayenne
> Freshly ground black pepper
> 4 tablespoons finely minced curly parsley

1. Place the garlic and oil in a bowl and set aside for at least 4 hours, stirring occasionally.

2. When ready to prepare the dish, place the shrimp in a large bowl. Gradually add the salt to the bowl, tossing the shrimp to evenly coat them. Set aside for 10 minutes.

3. Divide the oil and garlic between 2 large skillets over medium heat. Allow the garlic to cook until just golden at the edges. Stir half each of the paprika and cayenne into each skillet. Season with black pepper. Raise the heat to medium-high and divide the shrimp between the skillets. Stir the shrimp regularly, coating them with the oil, until they're barely cooked through, 2 to 3 minutes.

4. With a slotted spoon, quickly transfer the shrimp to heated serving dishes and spoon equal amounts of the garlic over and around each serving. Divide and sprinkle the parsley over each serving and then spoon in the remaining garlic oil. Sprinkle with additional salt if desired.

Pine Nut Cake

· · • · · ·

This nutty, fluffy crowd-pleaser can be made a few hours before the party and refrigerated.
Bring to the buffet table whole, then cut into slices and serve on dessert plates.

makes one 10-inch cake

for the sponge:
1 cup pine nuts, untoasted

12 large eggs, separated

1 cup granulated sugar

1 teaspoon vanilla extract

Grated zest of 1 lemon

½ teaspoon kosher salt

1 ½ cups sifted all-purpose flour

for the buttercream icing:
8 ounces (2 sticks) unsalted butter, at room temperature

8 ounces (1 cup) cream cheese, at room temperature

2 cups confectioners' sugar

4 to 6 tablespoons heavy cream, more as needed

1 egg yolk

½ teaspoon vanilla extract

2 teaspoons fresh lemon juice

Grated zest of ½ lemon

for assembly:
2 ½ cups pine nuts, toasted

1. Heat the oven to 375°F. Lightly butter and flour two 10-inch circles of parchment paper cut to fit two 10-inch springform cake pans. Place them in the pans—buttered sides up—and set aside.

2. Begin making the sponge: Process the cup of untoasted pine nuts in a food processor until it resembles smooth peanut butter, pausing once or twice to scrape down the sides of the bowl.

3. Using an electric mixer, beat the 12 egg yolks and 1/3 cup of the granulated sugar at medium-high speed until thick in texture, and light in color, and the batter forms a ribbon when the beaters are raised from the batter. Beat in the vanilla, lemon zest, and the puréed pine nuts until just blended. Reserve.

4. Clean the beaters well, and in a clean bowl, beat the egg whites with the electric mixer until frothy. With the mixer running, add the salt, and slowly pour in the remaining 2/3 cup of sugar. Continue to beat the mixture until the whites stand in soft peaks, drooping just a bit when you raise the beaters.

5. Gently fold the egg whites, one-third at a time, into the reserved yolk mixture. Keep the mixture light and airy; it is not necessary to entirely incorporate the whites before the next addition. In the same fashion, fold in the 1 1/2 cups flour in thirds, completely incorporating the mixture after the final addition. Divide the batter between the cake pans, place in the oven, and bake until a skewer inserted into the cakes comes out clean, 25 to 30 minutes. Place the pans on racks to cool completely. When cool, run a knife around each cake to make sure it won't stick, release the springform sides, remove the pan bottoms, and carefully peel off the parchment paper. Place the cakes back on the racks, and reserve.

6. Make the buttercream icing: With an electric mixer, cream the butter and cream cheese until fluffy, occasionally scraping down the sides of the bowl. Gradually beat in the confectioners' sugar, followed by a few tablespoons of cream and the egg yolk. Beat in the vanilla, lemon juice, lemon zest, and additional cream as needed to produce a spreadable icing. (You may make the buttercream in advance, and store it in the refrigerator, but allow it to warm slightly before use.)

7. Assemble the cake: Combine one-third of the icing with 1/2 cup of the toasted pine nuts. Place one cooled cake on a cake stand or plate. Evenly spread the icing with the pine nuts on top of the first cake. Top with the second cake, bottom side down. Evenly spread the remaining icing (which has no pine nuts) over the entire cake top and sides. Then cover the entire cake, top and sides, with the remaining 2 cups of pine nuts. When applying them to the sides, gently press them into the icing in small handfuls.

You've Got Options

If you want to really go for it, you can add even more nibbles to your tapas buffet, coming ever closer to imitating a big-time, well-stocked tapas bar in Spain. The following things are awfully easy to serve, once you find good examples of them:

Olive Oil. Spanish olive oil is some of the best in the world—particularly the oil from Andalucia, in the south, that's made from the Picual olive. This oil often has a lovely green aroma, like that of tomato vines or stems. One brand I particularly like is Nunez del Prado. Leave a few bottles of oil on the buffet table for random drizzling—or transfer to several small, colorful terra-cotta pitchers.

Olives. Tapas bars in Spain always offer olives. My favorite olives there (though they're a little tricky to find here) are the green, meaty ones called Manzanillas, which just happen to go beautifully with dry Manzanilla sherry. Another tasty choice is the small, brownish-green olive from the north called Arbequinas, more bitter than Manzanillas. A platter of olives, either one variety or mixed, will disappear quickly. Provide small dishes near the olive platter for discarded pits.

Almonds. Another tapas bar must is almonds—which always taste incredibly good in Spain, leagues beyond what we have here; they are at once lighter, crunchier, and much more flavorful. You can now buy the almond that's used in Spain, called Marcona, from the Spanish web sites **(see Where to Find It, page 30)**. To prepare them for the party, sizzle them quickly in a skillet with some medium-hot olive oil; 1 to 2 minutes is plenty, just until the color changes slightly. Remove the almonds from the pan with a slotted spoon and drain on paper towels. Sprinkle immediately with lots of sea salt. They will taste best about half an hour later.

Pimientos de Padrón. Many tapas bars in Galicia and elsewhere offer small green chiles that are completely addictive. They are picked up by the stems and eaten whole, at room temperature; usually the taste is mild and sweet, but every once in a while a hot one surprises you. Tienda.com **(see Where to Find It, page 30)** sells a California version, raw and fresh. After you buy them, all you have to do is sauté a single layer in a few tablespoons of olive oil in a heavy pan over medium-high heat. As soon as they brown slightly and puff up a bit—usually a minute or two—they're done. Remove to a platter, sprinkle with salt, and cool to room temperature.

Ventresca. Another glory of Spain is the astonishing canned tuna produced there—particularly the type known as "ventresca," which comes from the tuna's fatty, velvety belly. Just place the tuna on a platter straight from the can; garnish, if desired, with lemon slices, parsley, or olives. Some Spanish brands of ventresca I love are Albo Filetes de Atun Blanco, Ortiz "El Velero," and Escuris. Make sure you see the word ventresca on the tin.

Manchego in Oil. So many of the great cheeses made in Spain are available in the U.S. today, and you could put together a stunning assortment. If you must narrow it down to one, however, the one that comes closest to a tapas-bar staple is Manchego, the heroic sheep's-milk cheese of La Mancha in central Spain. Many tapas bars in Spain cut firm Manchego into triangle-shaped pieces, stack the pieces in a round glass bowl so it looks like a round of cheese reconstructed, then drench the cheese with good Spanish olive oil. I've seen these things sit on tapas bars for a few days or more. You might want to make yours the day before the party and let it sit at room temperature. If you wish, skip the oil routine—the cheese is delicious on its own, too. Try to find an aged example in which a caramel-like flavor often develops.

Set Dressing

Though it's impossible to generalize about the "typical" Spanish tapas bar, there are certain shared characteristics. At the top of that list would be informality; these are taverns, after all, with a clientele there to socialize even more than to eat or drink. This quality is easily translated at your party: include nothing stiff, nothing formal, nothing elegant. (This might be good advice when considering your guest list, as well.) Nestle your tapas bar in a corner of your space, so guests will have to rub shoulders while reaching for the food. Set up a few tables and chairs nearby. Cover them with newspapers, perhaps—*not* white tablecloths—a few foil ashtrays, a single rose in a small vase, a dish of salt, and a pile of toothpicks. (At some of the more down-and-dirty tapas bars in Spain, your check is determined by how many toothpicks you've used!)

Another ubiquitous tapas-bar quality in Spain is "sports-macho." These places are not exactly like sports bars in the U.S.; you're not likely to see "football" games on huge screens at the end of the bar, and Buffalo wings are eschewed in favor of bite-sized octopuses and baby eels. But, despite an un-sports-bar-like sophistication, photos and trappings of athletic events are often found—especially if you consider bullfighting an athletic event. I'd suggest some sports bric-a-brac at your tapas party, but I'd definitely cool it on the bull stuff. It doesn't translate.

The last tapas-bar quality is all but ineffable—I call it a certain decadence, but only in the most literal sense, and only if you understand that I'm willing to look upon it with favor. Decay and decline can actually be beautiful. There is a tragic sense of life in Spain, which is part of that great country's charm and beauty. I say: go ahead. Buy one large flower pot to sacrifice. Put it in a sturdy garbage bag, and break it into large pieces with a hammer. Scatter those pieces all around the room, or write the names of the specific tapas dishes on the terra-cotta shards with an indelible marker and place the shards next to their corresponding foods.

Table Dressing

The most exciting single thing at your party will be the "tapas bar" itself—the table upon which you lay your tapas. And in the spirit of authenticity and body-huddling, I do suggest that you create one table upon which all of your little Iberian-style jewels may be placed.

Cover that table with an amply sized cloth in a dark, solid color; green and blue are good as they're both food-friendly and fairly neutral. The excitement's in the food, remember. Now, many tapas bars in Spain present dishes at different levels, physically speaking, through the use of stands, countertop-toppers, and the like. Use what you have to accomplish this kind of multi-level effect. You can build sturdy "platforms" of varying heights under the cloth (this is why I advised using an "ample" one). Blocks, wood, upturned mixing bowls, or baking pans can be put to use in constructing the "stage." Even cardboard boxes, providing they're of substantial strength, serve the same purpose. Just make sure everything is heatproof! And speaking of stands, don't forget to give pride of place to your *jamonera*, or ham stand; make it central, and make it accessible from both sides.

On the buffet table, arrange the food attractively, but not obsessively. This isn't haute cuisine. Special terra-cotta dishes, called *cazuelas*, are available in this country **(see Where to Find It, page 30)**; they can be platters for your party, and will be useful additions, even after the party, to your *batterie de cuisine*. But white bowls and platters, either round or rectangular, are authentic, too.

Resist the temptation to use paper plates, no matter how nose-thumbingly informal they seem, because they're not practical for this party. Rent plates if you must, but provide your guests with something substantial to hold. If things go as planned, your guests will be standing while eating, and carrying on animated conversations! Something small—no more than 6 inches in diameter—works best. And don't underestimate the number of plates needed; several per person is recommended. Keep them nearby.

Where to Find It

Tienda.com

3701 Rochambeau Rd.
Williamsburg, VA 23188
757.566.9606 (tel)
888.472.1022 (toll free)
757.566.9603 (fax)
www.tienda.com
A comprehensive source of imported Spanish food, cookware, and other items, including jamon-carving stands.

The Spanish Table

1427 Western Ave.
Seattle, WA 98101
206.692.2814 (tel)
206.682.2814 (fax)
www.thespanishtable.com
Dedicated to all things Spanish and Portuguese, this company, with brick-and-mortar locations in Seattle, Berkeley, and Santa Fe, is the equivalent of one-stop shopping for your tapas party.

Smith & Hawken

(multiple locations)
4 Hamilton Landing,
Suite 10016
Novato, CA 94949
800.940.1170 (toll free)
www.smithandhawken.com
Glazed terra-cotta pottery, live olive trees for livening up your party space.

Surfa's Restaurant Supply and Gourmet Food

8825 National Blvd.
Culver City, CA 90232
310.559.4770
www.surfasonline.com
Usually stocks one of my favorite Spanish tunas, Albo Filetes de Atun Blanco, Ventresca.

Zingerman's

422 Detroit St.
Ann Arbor, MI 48103
888.636.8162 (toll free)
www.zingermans.com
Arguably one of the best food purveyors in the country, Zingerman's carries the Ortiz brand of ventresca tuna.

Grilled Pizza in the Backyard

With Red-Checkered Tablecloths *and* Dean Martin

A Party for 12

The Menu

Old-Fashioned Chunky Antipasto Salad with Salami and Provolone

White Clam Pizza

Pizza with Chicken Diavolo, Mozzarella, and Arugula

Gorgonzola and Caramelized Onion Pizza

Classic Pizza Margherita

Limoncello Granita

Polenta Cookies with Chopped Pistachio Nuts

Espresso

Everyone loves pizza—and everyone would love to be the host of a boisterous pizza party, with pie after glorious pie coming out of the oven to dazzle the guests. There's only one problem with this fantasy: it takes a restaurant pizza oven to create truly excellent pizza. Only the high heat of the professional models can cook pizza quickly, and blister the dough in just the right way. The 550°F on your home oven is just 60 percent or so of the heat you need for great pizza.

Great news, however. Thanks to American ingenuity, specifically the ingenuity of George Germon and Johanne Killeen at Al Forno in Providence, Rhode Island—the pizza world was given something new. Because of it, life will be forever improved for home pizza-makers! These two great restaurateurs hatched the idea of cooking pizza on top of a hot, smoky grill. They created it as a restaurant recipe, but as long as you've got a grill and a place to put it (like your backyard), you can cook pizza exactly as they do at the restaurant. Here's the big reason I'm so excited: this thin-crusted grilled pizza is some of the best pizza you'll ever taste, truly authentic and delicious.

Pizza itself is the focus of this simple outdoor party. Your guests will sample a version of New Haven's famous white clam pizza, go on to two "creative" pizzas, and conclude with a killer version of classic cheese-and-tomato pizza.

As long as we're celebrating American pizza ingenuity, I think it's a good idea to celebrate all the wonderful things about Italian-American food and culture. For me, this party echoes the good old days, the 1950s and 1960s, when Italian-American food got the respect it deserves. One taste of the old-fashioned chunky antipasto salad that kicks off this party, laden with crunchy hearts of iceberg lettuce, and you'll likely say—as I've been known to—"Exactly what is so great about radicchio?"

The
Plan

As your guests arrive, toss and dress the Antipasto Salad, and place it on your outdoor buffet table—which you've already set with plates, forks, and napkins. Invite guests to help themselves to salad, and to the loaves of crusty bread you've put out. A few bottles of good olive oil on the buffet would also be lovely. Set up a section of the table for do-it-yourself wine, beer, and soda—and lots of cold bottles of San Pellegrino!

Place a table near the grill on which you can roll out the pizza dough. Have 24 balls of dough ready to go. Have a bowl of olive oil and a pastry brush handy. As soon as the fire's very hot, start rolling. You will likely be able to get three pizzas on the grill simultaneously; place them over the fire, and begin the White Clam Pizza recipe. When the three clam pizzas are done, transfer them to a large cutting board you've set up on the buffet table. With a pizza cutter or a large, very sharp knife, cut each pizza into quarters, yielding a total of 12 pieces. Guests will serve themselves from the cutting board as you return to the dough-rolling station for three more clam pizzas.

The rhythm continues as you work your way through three chicken pizzas, three more chicken pizzas, three Gorgonzola pizzas, three more Gorgonzola pizzas, three tomato pizzas, and three more tomato pizzas. Keep the wine flowing and the salad bowl replenished.

Your work slows down as you pass out 12 bowls of Limoncello granita with spoons. Time to stoke up the espresso machine—and to pass cookies with the cups of coffee.

The Ingredient

The pizza dough itself is the heart and soul of the party. Just be sure to follow the recipe directions carefully. You'll be amazed at how good it is—and so will your guests!

Beverage Time

I was astonished, in Naples, when I asked the pizza pros there, "What's the best wine to drink with pizza?" "The best wine?" they asked, looking puzzled. "The best wine is Coca-Cola." Certain they were kidding me; I persisted. "No, really. What kind of wine do you like with pizza?" Guess what? They persisted, too. "We don't like wine with pizza," they said. "We drink Coca-Cola with pizza, or beer." So many Neapolitan pizza aficionados told me the same thing—and I saw so many actually do it—that I finally started to believe them.

And you know what? The bubbles of both Coca-Cola and beer really are good with pizza. Try it yourself. Put iced cans or bottles of both at your buffet table beverage station.

Despite the prevailing Neapolitan wisdom, however, I still like wine with pizza, too—as long as the wine is not too serious, and as long as it's served out of cheap tumblers. So offer guests a choice of either white or red. For white, I'd serve exactly what I drank for so many years in Italian-American restaurants with checkered tablecloths: Soave Bolla, from northern Italy. When it came to red in those restaurants, the *padron* would normally bring out a clear bottle filled with red wine, but unlabeled. "We make this in the garage," he would say. And if you wish to make your own garage wine for the pizza party, that'd be a great thing! But if you don't have the time and interest, just buy a few mega-bottles of Gallo Hearty Burgundy, and funnel them into clear glass bottles.

Whether you wish to claim them as your own winemaking efforts or not is up to you. I only know that I didn't see a lot of garages around the restaurants I used to go to.

The Recipes

Old-Fashioned Chunky Antipasto Salad with Salami and Provolone

. . ● . .

The following recipe instructs you to prep all of the vegetables and antipasto items and throw them into a big salad bowl; but if you'd rather prep these items in advance, just hold them separately and toss at the last minute. The garlic-salt-vinegar base needs to steep for at least an hour; you could do it 5 or 6 hours in advance if you wish. At the last minute—and only at the last minute—combine all elements, toss with olive oil, toss with vinegar, and serve.

serves 12

4 large cloves garlic

1 teaspoon kosher salt

$\frac{1}{2}$ cup red wine vinegar

4 teaspoons balsamic vinegar

3 large, heavy heads of iceberg lettuce

$\frac{3}{4}$ pound Italian salami, cut in $\frac{3}{8}$-inch slices

$\frac{1}{2}$ pound sharp provolone, cut in $\frac{1}{4}$-inch slices

24 stuffed green olives

24 black olives (in the style of your choice)

3 medium scallions, cleaned

3 tablespoons capers, drained

32 pepperoncini from a jar (also known as "Tuscan peppers")

$\frac{1}{2}$ pound marinated artichoke hearts from a jar, drained and cut into 32 pieces

$\frac{1}{2}$ pound roasted red peppers from a jar, drained and cut into about 4 dozen large squares

24 anchovy filets, each cut into 4 pieces

36 cherry tomatoes, halved

2 teaspoons dried oregano

$\frac{1}{2}$ cup fruity olive oil

Freshly ground black pepper

1. Smash the garlic cloves on a cutting board and sprinkle with the salt. Continue to smash and mince until a fine paste is formed. You should have about 2 teaspoons of paste.

2. Place the garlic paste in a mixing bowl. Whisk in the red wine vinegar and the balsamic vinegar. Let sit for at least 1 hour.

3. When ready to make the salad, core the iceberg lettuce heads. Discard the cores along with the outer leaves. Tear the yellow-green hearts into compact chunks that are each about 1 ½ inches square. You should have about 12 to 15 cups of inner heart chunks (the more inner heart you use, the better the salad will be). Place the chunks in a very large salad bowl.

4. Cut the salami slices into approximately 60 square-ish ¾-inch pieces. Add to the salad bowl. Cut the provolone slices into approximately 60 square-ish ¾-inch pieces. Add to the salad bowl. Add the olives, both green and black, to the salad bowl.

5. Cut a few inches off the darkest ends of the scallions. Discard. Cut the remaining scallions in half lengthwise, then coarsely chop them. Add the chopped scallions to the salad bowl along with the capers, pepperoncini, artichoke hearts, red peppers, anchovies, and cherry tomatoes. Toss the salad well to blend. Crush the dried oregano in your hand, and crumble it into the salad. Toss again, distributing the oregano well.

6. Add the olive oil to the salad, and toss well. Then add the reserved garlic-salt-vinegar mixture, tossing again. Toss with black pepper. Taste for seasoning, adjusting with salt and/or vinegar as necessary. Serve immediately.

Master Recipe for Pizza Dough

· · ● · · ·

One virtue of this grilled pizza recipe is that it takes little time and trouble to make the dough. Even neophyte dough workers can create a great crust quickly. One thing that helps is the "look" of the finished product; these pizzas are far from perfect rectangles. That removes the pressure! One of my favorite practitioners of grilled pizza is Vincent Scotto, a New York chef who used to work at Al Forno; his pizzas, from a recipe like this, look like rough, improvisational ovals. Spectacular!

makes enough dough for 24 pizzas, each one measuring approximately 6x10 inches

6 cups lukewarm water

3 tablespoons rapid dry yeast

¼ cup granulated sugar

½ cup kosher salt

½ cup plus 2 tablespoons extra-virgin olive oil

8 cups bread flour

8 cups all-purpose flour, plus additional as needed

1. Combine the water, yeast, and sugar in a large bowl, and let sit until the mixture looks foamy with bubbles on the surface, about 15 minutes.

2. Stir in the salt and olive oil.

3. Combine the flours. Add about ¾ of the combined flour to the yeast mixture. Stir the solids and liquid together; it's not necessary to knead. The mixture should be soft and sticky, but still firm enough to form into balls. If it's not firm enough, gradually add more flour. When the dough feels right, divide the dough into 24 balls.

4. Oil baking sheets. Place the balls about 2 inches apart on the baking sheets. Cover with plastic wrap or clean tea towels and let them sit at room temperature for 40 minutes.

5. To roll out the balls, dust a counter or cutting board with flour. Dust your rolling pin, too. You may have to flour the balls while rolling as they will be slightly sticky. Roll each ball into a rough rectangle that's about 6x10 inches. The shape of the rolled-out dough can be irregular. What's important is that the dough be about ⅛ inch thick.

6. Place the first piece of rolled-out dough on a platter, then cover with parchment paper or plastic wrap. Roll out another piece, cover with another sheet of paper or wrap, then roll out the third. You will cook the pizzas on the grill three at a time, so you can wait until the first three pizzas are cooked before you roll out the next three.

COOK'S NOTE: *I like to use the rolling pin as little as possible. Yes, I give the dough a preliminary pass with it, but I find that the more you stretch the dough by hand—sort of like the quintessential pizza-flinging guy at the pizzeria—the springier and flakier the finished product is. Remember: you're not looking for perfect rectangles!*

The basic technique in grilling pizza is to brown one side over a hot fire, then flip the dough over and place the pizza toppings on the already-browned side. You want the toppings to warm and/or melt before the underside of the pizza gets too brown. Once you've flipped the pizzas, it is a good idea to cover the grill so that the heat stays trapped inside and warms the toppings more quickly. If the undersides are cooking too quickly, you can always move the pizza to a "cooler" side of the fire as the toppings warm.

White Clam Pizza

. . . ● . . .

Several places in New Haven, Connecticut, are famous for this tomato-less, cheese-less, clam-laden pizza; it's also a specialty of Lombardi's in lower Manhattan, the first pizzeria ever opened in the U.S. (circa 1905). I love it because it's the pizza equivalent of one of my favorite dishes, linguine with white clam sauce. The following version puts the emphasis on the clams—raw clams, which don't get cooked very long so that they remain tender, and rich in clam flavor.

Do your prep about 2 hours before the party starts.

makes 6 pizzas

¾ cup extra-virgin olive oil, plus additional for brushing pizza
1 cup thinly sliced garlic
3 dozen live cherrystone clams, scrubbed
2 cups loosely packed, finely chopped curly parsley

1. Pour the ¾ cup olive oil into a medium sauté pan over medium heat. Add the garlic. Cook until the garlic is just starting to turn golden, about 5 to 7 minutes. Turn off the heat and set aside.

2. Shuck the clams, reserving the juice, and cut each clam belly into 4 pieces. When all the clams have been cut, add them to the garlic and oil. Moisten the mixture with a few tablespoons of reserved clam juice. Reserve and refrigerate if not using immediately.

3. Add the parsley to the clam mixture and blend well.

4. When you're ready to cook the pizzas, roll out 3 of the dough balls (instructions in Master Recipe for Pizza Dough, page 40). Brush one side of each pizza with a little of the extra olive oil. Place the pizzas, oiled side down, on the grill. Cook pizzas to brown the first side. Turn over, and spread the browned side of each pizza with one-sixth of the clam-oil-parsley mixture, spreading it out evenly. Cover the grill. Take the pizzas off the fire as soon as the undersides of the pizzas brown.

5. Bring the pizzas to the buffet table on a wooden board. Cut into 12 pieces. Let the guests eat while you return to the grill and prepare more pizzas.

Pizza with Chicken Diavolo, Mozzarella, and Arugula

· · ● · ·

This pizza is popular in Naples and has become popular here. The key is the fresh arugula leaves that get strewn on the pizza just as it comes off the heat, which causes the leaves to wilt a bit.

Begin your work on these ingredients about 3 hours before the party starts.

makes 6 pizzas

6 boneless chicken thighs, skin on

6 tablespoons extra-virgin olive oil, plus additional for brushing pizza

8 cloves garlic, finely minced

6 tablespoons fresh lemon juice

Crushed red pepper

Kosher salt

1 pound fresh mozzarella, thinly sliced, divided into 6 portions

2 bunches arugula, leaves only, washed and dried

1 ½ cups finely grated Pecorino Romano

1. About 3 hours before the start of the party, toss the chicken thighs with the 6 tablespoons of olive oil, the garlic, lemon juice, and crushed red pepper. Cover and refrigerate for 2 hours.

2. About 1 hour before the start of the party, season the thighs well with salt, and broil, skin side up, until the skin is brown and the chicken is cooked through, about 10 to 12 minutes. If the skin gets too brown before the chicken cooks through, flip the thighs over and cook on the other side. Remove the cooked chicken from the broiler, and let it rest for 10 minutes. Then cut the chicken into broad, thin slices. Reserve, covered, at room temperature.

3. When you're ready to cook the pizzas, roll out 3 of the dough balls (instructions in Master Recipe for Pizza Dough, page 40). Brush one side of each pizza with a little of the extra olive oil. Place the pizzas, oiled side down, on the grill. Cook pizzas to brown the first side. Turn over, and top the browned side of each pizza with one-sixth of the mozzarella. Salt lightly. Top the mozzarella on each pizza with the cooked slices of 1 chicken thigh. Cover the grill. Take the pizzas off the fire when the mozzarella has melted, making sure the underside hasn't burned. Immediately top each pizza with one-sixth of the arugula leaves. Sprinkle each pizza with ¼ cup Pecorino Romano.

4. Bring the pizzas to the buffet table on a wooden board. Cut into 12 pieces. Let the guests eat while you return to the grill and prepare more pizzas.

Gorgonzola and Caramelized Onion Pizza

· · ● · · ·

I love the sweet-sour-salty collision of flavors on this exciting pizza. Start working on the ingredients about 1 hour before the party starts.

makes 6 pizzas

2 pounds red onions

1 pound yellow onions

¼ cup unsalted butter

2 tablespoons extra-virgin olive oil, plus additional for brushing pizzas

3 tablespoons sugar

6 tablespoons red wine vinegar

Kosher salt

½ pound Gorgonzola dolce, refrigerated

2 cups very finely chopped curly parsley

1. Cut all the onions in half, and slice thinly. (This may look like a lot, but once cooked, the volume reduces drastically.)

2. Heat the butter and 2 tablespoons of oil in a large sauté pan over medium-low heat. Add the onions and cook, stirring occasionally, until the onions are soft and caramelized. This will take about 1 hour. Stir in the sugar and vinegar. Season with salt. Reserve.

3. Place the Gorgonzola in the freezer for a few minutes (it's easier to handle when it's very cold). Crumble the Gorgonzola, then return to the refrigerator.

4. When you're ready to cook the pizzas, roll out 3 of the dough balls (instructions in Master Recipe for Pizza Dough, page 40). Brush one side of each pizza with a little of the extra olive oil. Place the pizzas, oiled side down, on the grill. Cook pizzas to brown the first side. Turn over, and top the browned side of each pizza with one-sixth of the Gorgonzola, evenly distributed across the pie. Top the Gorgonzola on each pizza with one-sixth of the onions. Cover the grill. Take the pizzas off the fire when the Gorgonzola has melted, making sure the underside hasn't burned. Immediately top each pizza with one-sixth of the parsley.

5. Bring the pizzas to the buffet table on a wooden board. Cut into 12 pieces. Let the guests eat while you return to the grill and prepare more pizzas.

Classic Pizza Margherita

· · • ● • · ·

The pizza of pizzas—the most simple and traditional one—can be started half an hour before your guests arrive if you're not busy with other things.

About Pizza Margherita

Pizza goes back into antiquity in southern Italy. At least preliminary forms of it do, those made with oil and herbs and dough, but no tomatoes or cheese. It was in the 1600s that Italians started adding tomatoes to their oven-baked pies, and it was the peasants of Naples who were the first to tomato-ize their focaccia bread rounds.

In 1830, pizza took a giant step forward with the opening of the world's first pizzeria, Port'Alba, in Naples; the pizzas were cooked in an oven lined with lava from Mount Vesuvius, the very famous volcano. What many people don't realize is that what most of us call pizza—with cheese!—was born just over a hundred years ago, in 1889, when Queen Margherita Teresa Giovanni, the consort of Umberto I, King of Italy, paid a royal visit to Naples. Don Raffaele Esposito, who owned a place called Pietro Il Pizzaiolo, was asked to prepare a special pizza for the Queen. Esposito brought together the by-then-traditional tomatoes, as well as basil, but he shocked everyone by adding mozzarella. His rationale was not gastronomic; he wanted to make a visual reference to the flag of the newly united Italy. Obviously, to the pizza's red and green, he had to add some white! This pizza—which in the U.S. is known simply as "pizza"—is still known in Italy as Pizza Margherita, after the Queen. And to this day in Italy you have to ask for Pizza Margherita if you want cheese on your pizza.

makes 6 pizzas

> **2 (28-ounce) cans whole tomatoes in thick purée**
> **2 cups loosely packed, coarsely chopped basil leaves**
> **4 tablespoons finely minced garlic**
> **12 ounces Bel Paese, grated**
> **6 ounces sharp provolone, coarsely grated**
> **6 ounces Pecorino Romano, finely grated**
> **Olive oil, for brushing**

1. Drain the tomatoes and cut into ½-inch chunks. Mix them in a bowl with the basil and garlic. Set aside. You'll have about 3 cups.

2. Mix the cheeses together with your hands, blending them well. Divide into 6 equal portions.

3. When you're ready to cook the pizzas, roll out 3 of the dough balls (instructions in Master Recipe for Pizza Dough, page 40). Brush one side of each pizza with a little olive oil. Place the pizzas, oiled side down, on the grill. Cook pizzas to brown the first side. Turn over, and top the browned side of each pizza with one-sixth of the cheese mixture, well distributed across the pie. Top the cheese on each pizza with one-sixth of the tomato mixture (about ½ cup for each pizza), well distributed across the pie. Cover the grill. Take the pizzas off the fire when the cheese has melted, making sure the underside hasn't burned.

4. Bring the pizzas to the buffet table on a wooden board. Cut into 12 pieces. Let the guests eat while you return to the grill and prepare more pizzas.

Limoncello Granita

· · • · ·

Granita—flavored ice, scraped to make a spoonable dessert—is wildly popular in Italy. A form of it has long had popularity in the U.S., too; in cities all over America, many a Little Italy merchant drizzled syrup over shaved ice and called the concoction a "snow cone." That early 20th-century practice morphed into "Italian ices," still a popular American treat.

The following concoction is a perfect end to your grilled pizza party—light, refreshing, made with Limoncello, a sweet, lemony liqueur specialty of the Naples region. It, too, is wildly popular in Italy; among liqueurs there, only Campari gets served more often. The granita will take about 4 hours from start to finish. It could be made the morning of the party, as it's not going to freeze rock solid; just remember to check it every hour and rake it with a fork to keep the soft, flaky consistency. If you wish, you could garnish individual servings with fresh mint and/or slivers of candied lemon peel.

serves 12

3 cups Limoncello (the liqueur should be 26% to 28% alcohol)
3 cups water

1. Combine the Limoncello with the water and pour into a wide, shallow pan that fits into the freezer.

2. After half an hour, the mixture should be freezing around the edges. Use a fork to stir the frozen border into the liquid part at the center. Repeat this procedure every 45 minutes or so until all of the granita is frozen. Keep scraping and breaking up any parts that are frozen solid. It will take about 4 hours for the granita to freeze properly—at which time it should have a soft, flaky consistency. If you've prepared the granita before the party, keep it in the freezer in the wide pan—but keep checking it every hour or so, raking it with a fork, to make sure it doesn't solidify.

3. When ready to serve, spoon into serving dishes (about ½ cup of granita per dish). Serve immediately to beat the inevitable melting that will occur after a few minutes.

Polenta Cookies with Chopped Pistachio Nuts

· ˙ ● ● ● ˙ ·

You may be tempted to serve these delicious, buttery cookies with the granita, but I like them much better with a cup of espresso after the granita. I think they're best just a few hours out of the oven, but they're also very good when baked the day before.

makes about 3 dozen 1½-inch cookies

> ¼ **cup candied lemon peel, cut into ⅛–inch dice**
> **1 cup unsalted butter, softened**
> ¾ **cup sugar**
> **1 large egg yolk**
> **1 ½ cups all-purpose flour**
> **1 cup finely ground polenta**
> ¼ **teaspoon salt**
> ¾ **cup roughly chopped unsalted pistachios**

1. Heat the oven to 350°F. Line two baking sheets with parchment.

2. Cover the lemon peel with boiling water in a small bowl. Let it stand 5 minutes, then drain and pat the lemon peel dry with a paper towel. Set aside. (This process removes excess sugar.)

3. Using an electric mixer with the paddle attachment on medium speed, cream the butter and sugar until the mixture is light and fluffy. Add the egg yolk, flour, polenta, and salt, and mix until the mixture forms a soft mass. (Alternatively, place the aforementioned ingredients in the bowl of a food processor, and pulse until the mixture forms a soft mass.)

4. Stir in the lemon peel and pistachios by hand, blending evenly.

5. Using your hands, take about 1 tablespoon of the mixture and form it into a 1-inch ball. Place it on a baking sheet and flatten with the palm of your hand until the cookie is about 1/2 inch thick. Continue until all the dough is used, and all the cookies are flattened. You should have about 36 cookies, each one an inch away from the next; employ multiple cookie sheets if necessary. Don't worry if the cookies are not uniformly smooth.

6. Bake in the oven until the cookies start to turn golden, about 15 minutes. Cool on the cookie sheet for a few minutes, then transfer to a cooling rack. The cookies may feel soft, but they'll firm up as they cool. Store in an airtight container.

About Espresso Machines

You may well have an espresso machine that already makes you happy. If you do, simply make espresso for this party as usual.

However, if you're shopping around for a home espresso maker, I'd like to point out that I've fallen under the sway of the very fine new generation of espresso machines that require only capsules, or pods, of pre-ground coffee to make espresso. The results are startlingly restaurantlike—and the process couldn't be simpler!

One of my favorites is the FrancisFrancis espresso maker, produced by the great Italian coffee company Illy. (It's available in five models with five different styles, all making the same great cup of espresso.) You simply purchase Illy's E.S.E. servings (short for "Easy Serving Espresso" and known as "pods"), pop one in the machine, and press a button, and 30 seconds later you have a great individual cup of espresso, topped with the lovely, rich, copper-tinged foam called *crema*. Espresso for 12, at this party, can easily be done in this fashion in under 10 minutes.

You've Got Options

If you wish to dress up the buffet table, you could spread out small plates around the salad bowl containing many of the ingredients that are in the salad. Simply buy double or triple what you need for the salad—then create a small salami plate, provolone plate, olive plate, pepperoncini plate, artichoke heart plate, roasted red pepper plate, anchovy plate, and cherry tomato plate. Guests may fortify their salads with these fixin's, or may eat these antipasto items directly, possibly with bread and olive oil.

Set Dressing

This is a great backyard party even with no set dressing whatsoever. But there is one elaborate idea that, if you're up for it, would create an insanely celebratory environment for your grilled pizza. Autumnal Jewish celebrations for the festival of Sukkoth sometimes feature a "Sukkoth hut"—a rustic, outdoor "room." A company in North Carolina called The Sukkah Project **(see Where to Find It, page 52)** specializes in these easy-to-erect pavilions. With little trouble, you could convert one into something that looks like a grape arbor, replete with hanging fruit! If you're especially susceptible to the siren song of 1950s kitsch, shop rummage sales or craft stores for the soft, squishy plastic grapes that used to be the height of chic, and hang them from your arbor. Or you could hang lemons over the heads of your guests, as they do at one famous restaurant in Capri.

Plants will help set the scene; a profusion of containers featuring summer annuals will enliven any outdoor venue. Dwarf lemon trees would be perfect, evocative as they are of the Amalfi Coast. Check with your florist about renting them.

For your non-plant touches: Consider nesting red, green, and white mercury glass gazing balls in birdbaths, their colors mimicking the Italian flag. Speaking of the Italian flag—flutter one in a conspicuous place to let your guests know they've arrived at the right house. And one random touch that I especially like as set dressing is a fat and tired-looking bicycle resting (and rusting) off to the side—as if it awaits an emergency run to the local vineyard for more *fiaschi* of wine.

Table Dressing

I hardly have to tell you that red-and-white-checkered tablecloths are practically mandatory on your tables—a cheesy, nostalgic reminder of the days when a big night out meant red sauce on every chin and Frankie or Dean on every jukebox. If that's too much retro-recidivism for your more evolved tastes, use a white tablecloth (maybe layered with a red one), and add oversized red-and-white-checkered napkins.

Another must, in my book, are straw-covered bottles (or *fiaschi*) of Chianti—empty, but mounted with candles that have dribbled their wax down the sides of the bottles. These *fiaschi* could be ones that contained Chianti in a decade that's long ago and far away—or you could buy them today at a wine shop, in which case you might want to let your merchant know in advance that you're looking for them. When you open the bottles, taste the wine. You may want to drink it, or mix it with your Hearty Burgundy for your "garage wine," or spill it down the drain. But once the bottles are empty, insert candles in the openings and start making drips so the wax can do its decorative work on the bottles.

For a celebratory centerpiece, layer red and yellow and orange cherry tomatoes in a pretty clear glass bowl (such as a compote or trifle bowl), and top with decorative sprigs of fresh basil. Flank with small cellars of coarse salt. Or mound a colorful array of heirloom tomatoes in a bowl or basket, or on a platter. Strive for a mix of yellow, red, orange, purple, and green. Accent with color-compatible nasturtiums (also edible), preferably with leaves attached. Surround the centerpiece on the table with tall, beribboned vases containing long and thin *grissini* (Italian breadsticks).

Entertainment

This is too easy! How could you not invite a digitally recorded musical incarnation of Dean Martin to this party? He crooned the party's theme song in 1954: "When the moon hits your eye like a big pizza pie, that's amore." Of course, Frank Sinatra and Tony Bennett are welcome to come and spread their love, too.

If you have the space, while your guests are waiting for pizzas they could be engaged in one of Italy's, and Little Italy's, favorite outdoor pastimes: bocce! Though inspired by an ancient Egyptian game, the bocce we know today was invented by the early Romans (bocce is from the Latin *bottia*, meaning "boss"). The turn-of-the-century influx of Italian immigrants to America popularized the game here, and bocce ball sets are carried by most sporting goods stores. I even found a set that has battery-powered lights in the balls, facilitating play after sundown **(see Where to Find It, page 52)**.

Where to Find It

A.G. Ferrari Foods
14234 Catalina St.
San Leandro, CA 94577
877.878.2783 (toll free)
510.346.2100 (tel)
510.351.2672 (fax)
www.agferrari.com
Great source for all kinds of Italian gourmet products.

Gustiamo, Inc.
1715 West Farms Rd.
Bronx, NY 10460
877.907.2525 (toll free)
718.860.2949 (tel)
718.860.4311 (fax)
www.gustiamo.com
Another one of my favorite mail-order sources for Italian ingredients.

The Sukkah Project
Judith and Steve Henry Herman
c/o Steve Henry Woodcraft
4 Pine Tree Lane
Chapel Hill, NC 27514
919.489.7325 (tel)
703.852.3996 (fax)
www.sukkot.com
This company sells kits for outdoor dining structures. They come in various sizes, from 8x10 feet to 40x40 feet. Most can be assembled using only a screwdriver.

Tablecloths Online
Bright Hospitality, Inc.
P.O. Box 374
701 East Spring St.
Titusville, PA 16354
866.827.2303 (toll free)
866.827.7747 (toll free fax)
www.tablecloths-online.com
A large inventory of standard size tablecloths, including the ubiquitous red-and-white check; also offers the option of having a cloth custom-made to any size.

Shindigz by Stumps
One Party Place
South Whitley, IN 46787
800.348.5084 (toll free)
260.723.6976 (fax)
www.shindigz.com
Source of an Italian decorating kit with red, white, and green tissue balls, flag pennants, garlands, etc.

Smith & Hawken
(multiple locations)
4 Hamilton Landing,
Suite 100
Novato, CA 94949
800.940.1170 (toll free)
www.smithandhawken.com
Seasonally, this company carries bocce ball sets in its catalog and retail stores.

Frying High, Japanese Style

An Intimate Tempura Party with a Grand Sake Tasting

A Party for 6

The Menu

Grand Tasting of Sakes

Yellow Miso Soup with Bean Curd and Fresh Shiitake Mushrooms

Light and Crispy Tempura with Shrimp and Assorted Vegetables

Salted Seaweed Salad with Lemon and Freshly Grated Ginger

Quick and Spicy Cucumber Pickle

Tomato and Watercress Salad with Deep-Fried Tofu, Miso Dressing, and Black Sesame Seeds

Ponzu Dipping Sauce

Sesame-Chile Dipping Sauce

Green Tea Ice Cream

One of the intriguing things about food in Japan is its compartmentalization. If you want sushi, you go to a sushi bar. If you want grilled food, you go to a grill; if you want noodles, you go to a noodle shop. And if you want one of the great highlights of Japanese cuisine—the light, lacy, incredibly tasty deep-fried morsels known as tempura—you go, of course, to a tempura bar, where the chef will happily engage you for hours as he passes piece after miraculously fresh-fried piece to you over the counter.

It's a great type of dining, augmented by an array of small plates and side dishes that you can nibble on while waiting for your next shrimp. And it's a terrific type of restaurant experience that you can very easily reproduce at home!

The Japanese, of course, love to drink sake with tempura—and, in recent years, Americans have become more curious than ever about sake. Perfect! Get your party off to a roaring start with a sake tasting to tease the mind and whet the appetite. Then your guests can continue drinking their favorite sakes throughout the meal.

The Plan

This is one party where addressing the guests properly might be a good idea, following the Japanese love of propriety and decorum. How about sending out invitations—possibly hand-written on hand-made washi paper, folded into simple origami shapes (craft- and art-supply stores carry the materials). Or superimpose a reproduction of a Japanese woodcut (they're available in packs of eight) on a blank card. In either case, a fresh haiku, written by the host, might be just the thing to touch the hearts of the prospective guests.

Most of the parties in this book are visualized for 12 people—but not this one! Frying for 12 would be cumbersome, and acquiring the glassware for a 12-person sake tasting would be quite a task. Nope. This is a party for you and five other lucky people, who will have your full attention both as sake master and as chief deep-fryer.

You'll need to plan ahead some. The ice cream should be started the day before your party, and some of the salads will benefit from sitting a few hours.

This party unfolds entirely at one dining table—preferably in the kitchen, near your stove top. If you have an island in your kitchen, or a counter at which five people can sit (you, the tempura chef, will be standing), that would be ideal. Failing that, do you have the space to set up a table in your kitchen? Failing that, do you have a room just off the kitchen where your guests can dine?

As your guests arrive, seat them at the table, and offer them bowls of miso soup—to prepare their stomachs for the sake to come. You could wait until all five guests are assembled, or, if they arrive in staggered fashion, you could offer each one a bowl of miso as soon as he or she sits down. Already on the table will be eight white-wine glasses at each place, so that each guest will be able to taste and compare the eight sakes chilling in your refrigerator. As you'll see later, you can cut this number of sakes down as you see fit.

When the miso bowls have been cleared, it's time to start tasting sake (see Beverage Time, page 57). The next order of business, after the tasting, is this: clear the glasses, leaving each guest with one glass, or perhaps a fresh sake cup for the sake that will be drunk with the meal. Also, this would be the moment to present each guest with three small plates (the Salted Seaweed Salad with Lemon and Freshly Grated Ginger, the Quick and Spicy Cucumber Pickle, and the Tomato and Watercress Salad with Deep-Fried Tofu, Miso Dressing, and Black Sesame Seeds), and two smaller bowls (with the Ponzu Dipping Sauce and the Sesame-Chile Dipping Sauce).

You, of course, will head to the fryer and create miracles (full details below)—vegetable miracles first, followed by shrimp miracles. Every time you have at least five fresh-fried pieces of tempura ready to go, place them on a Japanese platter lined with absorbent paper and pass it over the counter to your guests, or deliver it to their table and serve. If you're working with two fryers, as suggested below, you may be able to serve as many as 12 pieces of tempura simultaneously.

When your guests are sated—and, with the quantities suggested below, they will be!—pull your green tea ice cream out of the freezer, spoon it into bowls, and finally, relax with your company.

It's an active night for a host, but the intense activity at the stove is balanced by the absence of other things to worry about. This is an intimate party, not a sprawling one, and everyone's attention will be focused on two things only: sake and tempura. And finally, on you—the miracle worker who created such a memorable event.

The Ingredient

Shrimp headlines this event. The shrimp tempura recipe will be excellent with any shrimp you use; but if you serve your guests absolutely killer shrimp, the kitchen will practically levitate.

The best shrimp I know of in the U.S. are Louisiana Head-On White Shrimp, often available from a middleman company in upstate New York called Farm-2-Market **(see Where to Find It, page 78)** that arranges deliveries from fishermen to retail consumers. The extraordinary shrimp I get through them are the shrimpiest shrimp I've ever tasted. The greatest thing about them is that they taste seasoned—super-sweet, quite salty—but they're not! They make absolutely astonishing shrimp tempura. Of course, each shrimp will give you one extra task to perform: the removal of the head. But this is a simple operation (just twist it off), and if you gather the heads and make a stock of them, you'll have an amazing shrimpy broth for another party!

Beverage Time

Sake (SAH-kay) is usually translated as Japanese rice wine—though most authorities say its production is more like the production of beer than of wine. Delicious stuff. Great with Japanese food. And one of the most confusing subjects in the whole gastronomic universe.

Three things, above all others, make it confusing. One is the incredible variety of sake; it would take a lifetime to master all the nuances in sakes owing to production methods, brewery differences, regional styles, and on and on. The second problem is the scope of those differences: it's not huge. The range is much more subtle than the range of variations in, say, wine. It doesn't take much expertise to discern the difference between a Chablis from Burgundy and a Cabernet from Napa Valley—but you really have to pay attention to find the differences between a Taru from Nada and a Daiginjo from Niigata! Lastly, there's the labeling problem. Sake labels are confusing even if you're fluent in Japanese—but the English-only reader is totally lost!

There are many ways to mentally organize the world of sake—that's one reason why it's such a difficult world to master. So I'm going to suggest a very simple, very basic breakdown as the basis for your tasting. I'm going to recommend eight different kinds of sake to have in your sake tasting, but please feel free to cut it down to six, or four, or any number with which you feel comfortable.

There is a type of sake called **junmai**, which makes up only about 20 percent of all sakes—which happens to be the top 20 percent of all sakes—and, by the way, represents most of the sake that's available in the U.S. Junmai sake is a "pure" product, brewed from three ingredients only: rice, water, and **koji** (the yeast that begins the fermentation process). At the other end of the quality continuum is **futsushu** sake, which normally has alcohol added to it to increase the yield; it may have sugar and acid added to it as well. The pure taste that sake lovers appreciate in junmai is not as apparent in futsushu.

The first four sakes in the tasting revolve around this issue of junmai/not junmai.

So, for starters, acquire a bottle of futsushu, the non-junmai, for your Sake #1, to get a ground-level view of sake. Some of them are quite nasty, but many are quite pleasant. None will have the refinement of junmai sake—a good first lesson to learn. For Sake #2 at your tasting, acquire a basic junmai with no further designations on it so you can compare it with the futsushu.

Aha! Time to start paying careful attention. For it is in the aforementioned "further designations" of junmai that things start getting complicated; there are several junmai sub-categories.

To understand them, you must learn something about the milling of rice. Grains of rice, from which sake is made, have a hull that is typically milled away in rice production (if it's not, you get brown rice). In sake production, the hull is not desirable because it may create off flavors in the sake, and it certainly won't produce a refined sake. But milling the hull away is labor intensive and costly, so the more that's "polished" away, the higher the price of the sake and, theoretically, the better the sake.

Now follow closely. With the type of sake called **Junmai Ginjo**, you are guaranteed that at least 40 percent of the rice itself was "polished" away before the sake was made. This will be Sake #3.

If you buy a type of sake called **Junmai Daiginjo**, you are guaranteed that 50 percent of the rice was "polished." This will be Sake #4. (To me, this is one of the best categories—usually very light and dry, plus fragrant and complex.)

Please note: there are also ginjos and daiginjos out there that are **not** junmais! These are known as **honjozo sakes**, though they're not always labeled that way. (They may simply say "Ginjo" or "Daiginjo.") These sakes typically have just a little bit of alcohol added to improve flavor—but that eliminates them from the junmai category. I told you this was complicated! So let's just skip those for the purposes of this tasting.

Four sakes will round out the tasting. I now ask you to break out of the junmai mental frame, for the following types of sake could be anywhere on the junmai scale (junmai, junmai ginjo, junmai daiginjo), or not on the junmai scale at all! But each type is distinctive:

Sake #5: **Genshu sake**. This is a very rare sake, though it is available in the U.S. Its chief point of difference is that it is never diluted (many sakes have water added to them), and its alcohol content is, therefore, high. Many sakes hover at about 15 or 16 percent alcohol; genshu usually goes up to at least 18 percent.

Sake #6: **Nigori sake**. This is one of my favorites—sake that has not been filtered, which means it's cloudy. I love the slightly richer texture.

Sake #7: **Taru sake**. Another one of my favorites—sake aged in cedar casks (a tradition going back to 1659). The resulting sake has a complex taste, usually appealing to inveterate wine drinkers. I especially love the one produced by Kikumasamune in Japan, which is a junmai.

Sake #8: **Nama sake**. This sake has not been pasteurized, so it must be refrigerated, giving it a fresh, lively quality. Nama sake can be junmai, junmai ginjo, junmai daiginjo, or other designations. For this tasting, it doesn't matter which designation you get—as long as your Sake #8 is a nama-sake, so you can experience the freshness.

Now that you have my suggestions for eight sakes in the sake tasting, a big question follows: how will you know which is which? For as I've indicated, clear labeling for the English-speaking consumer is obviously not a priority in the Japanese sake industry.

Here is my best advice: contact a company in New Jersey called Wine of Japan Import **(see Where to Find It, page 78)**. They import many sakes—and they not only strive for clear labeling, but will provide you with product cards for their individual sakes that give you a great deal of information! They have even created charts for each sake to show you the relative dryness-sweetness and lightness-richness of what's in each bottle. They do not sell sakes directly to retail customers, but they can advise you on local retail sources for their sakes. Another importer to consult is Japan Prestige Sake, in Los Angeles **(see Where to Find It, page 78)**. Call them for information on retail outlets in your locale.

One sake that is not imported by either Wine of Japan or Japan Prestige Sake is my beloved Kikumasamune Taru Sake. It is distributed in the U.S. by Mutual Trading Co. in Los Angeles—but they are wholesalers, and do not have a license to sell to the public. You can, however, check with them about availability. You can also consult the Kikumasamune website **(see Where to Find It, page 78)**.

Whichever sake you buy, make sure it's fresh. About a year or so after bottling, most sake begins to deteriorate.

As to the mechanics of your sake tasting: you can make this easy or difficult. I vote for easy.

Oh, sure, there are centuries of sake ritual that you might want to draw on as you organize your tasting. There's much ado about cups, for example; you can buy sake cups made of porcelain, ceramic, or metal. You might want to look into the coolest of sake cups—square wooden blocks (known as *sake masu*) used exclusively for cold sake. It takes a little work, however, to line up your mouth just right with the square-cornered block, so these may not be the best tasting vessels—for starters, you'd need 48 of them!

At my sake tasting parties, the sake is treated as if it were white wine. That means it'll be drunk from wine glasses, at least during the tasting, which makes it easier to see and sniff the sake. And it will be drunk cold. Years ago, we all somehow got the message that sake is meant to be drunk warm, or even hot. And there is an old tradition in Japan of doing that—along with a tradition of drinking sake cold. But things have changed greatly: the modern generation of sake aficionados in Japan swears by cold sake—with 50°F usually considered to be the ideal temperature.

Place your sakes in the refrigerator 2 to 3 hours before the party starts. If you have eight sakes, put out eight white-wine glasses at each of the table settings. A way to make the tasting run smoother is to attach a little piece of tape or tag to each glass, giving it a number; each guest, then, would have glasses numbered 1 through 8. Make sure to leave a little room at each setting for the bowl of miso that everyone will drink before the sake tasting starts.

After the miso has been finished, remove the miso bowls and get the tasting started! Pull sake #1 from the fridge and pour a little bit (no more than 2 ounces or so) into each guest's glass #1. Continue with the rest of the sakes until everyone has 8 sakes. Because you've read this chapter—you're the group leader. Explain what the categories are, and encourage your guests to give responses to the sakes. If you'd like to make this all a little more "serious," furnish pads and pencils for your guests. Ask them to give a score to each sake, perhaps on the scale of 1 to 20 from worst to best. The guests will keep those scores private—until the end. Then, you can go around the table, asking everyone's score for each sake. When you tally up the scores, one sake will likely get the highest total—the winner!

As you shift from sake tasting to tempura dinner, it's probably best to remove all 48 glasses from the table. Furnish each guest with one new glass or one sake cup. During the course of the meal, all of the remaining sake will be available in the refrigerator. Invite your guests to help themselves, since you'll be busy frying.

I think when your guests drink their first sips of sake with the dinner, after the tasting, it's time to say *kampai!*—the Japanese equivalent of "bottoms up."

The Recipes

Yellow Miso Soup with Bean Curd and Fresh Shiitake Mushrooms

· · · ● · · ·

This starting soup will be delicious any way you serve it—but it would be really special in *wan,* the small Japanese bowls with matching lids (generally black lacquerware, but sometimes ceramic or porcelain).

makes 6 servings

2 tablespoons vegetable oil

6 medium shiitake mushrooms, stems removed, caps sliced ¼ inch thick

Kosher salt

6 cups Dashi (page 63)

½ cup plus 1 tablespoon yellow miso paste (*shinshu-miso*; see Where to Find It, page 78)

4 ounces soft bean curd in small dice, at room temperature

3 scallions, sliced very thinly on the bias

1. Heat the oil in a medium skillet over medium heat. Add the mushrooms and gently cook without browning them, stirring occasionally, until tender and just cooked through, about 5 minutes. Season lightly with salt, remove from the heat, and set aside.

2. Bring the Dashi to a bare simmer in a medium saucepan. Stir in the miso paste, mashing it against the sides of the pot to help it dissolve. Keep the soup at no more than a bare simmer.

3. Divide the mushrooms, bean curd, and scallions among six small soup bowls. When ready to serve, divide the soup among the bowls, top with lids if possible, and pass immediately.

Dashi

· · ● · ·

Dashi is essential in the Japanese kitchen. It is a stock, basically, made from dried seaweed and dried tuna (bonito), that is used in a wide range of Japanese dishes.

This recipe yields more than you will need for the miso soup in this party, but you'll need some for the dipping sauces. Keep the extra dashi on hand for more soup later on. Dashi can be stored in the refrigerator for up to a week, or frozen for about a month.

By the way, perhaps the only acceptable powdered stock of any kind I've ever used is dashi powder, a wonderful shortcut available at all Japanese groceries (as is the konbu and dried bonito you'll need to make dashi from scratch).

makes 2 quarts

8 cups plus ¼ cup cold water
2 ounces konbu (giant kelp)
2 ounces dried bonito flakes

Place 8 cups of water and the konbu in a large saucepan over medium heat and bring just to a simmer. Immediately add ¼ cup of cold water and stir in the bonito flakes. Return to a bare simmer and immediately turn off the heat. Let the mixture sit for 2 minutes. Discard the konbu and strain the liquid through a fine mesh sieve.

Light and Crispy Tempura with Shrimp and Assorted Vegetables

· · ● · ·

With tempura, you make frying the entertainment at your party.
It's unusual, innovative—and scrumptious!

makes enough for 60 pieces of tempura

3 scant cups all-purpose flour, plus about a cup extra for dusting
  vegetables and shrimp
1 cup potato starch
½ teaspoon baking soda
4 cups ice water
1 jumbo or extra-large egg yolk
Vegetable oil for deep-frying
Vegetables for Tempura (page 67)
Kosher salt
Shrimp for Tempura (page 68)

1. Before your guests arrive, mix together the 3 scant cups of flour, potato starch, and baking soda. Divide the mixture evenly between two large mixing bowls using a measuring cup (you should have about 2 cups of mixture in each bowl). Place the extra dusting flour on a plate.

2. Place the ice water in a clear pitcher or large Pyrex measuring cup, and, using a fork, beat in the egg yolk until the yolk is well incorporated. Keep the water-yolk mixture refrigerated at all times (except when you're using it).

3. At cooking time, place the vegetable oil, several inches deep, in one or two wide cooking vessels (two woks would be ideal) over medium-high heat. Heat the oil to 335°F.

4. Pour 2 cups of the water-yolk mixture into one of the mixing bowls containing the flour–potato starch mixture. Stir—not too vigorously—with chopsticks, just mixing the liquids and solids together, about 30 seconds. The finished tempura batter should be lumpy and approximately the consistency of heavy cream. If you need to thin it, do so with a little tap water. (Reserve the other bowl of flour–potato starch mixture for later, and return the water-yolk mixture to the refrigerator.)

5. When the oil is at 335°F, pick up 1 vegetable piece with chopsticks, dust it lightly with flour, dip it in the tempura batter briefly, then add the vegetable piece to the hot oil. Make sure it doesn't stick to the bottom or sides. Perform the **batter-drizzle technique:** pick up a little extra batter with the tips of your chopsticks, and drizzle it over the vegetable in the oil. Repeat one or two more times, drizzling evenly over the vegetable and occasionally letting the batter drip off into the hot oil; this will create a lacy edge on the finished piece of tempura. Turn the vegetable over after a minute or so; finish cooking for 1 minute on the other side. After a total of about 2 minutes of cooking time, the piece should be cooked on the inside, light-yellow on the outside, and crispy. Drain on paper towels, salt, and serve. Make sure to scoop up any loose bits of batter from the oil with a spider or slotted spoon.

> COOK'S NOTE: *You can have more than 1 piece of tempura going at a time, perhaps as many as 6 pieces in a large wok, and if you have two large woks with hot oil, 12 pieces simultaneously! Start slowly, but you will soon get into the rhythm. You may want to use a spider or tongs for efficiency. Try to keep the oil at an even 335°F.*

6. Keep frying vegetable pieces until you have run out of vegetables and/or batter. It's time to switch to shrimp tempura!

7. Remove the water-yolk mixture from the refrigerator, and pour 2 cups plus 6 tablespoons of it into the second bowl of the flour–potato starch mixture. Stir—not too vigorously—with chopsticks, just mixing the liquids and solids together, about 30 seconds. The finished tempura batter should be lumpy, and approximately the consistency of thin cream. If you need to thin it, do so with a little tap water.

8. Scoop up loose batter bits from the oil and discard. Turn up the heat, and bring the oil to 350°F.

9. When the oil is ready, pick up a shrimp with chopsticks, dust it lightly with flour, dip it in the tempura batter briefly, then add the shrimp to the hot oil. Keeping it submerged with your chopsticks, quickly drag it a few inches through the hot oil two or three times. Release it; make sure it doesn't stick to the bottom or sides. Perform the **batter-drizzle technique** (see step 5). Do *not* turn the shrimp. After a total of about 2 minutes cooking time, the shrimp should be cooked on the inside, light-yellow on the outside, and crispy. Drain on paper towels, salt, and serve. Make sure to scoop up loose bits of batter from the oil with a spider or slotted spoon. As with the vegetable pieces, you can fry several shrimp at the same time once you get into the rhythm. Try to keep the oil at an even 350°F.

About Tempura

One great feature of a tempura dinner is that so much of it is done in advance. You will have all of your vegetables cut and ready to go. You will have your shrimp prepped. You will have two mixing bowls of your premeasured flour-potato-starch–baking soda mixture, and you will have already made the water–egg yolk mixture that gets poured into them. There's little to do at the last minute, except to start frying.

Now, some cooks are skittish about deep-frying—but with a deep-fry thermometer in hand, there's no need to be. Monitor that temperature on the thermometer, keep the temperature steady by turning the heat up or down, and you'll have no frying problems.

The first course is assorted tempura vegetables. They take more cooking time than shrimp do—and, accordingly, they cook at a lower temperature with a slightly heavier batter. This is great!—you just start the cooking at the lower temperature, 335°F, using the regular batter.

When it's time to move on to the shrimp, you raise the temperature to 350°F and you mix a new batter that has more water in it, making it a bit lighter. Simple!

Most tempura recipes omit key pieces of information that tempura chefs use in creating their lacy, airy, delicate creations. This one does not. One of the best tempura chefs I know in America—who cooks at Sachi, a superb Japanese restaurant/sushi bar on the Upper East Side of Manhattan—took me into his kitchen and showed me his secrets. So I'm sharing his **batter-drizzle technique** for creating a lacy coating, his shrimp-manipulating technique to ensure texture and straightness, and his shrimp-dragging technique to guarantee the right look. He also stressed, in the strongest terms, that making good tempura means scooping up loose batter bits out of the deep oil continually, obsessively!

When you're ready to serve your first pieces of transcendent tempura, the set-up of this party makes it a breeze. Place at least five pieces of tempura on a small platter, perhaps on absorbent paper, and pass it to your five seated guests (who, ideally, are either at your kitchen counter or at an in-kitchen table). They will have dipping sauce on the table as well as Japanese side dishes to munch on. Your job: just keep the tempura coming. Ideally, every 2 minutes or so there'll be 12 new pieces to offer. If your guests show even the slightest flagging of appetite—quick! Switch to shrimp!

Vegetables for Tempura

You'll want at least 4 different vegetables, but 6 or even 8 would be so much more fun! How many pieces should you prepare overall? For six people, you could get away with two dozen pieces—but for my kind of crowd, I'd be ready to go with 50 or 60.

Zucchini. Choose smallish zucchini. Cut off the ends, leaving a cylinder that's about 4 inches long. Stand the cylinder on one of its round bottoms (choose the wider of the two). Starting at the top and cutting downward toward the counter, cut off an $1/8$-inch slice of skin on two opposite sides and discard. Now cut the remaining block of zucchini into rectangles that are $1/4$ inch thick (they will have a strip of skin on the outside, and seeds in the center).

Sweet Potato. This is one of the great tempura candidates. Peel and cut the potato into $1/8$-inch rounds. You may substitute regular white potato, which will give you a french-fry taste.

Snow Pea. This makes delicious tempura, but there are two tricks you should know. First, dampen the pea pods with a little water so they'll take the initial flour dusting. Second, when the pea pod tempura comes out of the hot oil, cut it with a very sharp knife, on the diagonal, into 3 or 4 pieces, cutting swiftly and deftly to keep the coating on.

String Bean. Follow the directions for snow peas.

Japanese Eggplant. Cut the eggplant, skin on, into $1/4$-inch slices. Or try this much more interesting cut. Buy small Japanese eggplants that weigh about 3 ounces each. Cut off the stem end and halve the eggplant lengthwise. With the cut side of one half on the counter, make four cuts the long way, keeping the flesh attached at the stem end, to create a fan. Spread the fan out with your fingers. Repeat with the other eggplant half. When flouring and battering, keep spreading the fan out, making sure that all exposed flesh gets coated.

Onion. Slice an onion (preferably a sweet one) very thinly and toss into tangles. Pick up about 2 tablespoons of tangle, and proceed with flouring and battering. When the tangle hits the oil it will spread out a bit.

Enoki Mushroom. Treat these long, thin mushrooms like onion slices: just force 'em into a tangle. You'll be amazed at the depth of flavor.

Shiso. If you can find shiso leaves (sometimes called perilla)—a Japanese herb that tastes like minty pine—you can make one of the most exciting tempura items! Flour and batter lightly on *one* side, then pop into the oil.

Nori. Nori, the dried sheet of compressed seaweed used so often at the sushi bar, makes great tempura. Cut a strip that's about 1 by 2 inches. As with shiso, flour and batter on *one* side only.

Shrimp for Tempura

The ideal in shrimp tempura—which you can see in any good Japanese restaurant—is a straight shrimp, not at all curled. This takes a little work—and a few tips from Sachi.

First, buy shrimp that run about 24 to the pound. Then you can easily do the math: if you'd like to serve each guest 8 shrimp, you'll need about 2 pounds.

Peel off the shells, but leave the tail section intact. The trick is to remove a small piece of shell that looks like a thorn; it's right over the spot where the tail meets the shrimp flesh. Just pick it off. This little piece holds water, which is not good for the frying. Similarly, the ends of the tail hold water. Lay the shrimp on the counter, and with a sharp knife, diagonally cut off the bottom $1/8$ inch of the tail; you will likely see water being expelled as you do.

Place the shrimp on its side on the cutting board, with the "back" of the shrimp to your right (if you're a righty!). With one hand, hold the flat side of the blade of a chef's knife along the vein side of the shrimp; working with your other hand, push the shrimp up against the blade, lining it up against the blade and straightening the shrimp in the process. Make a slit along the vein side of the shrimp, and use the knife to pick out the vein.

Time to enforce the straightening. Pick up the shrimp, and place it de-veined-side down on the cutting board. With the knife, make four even gashes on the underside of the shrimp (where the legs were); each gash should be about $3/8$ inch thick. Now turn the shrimp over, so the de-veined side is on top. Use the first two fingers of both hands to press firmly on the tail end, until you hear a little crack. Move your fingers up the shrimp and crack it again. Crack it two more times, moving toward the head end of the shrimp. Now wrap your fingers around the shrimp, which is still de-veined side up on the board, squeezing hard from both sides toward the center. You will end up with a long, straight, slightly compressed strip of shrimp. It is now ready for flouring and battering.

Salted Seaweed Salad with Lemon and Freshly Grated Ginger

· · • ● • · ·

Seaweed is a wonderful side dish in Japanese meal—slight, delicate, usually with the subtlest taste of the sea. But there are many kinds of seaweed out there. For this salad, I strongly urge you to acquire one remarkably springy, frilly, fresh-tasting green seaweed imported from Japan.

makes 6 servings

1 (500–gram) bag salted tosaka ao, or about 3 very loosely packed cups of another seaweed (see Cook's Note)

1 tablespoon rice wine vinegar

2 teaspoons fresh lemon juice

1/2 teaspoon kosher salt

1 teaspoon sugar

1/2 teaspoon finely grated fresh ginger

1 1/2 teaspoons Japanese soy sauce

4 teaspoons Japanese or Chinese sesame oil

1 tablespoon sesame seeds, toasted until golden brown in a hot skillet

1. Rinse the seaweed in a large bowl in three or four changes of cold water, swishing it around to release the salt. Cover with water and set it aside to soak for 10 minutes. Drain, and then thoroughly squeeze the seaweed between clean kitchen towels to remove all excess moisture. Return to a dry mixing bowl.

2. Prepare the dressing: Whisk the vinegar, lemon juice, salt, and sugar together in a bowl until the crystals dissolve. Add the ginger, soy sauce, and sesame oil, whisking to incorporate.

3. When ready to serve, toss the seaweed with most of the dressing and half of the sesame seeds. Taste and add more dressing to suit your taste. Divide among six small salad bowls, sprinkle each portion of seaweed with the remaining sesame seeds, and serve immediately.

> COOK'S NOTE: *I am crazy about green (ao) tosaka seaweed, prepared by the Kaneryo company, exported from Tokyo by the Central Trading Co. It is heavily salted, packed in a plastic bag, and sent to the U.S. frozen. I buy mine at the great Japanese store Katagiri in New York City, where it's on the refrigerator shelf already defrosted* **(see Where To Find It, page 78)**. *If you buy it, you can store it, defrosted, in your refrigerator for a couple of weeks.*

Quick and Spicy Cucumber Pickle

· · • · · ·

makes 6 servings

4 medium Kirby cucumbers (each about 4 to 5 inches long), washed and cut into ⅛-inch rounds

1 ½ tablespoons kosher salt

¾ cup rice wine vinegar

2 generous tablespoons dried bonito flakes

2 ¼ teaspoons sugar

2 scallions, sliced very thinly on the bias

Hot Japanese chile-sesame oil

1. Place the cucumbers in a mixing bowl and sprinkle with the salt, tossing well to combine. Gently massage the salt into the cucumbers for about 1 minute and set aside.

2. Combine the vinegar, bonito flakes, and sugar in a small saucepan and bring just to a simmer over medium-high heat, stirring to dissolve the sugar. Cool the mixture quickly by placing the pan in a bowl filled with ice. Set aside.

3. Transfer the cucumbers to a small glass or ceramic dish, discarding any liquid left behind in the bowl. Pour the vinegar mixture over the cucumbers and marinate them in the refrigerator for at least 2 hours, turning the pieces over once or twice.

4. To serve, lift the cucumbers from the marinade, briefly shaking the slices to remove any excess liquid. Place the cucumbers on small serving plates, overlapping the slices in an attractive pattern (a small circle works nicely). Top the cucumbers with a bit of sliced scallion and a light drizzle of chile-sesame oil.

Tomato and Watercress Salad with Deep-Fried Tofu, Miso Dressing, and Black Sesame Seeds

· · • · ·

makes 6 servings

2 pints grape tomatoes, halved

Scant 5 cups of watercress (measured after thick stems are removed)

6 ounces deep-fried tofu, cut into 1/3 x 3/4-inch rectangles (see Cook's Note)

1 tablespoon plus 1 teaspoon black sesame seeds

3/4 cup Miso Dressing, or more (page 72)

Combine the tomatoes, watercress, tofu, and 1 tablespoon black sesame seeds in a large mixing bowl. Add the Miso Dressing, tossing thoroughly to coat. Taste and add a bit more dressing if desired. Distribute the salad evenly among six small plates and sprinkle each with the remaining black sesame seeds. Serve immediately.

> COOK'S NOTE: *Deep-fried tofu (sometimes labeled fried tofu) is available in Japanese markets; it comes in two styles: thick cakes and thin sheets. You want the thick cake (called atsu-age or nama-age in Japanese), usually sold in a 12-ounce brick in the refrigerated section. Many Japanese chefs prepare the tofu by soaking it quickly in boiling water (just a few seconds to remove excess oil), and then blotting it dry with paper towels. I find this step unnecessary, especially for this salad.*

Miso Dressing

· · · ● · · ·

makes 1 1/4 cups

3 tablespoons yellow miso paste (*shinshu-miso*; see **Where to Find It, page 78**)

3/4 teaspoon finely grated ginger

1 tablespoon soy sauce

1 tablespoon sugar

Pinch of cayenne

1 1/2 tablespoons rice wine vinegar

Generous 1/2 cup vegetable oil

1 teaspoon Japanese or Chinese sesame oil

Scant 1/2 cup water

Combine all of the ingredients in a blender jar and process for 30 seconds. The dressing can be made up to 1 week in advance and stored, tightly covered, in the refrigerator. If the mixture has separated slightly, process briefly before using.

Ponzu Dipping Sauce

· · · ● · · ·

makes 1 3/4 cups

6 tablespoons mirin

1/8 teaspoon kosher salt

6 tablespoons soy sauce

6 tablespoons rice wine vinegar

1/4 cup fresh lemon juice

Finely grated zest of 1 lime

2 tablespoons fresh lime juice

1/4 cup Dashi (page 63)

1. Place the mirin in a small saucepan over medium-high heat and reduce to 3 tablespoons. Set aside to cool slightly, about 10 minutes.

2. When the mirin has cooled, whisk in the remaining ingredients until the salt is dissolved. Let the mixture sit for at least 2 hours to allow time for the lime zest to flavor the sauce. Strain the mixture through a fine mesh sieve before serving.

Sesame-Chile Dipping Sauce

• • • ● • • •

makes 1 1/2 cups

2 tablespoons plus 2 teaspoons sugar

1/2 cup rice wine vinegar

2 tablespoons plus 2 teaspoons chile-bean paste (see Cook's Note)

2 teaspoons finely grated ginger

1/2 cup Dashi (page 63)

1/4 cup soy sauce

4 teaspoons Japanese or Chinese sesame oil

4 teaspoons hot Japanese chile-sesame oil

1. Whisk the sugar into the vinegar in a small bowl until dissolved.

2. Working over the bowl, push the chile-bean paste through a fine mesh strainer to remove the rough solids. Collect any paste that has caught on the underside of the strainer and whisk it into the bowl. Whisk in the remaining ingredients. You may make this sauce in advance, but whisk again before serving.

> COOK'S NOTE: *Chile-bean paste is a Chinese specialty that works wonderfully well in this dipping sauce. My favorite brand is Lee Kum Kee; other brands I've used are Lan Chi and Oriental Mascot. Lee Kum Kee is widely distributed. Check the ethnic foods section of grocery stores. Or,* **see Where to Find It, page 78**.

Green Tea Ice Cream

. . • ● • . .

Green tea ice cream, called *maccha* ice cream in Japan, takes its name from the expensive green tea powder used in traditional tea ceremonies. But I find that bags of green tea from a large commercial producer also give you an enormous green tea flavor—if you use enough tea bags. In fact, the following recipe makes the best green tea ice cream I've ever tasted.

You need to start this the day before your party.

makes 1 quart

> **2 cups half-and-half**
> **1 cup heavy cream**
> **1 cup sugar**
> **⅛ teaspoon salt**
> **½ teaspoon vanilla extract**
> **20 green tea bags (see Cook's Note)**

1. Combine the half-and-half and the heavy cream in a medium saucepan and bring just to a simmer over medium-high heat, taking care to prevent the liquids from boiling over.

2. Turn off the heat and immediately add the sugar and salt, stirring briefly to dissolve. Stir in the vanilla and the tea bags and let the mixture cool to room temperature, occasionally stirring and gently pressing on the tea bags to help extract their flavors. When cooled, store the mixture (including the tea bags), tightly covered, in the refrigerator overnight.

3. The following day, pass the mixture through a sieve set over a bowl, gently pushing on the tea bags to release their liquid. Tear open one of the spent teabags; remove ¼ teaspoon of loose tea leaves, and stir them into the ice cream base. Freeze in an ice cream maker according to the manufacturer's instructions.

> COOK'S NOTE: *The tea I used to make this recipe was Celestial Seasonings green tea, available in most supermarkets.*

You've Got Options

There's plenty to eat at this meal, so I say it's not absolutely necessary to serve rice. However, rice is a Japanese tradition with tempura—and it would be a lovely diversion for your guests as they eagerly await their next little bits of deep-fried heaven.

Happily, there is one super-easy way to take care of your rice needs at this party: cook the rice in an electric rice cooker! These gadgets are really handy, really easy, and really do a great job. You just place rice in the chamber (up to a measured line on the side), along with water (again, up to a measured line on the side). Press a button, and, 40 minutes later, your rice is ready to place in individual bowls for serving to your guests. Best of all, the cooker holds your rice perfectly for hours, so you can keep going back to it for seconds and thirds. There is one rice cooker, made in Japan and widely available here, that I prefer over all the others I've tried: the Zojirushi Model #NS-JCC10.

I prefer Tamaki Gold rice, a California premium short-grain rice produced by the Williams Rice Milling Company in Williams, California. It cooks up slightly sticky, with amazingly luminous, chewy pearls of rice. If you'd like to gild the lily, you can top the rice with something I call "Japanese sprinkles"—*furikake,* which is a crunchy assortment of seaweed bits, often with sesame seeds and bits of dried fish added. Absolutely delicious! A brand I like is the Urashima Furikake—which, along with the Tamaki Gold rice, is available at Katagiri **(see Where to Find It, page 78).**

Table Dressing

At your table, define each guest's place with a tray—wood, lacquerware, bamboo, or rattan. Or use placemats, preferably ones made of natural materials. An underlying cloth is optional.

Even such humble table accoutrements as chopstick rests (called *hashioki*) can be enchanting on the traditional Japanese table. Try to find polished river stones, available by the bagful, to use as chopstick rests. Chopsticks, called *hashi* in Japanese, can be tasteful and colorful.

For the miso soup, it would be great to use the lidded soup bowl called a *wan*; I prefer it in lacquerware. Alongside, you'll need a deep soup spoon, which can be made from the same material.

For the tempura, rectangular plates would be sensational, perhaps made of ceramic. I don't know if it's due to the recent proliferation of sushi bars in this country, but Americans have definitely discovered the uncommon beauty and geometric appeal of Japanese-inspired ceramics. Food looks great on them! Import stores are a good source, but local art cooperatives often have stunning and unique examples in a variety of price ranges. (I especially keep a lookout for *raku*, the distinctive crackle-finish pottery that seems to depend as much on chance as on the artist's skill.)

Keep this in mind when you're shopping: most everyday sets of sakeware and dinnerware come in odd numbers! Some say it's a direct influence of Shinto principles: perfection should be attempted only by the gods, and humans striving to achieve that state—as evidenced by even numbers—only attract the gods' wrath.

Seasonality informs the Japanese table. You should be mindful of that when selecting colors, materials, and floral arrangements for your party. Spring/summer? Cherry blossoms, forsythia, Japanese iris, greens and blues. Fall/winter? Branches of Japanese maple, boughs of white pine or cedar, maybe even in a cast iron or stoneware teapot with three or five well-chosen blooms.

A whimsical touch at each guest's place would be an origami bird or perhaps a Japanese fan. And don't forget to pass out the hot towels at the beginning of the meal! I recommend passing them a second time as well, as you pass from vegetable tempura to shrimp tempura, keeping fingers grease-free.

A lot of glassware and tableware are required for this party. Here's a checklist.

- **48 white wine glasses for the tasting**
  (*or 6 glasses for each sake you will pour*)
- **6 sake cups** (*sake masu*)
- **6 miso bowls with lids** (*wan*)
- **18 small plates for the salads**

- **12 small bowls for the dipping sauces**
- **Platters for serving tempura**
- **6 small plates for the tempura**
- **6 small bowls for the ice cream**

Set Dressing

Japanese homes are very austere by Western standards, so "clutter control" should be your watchword. Tuck away those things that aren't servicing the party's theme or contributing to your guests' comfort and enjoyment.

A great touch would be to use bamboo fencing or shoji screens, iconic of Japanese culture, to hide anything that distracts from the serene, Eastern aesthetic you're trying to emulate. A less expensive option would be common matchstick bamboo roll-up blinds to establish the illusion of a private Japanese dining room. Or hang simple curtains, made with cloth printed with an Oriental motif, and suspended from bamboo rods.

In a Japanese home, tatami mats (woven floor mats with cloth-bound edges), would define the dining space. Tatami mats come in a standard size, 3x6 feet. One mat on the floor, somewhere in the kitchen/dining area, would get the point across beautifully. Shoji lamps, which work especially well in corners, or rice-paper globes slipped over existing fixtures, could provide light and cultural exclamation points.

It would also be fun, if possible, to leave out on countertops a few "cocktail table" books on Japanese arts—such as the great art of woodblock printing (look for the name Hiroshige). These might spark lively conversation, especially after eight sakes!

Traditional Japanese garden elements could be part of the party's landscape as well. The simplest touch would be potted, miniature Japanese trees—bonsai, cherry, or Japanese maple.

Where to Find It

Farm-2-Market
P.O. Box 124
Trout Town Rd.
Roscoe, NY 12776
800.663.4326 (toll free)
607.498.5275 (fax)
www.farm-2-market.com
Great source for outstanding
shrimp and seafood.

Wine of Japan Import, Inc.
235 West Parkway
Pompton Plains, NJ 07444
973.835.8585 (tel)
973.835.9097 (fax)
www.wineofjapan.com
Excellent importer of Japanese
sake, and disseminator of sake
information.

Kikumasamune
www.kikumasamune.com
Website provides information on
local availability of their sakes
around the country.

Kiku-Masamune Sake Brewing Co., Ltd.
431 Crocker St.
Los Angeles, CA 90013
213.626.9458 (tel)
213.626.5130 (fax)
Importers of Taru Sake; call for
availability.

www.sake.nu
A website devoted to sake. If
your local laws allow, you may
be able to buy sake from it.

True Sake
560 Hayes St.
San Francisco, CA 94102
415.355.9555 (tel)
www.truesake.com
Great retail store that stocks
over a hundred sakes.

Japan Prestige Sake
(Main Office)
446 E. Second St.
Los Angeles, CA 90012
213.625.1621 (tel)
213.625.1623 (fax)
This importer brings over 150
sakes to the U.S., and in my
experience, is an excellent
source of information.

Katagiri & Co.
224 East 59th St.
New York, NY 10022
212.755.3566 (tel)
212.752.4197 (fax)
www.katagiri.com
Fabulous Japanese grocery, with
a wide selection of products
from the mundane to the eso-
teric. Excellent source for tosaka
seaweed and *shinshu-miso*.

I-Clipse, Inc.
dba Pacific Rim Gourmet
4905 Morena Blvd.,
Suite 1313
San Diego, CA 92117
800.910.WOKS (toll free)
www.pacificrim-gourmet.com
A fine online source for Asian
ingredients.

Mrs. Lin's Kitchen
2415 San Ramon Valley Blvd.,
#4-188
San Ramon, CA 94583
925.830.9053 (tel)
925.830.9055 (fax)
www.mrslinskitchen.com
An online emporium of sake
sets, Asian tableware, cookware,
groceries, and more.

Sabi
8606 Melrose Ave.
Los Angeles, CA 90069
310.659.9838 (tel)
310.659.9839 (fax)
www.sabistyle.com
A store for the upscale Asian-
influenced Western home,
carrying lacquerware, ceramic
dinnerware, chopsticks, bowls,
sakeware, and more.

Oriental Furniture
810 Worcester Rd.
Natick, MA 01760
800.978.2100 (toll free)
www.orientalfurniture.com
Carries a large selection of
shoji screens, shoji lamps, art,
and furniture.

Japanese Style, Inc.
16159 320th St.
New Prague, MN 56071
877.226.4387 (toll free)
952.758.1922 (fax)
www.japanesegifts.com
A specialty purveyor of Japanese
gifts, clothing, garden-related
products, dishes, and party
supplies.

Tunisia for Twelve
A Grand Couscous Party

A Party for 12

The Menu

Coupe de Figue with Sparkling Wine

Maghreb Olives

Deep-Fried Brik with Tuna, Capers, and Egg

Spicy Couscous with Homemade Lamb Sausage,
Vegetables, Chick Peas, and Mint

Ras el Hanout

Harissa

Medjool Date and Almond Wands with Rosewater

Couscous—a steaming plate of light, fluffy pellets of buttered pasta, paired with warmly flavored stews of meat and vegetables, with or without fruits, with ample condiments on the side—is simply great party food. The very muchness of it all is cause for celebration! But many people in the U.S. who prepare couscous for their families, or for a crowd, think of one nation only when dreaming of a couscous dinner: Morocco. Undoubtedly, it was Paula Wolfert, food goddess and author of *Couscous and Other Good Food from Morocco*, who, with this fabulous book, created the knee-jerk Moroccan couscous reaction here. Well, no one can deny the wonderfulness of Moroccan couscous—but there are other options, all along the fascinating northwest coast of Africa, an area known as the Maghreb.

The French, for example—who, as occupiers, know a thing or two about the region—are ga-ga for couscous at the many restaurants in Paris devoted to this dish. There, however, you are more likely to find Algerian-style couscous than

Moroccan-style: spicier, less sweet, with the almost automatic addition of the great lamb sausage called merguez. In Tunisia, the small country with the most easterly position on the coast of the Big Maghreb Three (Morocco, Algeria, Tunisia), merguez sausage is just as indigenous. Here, the dish is called "kouski," and it gets richer, and even spicier, with the addition of Tunisia's fiery chile paste, harissa.

To much of the Western world, Tunisia is a bit of an enigma; our impressions of it are muddled with those of Egypt, Libya, and Algeria, with a few scenes from the movie *Casablanca* thrown in. Indeed, Tunisia, on the southwest shore of the Mediterranean basin, is a conflation of many cultures: Carthaginian (of course; Tunisia was ancient Carthage), Roman, Phoenician, Turkish, Moorish, Berber, Italian, and French.

But finding some clarity is just one exciting, exotic, spicy party away.

The Plan

This is a good party for when you have lots of time the day before. On that day, you begin by making harissa and ras el hanout. Then you make the vegetable stew for the couscous, and you blend the mixture for the lamb sausage. On the day of the party, your labors will be lighter.

The party itself is also an easy one. The first course—stuffed, deep-fried pastry triangles with runny egg inside—is a stand-up, pass-around affair. After that, it's to the table—where each diner will be served a steaming bowl of buttered couscous, spicy vegetables, and rich lamb sausage, with communal oils and condiments at hand. Extra helpings of the stew and merguez will sit on the table, possibly in the covered, conical pots known as tagines. More grains of couscous may be required as well, late in the meal, in which case you'll make it fresh, and hot, in 5 minutes.

The Ingredient

This particular party derives its strength from a subtle gathering of elements, a true harmony, it is hoped, of aromas and flavors. The element that will stand out for most people, however, is merguez, the reddish, juicy lamb sausage that rides atop the couscous. The French have developed a passion for this sausage, and it is quite common all over France. Because of that, people in the U.S. who sell French comestibles sell merguez as well. You can buy a very good merguez from D'Artagnan, in New Jersey **(see Where to Find It, page 101)**.

A better idea is to make your own spectacular merguez. Fear not: I'm not asking you to get a sausage stuffer and put this merguez in casings. The mixture itself is delicious, and merely forming it into sausage-like shapes, without casings, and sautéing it until it's crunchy and juicy, is guaranteed to draw the oohs and ahs.

Beverage Time

I have nothing but respect for our Muslim brethren who, following the teachings of Mohammed, shun alcohol. But I also have nothing but understanding for the many Muslims in North Africa who choose to drink wine. After all, Tunisia was a French protectorate from 1881 until 1956, and while Arabic is the official language, French is widely spoken. With influence from La Belle France, there is, in fact, a good deal of wine produced in Tunisia, Morocco, and Algeria. So the high spirits offered at this party are breaking no cultural taboos. And speaking of France—and considering the difficulty of finding a great little Tunisian red in the U.S.—it seems altogether appropriate to kick off this revel with some of the sparkling wine that often makes its way down to the north coast of Africa.

The other spirit widely produced in Tunisia is *boukha*, a kind of eau-de-vie made from figs. I have not been able to locate this in the U.S.—but I did follow the Franco-Tunisian spirit, and created a fig-and-wine cocktail to kick off this party.

If any of your guests are thinking anti-fig thoughts, the sparkling wine could be served on its own. With or without the fig additions, sparkling wine could be the beverage of choice for the duration of the meal; it does extremely well with light-ish foods that are a little spicy, a perfect description of the main couscous dish. It's also superb with things that are deep-fried, like the opening Brik.

On the other hand, after the cocktail hour, and after the Brik, it might be fun to switch to red wine, for which there is a Tunisian tradition. Something purple and fruity, not tannic and bitter, will merge seamlessly with the spicy vegetables of the main course. Very young Beaujolais is a possibility, as is the Californian wine known as Gamay Beaujolais (Beringer makes a "Nouveau" version every year that's quite good, and perfect drinking throughout the winter and spring after the harvest). "Novello" wines from Italy are increasingly popular; Torre di Luna and Mionetto are two of my favorites. There are good wines like these coming out of Spain now, some of them in the Somontano denominacion. And you can always rely on young, inexpensive Shiraz from Australia to be a food-matching wonder. Don't spend a lot on this (for there are much more expensive, and much less appropriate, Aussie Shirazes available). A few of my favorite low-cost ones are Rosemount, Deakins Estate, and Banrock Station.

The Recipes

Coupe de Figue with Sparkling Wine

● ● ● ● ● ● ●

This delicious cocktail is made with dried figs. Just be sure to buy good ones, though—which is to say, dried figs that are soft and sweet. For the sparkling wine, buying the best is not a necessity. There are good sparkling wines from France other than Champagne that cost much less—as well as good and inexpensive ones from Italy, Germany, the U.S., and Australia. Probably the best overall choice—price and quality factored in—is cava from Spain; a brand called Cristallino is a great value. This cocktail will give you only a little fizz, so don't look for aggressive bubbles in the finished product.

makes 12 cocktails

> **1 pound dried figs, tough tufts snipped off**
> **3 bottles (750 ml each) sparkling wine**
> **4 (1 x 3-inch) strips of lemon zest**
> **12 slices of fresh fig, if in season**

1. Chop the dried figs coarsely.

2. Working in batches, process the figs in a food processor, along with 8 cups of sparkling wine, until the figs are finely minced. Stopper tightly the sparkling wine that remains, and hold it in the refrigerator.

3. Pour the fig mixture into a pitcher. Add the lemon zest and stir well with a wooden spoon. Cover with plastic wrap and hold in the refrigerator for about 24 hours.

4. When ready to prepare the cocktails, strain the fig mixture into another pitcher, pressing down on the solids in the strainer with a wooden spoon. Discard the solids; you will have about 6 cups of fig wine.

5. Pour 4 ounces of fig wine into a small wine glass. Top with just a few drops of reserved sparkling wine, and whip the mixture until it froths a little. Garnish with a fresh fig slice, if possible, and serve immediately. Repeat until a dozen drinks are made.

Maghreb Olives

• • ● • •

North Africa is famous for its black, wrinkled, oil-cured olives, with a taste almost reminiscent of licorice or prunes. If you have an excellent batch of olives in that style—such as the least bitter oil-cured olives I've ever tasted, Sun-Dried Mission Olives with Olive Oil, California Harvest, from Grapevine Trading Co. **(see Where to Find It, page 101)**—you don't necessarily need to do anything to them. But a little marinade with some typical flavors of the Maghreb will make them even livelier. Lay out the olives in bowls (with accompanying dishes for pits) all around the party venue.

serves 12

> **2 pounds black oil-cured olives**
> **1 to 3 teaspoons crushed red pepper**
> **1 to 3 teaspoons Ras el Hanout (page 93)**
> **¼ cup fruity olive oil**

Combine the olives with the crushed red pepper and Ras el Hanout, mixing well. (It's your choice between a light amount and a heavy amount.) Toss with the olive oil. Hold or serve.

Deep-Fried Brik with Tuna, Capers, and Egg

. . ● . . .

Brik, or brek, is Tunisia's classic snack, and a delicious way to kick off your party. If you're familiar with Indian samosas, you have the basic idea: a stuffed, deep-fried, savory pastry. But there are great differences from samosa. In Tunisia, they use an extremely thin pastry called *malsouqua*; it is made by dabbing a wet dough on the hot underside of what looks like a gigantic wok. Only the ghost-like film that adheres becomes the pastry! It is not available in the U.S. I use my favorite brand of egg roll skins, which yield remarkably moist, bubbly, crispy results: Golden Dragon, manufactured by Nanka Seimen in Los Angeles, California, and available online from I-Clipse (see **Where to Find It, page 101**).

As for the filling, you'll find that the flavors of North Africa are more subdued than the flavors of India; this particular stuffing, with its tuna, capers, and grated cheese, shows a distinct Mediterranean flair. Most exciting, and most Tunisian, of all, is a whole, raw egg slipped inside each brik; when you fry the pastry just right, you have a runny yolk inside moistening the filling. It's great! To emphasize the egg's presence at the center of the brik, I like to cut the finished briks in half, which exposes the runny yolk. They must be quickly turned yolk side up, and served.

One way to serve them is to simply pass them around by hand, immediately after you've cut them. But I can think of a more amusing way. Acquire one of those quaint English toast holders, in which a number of triangles of toasted bread snuggle in the slots—and fill the slots with cut briks instead! Your guests will love your quirky ingenuity.

makes 48 brik halves

4 (6-ounce) cans good-quality Mediterranean tuna in olive oil

1 ¾ cups minced onion

¾ cup chopped cilantro leaves

¾ cup small capers, rinsed and drained

¾ cup freshly grated Parmigiano-Reggiano or Grana Padano

¾ teaspoon freshly ground black pepper

¼ cup unsalted butter, at room temperature

¼ cup extra-virgin olive oil

2 teaspoons mild Louisiana hot sauce, plus additional as needed

Kosher salt

24 Chinese square egg roll wrappers (preferably Golden Dragon,
measuring 6 ¾ x 6 ¾ inches)

24 medium eggs

Olive oil, for frying

Harissa Table Sauce (page 95)

1. Mash the tuna with a fork in a large bowl and combine well with the onion, cilantro, capers, cheese, pepper, butter, olive oil, and hot sauce. Add salt.

2. Lay a square egg roll wrapper on the counter. Bring together two opposite corners of the square to form a triangle. Return the corners to their original positions, leaving behind a crease at the center of the square to serve as a guideline. On the triangular area just below the crease, which is half of the egg roll skin, center 3 tablespoons of the tuna filling. Make a shallow well to accommodate a raw broken egg, keeping the filling half an inch from the perimeter of the wrapper. Carefully break an egg into the well, and top with hot sauce. Using the egg white that has probably leaked a bit from your well, smear a thin layer along the outer ½ inch of the wrapper. Enclose the filling by bringing the two opposite corners to meet once again, creating a triangle. Seal the edges, working out the air pockets as you go. Set aside without flipping over. Repeat with the remaining wrappers.

3. Pour ½ inch olive oil into two large skillets and heat the oil to 360°F. Working in batches, carefully place the pastries in the oil and fry them until golden brown and crispy, about 1 minute per side (the egg yolk should still be runny). Drain the pastries briefly on paper towels, cut them in half with a very sharp, serrated knife, and immediately turn them cut side up. Top each half with a bit of Harissa Table Sauce. Pass the pastries by hand, or in English toast holders.

Spicy Couscous with Homemade Lamb Sausage, Vegetables, Chick Peas, and Mint

· · · · · ·

About Couscous

There's lots of confusion over the word "couscous." For starters, people often think it's a type of grain; it's really just a tiny type of pasta, sometimes made from semolina, sometimes made from other grains (like barley). Then comes the real confusion: the word "couscous" can refer either to the pasta itself or to the big-deal dish of pasta, stew, and condiments that is so beloved in the Maghreb and in Parisian couscous restaurants.

Now, you could go to considerable trouble to serve that pasta to your guests—and I'm all for trouble when it's warranted. You could make your own semolina pasta; you could also buy semolina pasta and go through a sequence of "wetting, drying, raking, aerating," as Paula Wolfert calls it, to achieve, theoretically at least, the perfect texture. Then, you could steam your couscous in a special pot called a *couscousiere*, over the fragrant vegetable stew you'll be serving. This drives a little more flavor into the couscous. But there's a problem; the theories, for me, never yield enough real-world results for me to commit myself, especially for a large party, to the old-fashioned way of doing things. Paula, forgive me, but I like to cook the stew in one vessel, sizzle the merguez in another, and in a third vessel steam up in 5 minutes (5 *minutes!* think of it!) the light and lovely, boxed, precooked semolina couscous so widely available today.

This dish overflows with dining delights: ten types of vegetables are involved, excellent homemade lamb sausage, bright-red homemade harissa to fire things up, fresh mint, and, if desired, a contribution from Morocco: a drizzle of argan oil, an ancient condiment with a wildly funky flavor made from the argan nut, found only in Berber territory in the Atlas Mountains. Oh yes, and there's couscous, too (the pasta).

You start this the day before.

½ cup extra-virgin olive oil

2 medium onions, finely chopped

2 heads garlic, cloves thinly sliced

6 tablespoons Ras el Hanout (page 93)

6 tablespoons Harissa (page 94)

3 tablespoons kosher salt, plus additional as needed

1 ½ teaspoons Aleppo pepper (**see Where to Find It, page 101,** or substitute ¼ teaspoon cayenne and 1 ¼ teaspoon sweet paprika)

4 tablespoons tomato paste

12 cups chicken broth

10 small potatoes (about ¾ pound), halved

2 large eggplants, stemmed and cut into 1-inch cubes

7 medium carrots, peeled and cut into 2-inch lengths

4 medium turnips, peeled and each cut into 8 wedges

1 large celery root, peeled and cut into pieces about the size of the wedged turnips

1 pound green beans, trimmed

3 medium zucchini, halved lengthwise and cut into 2-inch lengths

4 cups cooked and drained chick peas (or canned ones)

8 tablespoons (1 stick) unsalted butter

6 pounds Homemade Lamb Sausages (page 96, or store-bought merguez sausages)

½ cup coarsely chopped mint leaves

18 cups hot steamed couscous (see Cook's Note)

Harissa Table Sauce (page 95), for serving

Moroccan argan oil for drizzling, optional (**see Where to Find It, page 101**)

1. Warm ¼ cup of the oil in each of two large stockpots over medium-high heat. Divide the onions and 1 head of the sliced garlic between the two pots. Reduce the heat to medium and cook, stirring occasionally, until the onions and garlic are just golden at the edges. Divide the Ras el Hanout, Harissa, salt, Aleppo pepper, and tomato paste between the pots. Add a splash of broth to each, briefly whisking to dissolve the tomato paste, and then divide the remaining broth between the pots. Bring to a boil over high heat, reduce the heat to medium, and allow the broth to simmer gently for 15 minutes.

2. Divide the potatoes, eggplants, carrots, turnips, and celery root between the pots; return them to a simmer and cook, stirring occasionally, for 20 minutes. Divide the green beans, zucchini, and chick peas between the pots, and simmer, partially covered and occasionally stirring, until all the vegetables are tender, about 20 minutes more.

3. Just before the vegetables are done, melt the butter in a large skillet over medium-high heat and add the remaining 1 head of sliced garlic. Cook, stirring occasionally, until golden at the edges. When the vegetables in the pots are tender, divide the garlic and butter between the two pots, stir well to combine, and taste for salt. Let cool, then cover and refrigerate overnight.

4. The next day, when ready to serve, bring the vegetables back to a simmer and sauté the merguez, page 96.

5. To serve, mound hot vegetables in the center of a wide, shallow soup bowl. Top the vegetables with 3 merguez sausages, and sprinkle with chopped mint. Surround the vegetables with 1 1/2 cups hot couscous in a fluffy ring. Repeat until 12 bowls are made. Serve immediately. Bring extra vegetables with sauce to the table, topped with extra merguez. Serve bowls of HarissaTable Sauce. Keep a bottle of Moroccan argan oil on the table for drizzling, if desired.

> COOK'S NOTE: *I use a very widely distributed brand of tiny semolina couscous called "Near East, Original Plain." You'll need 4 (10-ounce) boxes for this recipe. Simply follow the instructions on the box by cooking the grains with water, salt, and butter.*
>
> *Be prepared should your guests request more couscous; it takes only 5 minutes to cook once the water boils. So, pre-boil the water! For another 10 cups of steamed couscous, you would have ready a pot of 4 cups water, 1 teaspoon salt, 2 tablespoons butter, and 2 boxes of couscous. Keep the water just below the boiling point as the main course begins, then bring to a boil when you see you need more couscous. A new, steaming platter is just minutes away.*

Ras el Hanout

· · · ● · ·

The famous spice blend of Morocco—the name of which means something like "top of the shop"—is not a Tunisian ingredient, but I couldn't resist bolstering the rich and spicy Tunisian flavors of the couscous with a little Moroccan TLC. The best place to buy ras el hanout is in an open street market in Morocco, where startling things are blended together—including substances like Spanish fly, thought to be aphrodisiacal (great for parties)! You can buy ras el hanout in the U.S., too (minus the aphrodisiacs), notably from Kalustyan's, the formidable New York spice purveyor **(see Where to Find It, page 101)**. But no two ras el hanout blends are ever the same. I formulated the following one, heavy on aromatic spices, for use in the couscous vegetables in this party. You'll notice a similarity between these ingredients and the spices of Indian food—but in Morocco, and the Maghreb in general, spicing is subtler and less bold than spicing in India.

makes about ¾ cup

3 tablespoons ground cinnamon

2 tablespoons ground coriander seed

1 tablespoon ground anise seed

1 tablespoon ground fennel seed

1 tablespoon ground cumin

1 tablespoon ground black pepper

1 ½ teaspoons ground allspice

1 ½ teaspoons ground green cardamom

1 ½ teaspoons ground nutmeg

1 ½ teaspoons ground ginger

¼ teaspoon ground cloves

Combine all the ingredients in a mixing bowl. Store in an airtight container for up to 6 months.

Harissa

· · ● · · ·

It was probably the Tunisians who first created harissa, a fiery, wonderfully fragrant paste made from dried chiles and, most typically, coriander seeds and caraway. *Harasa,* the Arabic word meaning "to grind," is the likely source of harissa's name; the paste is traditionally made in a mortar and pestle. I have found an easier way to make harissa, which includes soaking and a go-round in the food processor. The result, though a little chunkier, is brighter in color and fresher tasting than most mortar-made harissas.

makes 1 1/2 cups

8 ounces dried baklouti chiles (see Cook's Note)

6 tablespoons coriander seeds

3 tablespoons caraway seeds

4 teaspoons kosher salt

8 garlic cloves

8 tablespoons olive oil

1. Bring about 2 cups of water to a simmer.

2. Remove stems and seeds from the chiles. Place the chiles in a bowl and cover with the hot water. Soak for 10 minutes. Strain the chiles, reserving the soaking water. Place the chiles in the work bowl of a food processor.

3. Meanwhile, spoon the coriander seeds, caraway seeds, and salt into a large mortar. Grind with a pestle for a few minutes, or use a spice grinder, until the seeds are a fine powder. Transfer the spice mixture to a food processor. Add the garlic, olive oil, and 5 tablespoons of the reserved chile-soaking water. (Reserve the remaining water for Harissa Table Sauce, page 95.) Process until the mixture is a mostly smooth paste, about 2 minutes.

> COOK'S NOTE: *Dried Tunisian baklouti chiles—red, medium-wide, and a few inches long—are the traditional chiles for harissa. Their taste is perfect for this dish. You can obtain them from Kalustyan's* **(see Where to Find It, page 101)**.
>
> *You can also substitute any flavorful, medium-hot, medium-sized dried red chile that you can find (except chipotles).*

Harissa Table Sauce

· · ● · ·

This thinner version of harissa is ideal for guests to drizzle on their couscous.

makes about 2 cups

12 tablespoons Harissa (page 94)
¾ cup chile-soaking water (reserved from Harissa)
2 tablespoons olive oil
2 tablespoons white wine vinegar
Kosher salt

1. Combine ingredients thoroughly.

2. For serving, transfer to a cruet or small bowl.

Homemade Lamb Sausages

• • ● • •

(Merguez)

These spicy links are best started the day before cooking.

makes about 50 sausages

6 pounds fatty ground lamb (see Cook's Note)
10 large cloves garlic, very finely minced
3 tablespoons kosher salt
1 teaspoon cayenne
1 tablespoon freshly ground black pepper
5 tablespoons Harissa (page 94)
½ cup finely chopped flat-leaf parsley
Olive oil, for frying

1. Thoroughly combine all of the ingredients, except the olive oil, in a large mixing bowl. Cover. Refrigerate overnight.

2. When ready to serve, break off small pieces of the mixture and roll them between your palms into cylinders that are slightly wider and longer than breakfast sausages.

3. Fry the links in olive oil over medium-high heat until browned on all sides, but still a bit pink in the center of the sausage. Serve immediately on plates of couscous.

> COOK'S NOTE: The truth is—the fattier the lamb, the better these sausages will taste. When I make this recipe, I let my butcher know a few days in advance that I'll be needing 2 pounds of lamb fat; most butchers just throw away their trimmings. Then I ask the butcher to make me 6 pounds of ground lamb that consists of 4 pounds regular ground lamb mixed with 2 pounds of the ground lamb fat.

Medjool Date and Almond Wands with Rosewater

· · • · ·

These long, wonderful "wands"—loosely based on a Tunisian dessert called *makroudh*—are split in half before serving, because the rich flavor of Medjool dates comes through better that way.

Medjools **(see Where to Find It, page 101)**, originally from Morocco, are one of approximately 600 varieties of dates in the world. Date mavens call them the Rolls-Royce of dates; they are plumper and deeper in flavor than other varieties, though not as sweet as some. Good! There's plenty of other sugar to go around in this recipe, which ends up tasting something like an exotic, elongated Fig Newton.

Rosewater is available in health food and specialty food shops.

makes 36 "half-wands"

for the dough:

3 cups all-purpose flour

1 ½ teaspoons baking powder

1 ½ teaspoons baking soda

1 ½ teaspoons sugar

¾ teaspoon kosher salt

1 ¼ teaspoons finely grated lemon zest

9 tablespoons unsalted butter, melted

for the date filling:

1 pound Medjool dates, pitted

2 tablespoons extra-virgin olive oil

1 teaspoon finely grated orange zest

½ teaspoon ground cinnamon

¼ teaspoon ground ginger

Big pinch ground cloves

1 cup water, plus additional as needed

for the rosewater syrup:

1 ½ cups sugar

1 ½ cups water

2 teaspoons fresh lemon juice

3 tablespoons honey

2 teaspoons rosewater

for assembly:

¾ cup chopped almonds, plus
    additional for garnish
Olive oil, for frying

1. For the dough, combine all the ingredients, except the butter, in a mixing bowl. Work in the melted butter along with small additions of water (best achieved by wetting your hands as you work), until the dough just holds together. Pushing firmly with your palms, knead the dough for 5 minutes into a soft, smooth ball. Wrap tightly in plastic wrap and refrigerate at least 30 minutes.

2. For the filling, place all the ingredients in a medium saucepan. Bring to a gentle simmer, stirring to combine. With the pan still on the heat, use a wooden spoon to mash the dates into a paste, adding water as necessary to help soften them (you may need as much as 1/2 cup more). When the water has been absorbed, remove from the heat. Let cool slightly, then fit a pastry bag with a 1/2-inch tip (see Cook's Note), fill the bag with the date filling, and set aside.

3. To make the syrup, combine the sugar and water in a medium saucepan and bring to a boil over high heat. Reduce the heat to medium and let the mixture bubble, until just slightly thicker than maple syrup, about 10 minutes. Stir in the lemon juice, honey, and rosewater. Rewarm before serving.

4. To assemble, break off a golf ball–sized piece of dough. Flatten this ball into a thickness of just over 1/16 inch, making the piece large enough to allow you to cut out a 3x7-inch rectangle with a pastry cutter or a knife. Return the scraps to the larger piece of dough. Position the rectangle on the counter with a long side facing you. Sprinkle 2 teaspoons of almonds along the long side of the rectangle closest to you, leaving a 1/2-inch margin on that long side and at both ends. Press the almonds into the pastry firmly enough to hold them in place.

5. Pipe the date filling directly over the almonds, beginning and ending at the 1/2-inch margins on the sides. Lightly moisten the edges of the dough with water, and roll each package up like a cigar, rolling away from you, until you have a 7-inch cylinder with date filling inside. Press lightly on the long seam to seal. Now, pinch both ends to completely seal each package. Repeat with the remaining dough until you've made 18 cylinders. Refrigerate, covered, for up to a day.

6. On the day of the party, pour 1 inch of oil into a medium skillet, and heat to 350°F. Fry the pastries in batches until golden brown all over, 2 1/2 to 3 minutes. Transfer to a rack to cool.

7. To serve, use a serrated knife to cut each pastry in half lengthwise. Place on a serving platter, cut sides up. Drizzle with warm rosewater syrup, sprinkle with additional almonds, and serve.

Cook's Note: If you don't have a pastry bag, you can use a sturdy sealable plastic bag snipped at one corner.

You've Got Options

At the end of the meal, you might want to consider sweetened, hot green tea—brewed from gunpowder green tea, infused with fresh mint leaves, and garnished with toasted pine nuts.

Set Dressing

If you feel like going for it, this party could be a Maghreb fantasy. If you don't, just try to express the flavor of these design motifs in your own way. A large tent would be the dream venue, its floor stabilized with plywood (rental companies do this for a charge) and lavished with rugs and cushions. Indoors, the same effect could be accomplished with fabric (yards and yards and yards of it), radiating, tent-like, from a hoop suspended from the middle of the ceiling, the fabric discreetly tacked to the walls. Simplest of all would be the purchase of a large paper globe, ubiquitous in import stores. More expensive but more elegant versions are available from online purveyors **(see Where to Find It, page 101)**.

Walls? Think about the vintage travel posters that are available from online companies, or the prints of Tunisian scenery by Paul Klee **(see Where to Find It, page 101)**.

Press low tables into service and drape them with rugs, or fabrics, heavy on the paisleys and arabesques. Drag out all the ottomans, poofs, and hassocks you can find (either in your house or in your neighbors').

Table Dressing

I love the idea of an oversized white cloth—a bedsheet might even work—completely covering the table, with enough excess to generously knot the cloth at the sides. Top it with a beautiful kilim runner in a geometric-print fabric. (Geometric forms predominate in art and architecture in North African countries because depiction of human or animal forms in art was prohibited for religious reasons.)

Wherever possible, energize things with cerulean or sapphire blues, punctuated by gold and earthy tones (such as ochre and burnt sienna). Copper serving pieces that reflect light and colorful pottery—as well as arrangements of lemons, lemon leaves, and figs—would complement the food beautifully.

For height and drama on the table, consider amphora-like vases filled with olive branches or palm leaves or even gold-painted tree branches.

Entertainment

For music, Dizzy Gillespie's "A Night in Tunisia" is an obvious choice. But if you wish to probe more deeply into the ethno-gastro-musicological mysteries of Tunisia, you might want to log onto www.focusmm.com/tunisia. This site will give you insight into Tunisia's indigenous traditional music known as *malouf*, which means "that which is normal."

There's one obvious choice for post-couscous entertainment: find "Belly Dancer" in the Yellow Pages and go ahead and hire one. For those who don't wish to go as far as in-person gyration, the fine Tunisian/French film *Satin Rouge* chronicles a widow's journey of self-discovery through belly dancing, and might be shown after dinner on a big-screen TV.

Before your guests leave, offer the women a farewell rub of argan oil (Moroccan nut oil); it is supposedly a good way of inducing a tan. Paradoxically enough, it is also said to be a cure for oily complexions. You might also consider sending your guests off with jars of preserved lemons as party favors.

Where to Find It

D'Artagnan
280 Wilson Ave.
Newark, NJ 07105
800.327.8246 (toll free)
973.465.1870 (fax)
www.dartagnan.com
A source of authentic merguez lamb sausage.

Grapevine Trading Company
59 Maxwell Ct.
Santa Rosa, CA 95401
800.469.6478 (tel)
800.469.6808 (fax)
www.grapevinetrading.com
Good source for olives and other Mediterranean-style foodstuffs from California.

Kalustyan's
123 Lexington Ave.
New York, NY 10016
800.352.3451 (toll free)
212.685.3451 (tel)
www.kalustyans.com
Great source for argan oil, Aleppo and Baklouti peppers, and spices.

Western Date Ranch
P.O. Box 10210
Yuma, AZ 85366
928.726.7006 (tel)
928.317.0950 (fax)
www.medjooldates.com
The source for dates.

I-Clipse, Inc.
dba/Pacific Rim Gourmet
4905 Morena Blvd.
Suite 1313
San Diego, CA 92117
800.910.WOKS (toll free)
858.274.9013 (tel)
858.274.9018 (fax)
www.pacificrim-gourmet.com
An online source for Golden Dragon Egg Roll Skins.

Art.com
10700 World Trade Blvd.
Suite 100
Raleigh, NC 27617
800.952.5592 (toll free)
919.831.0015 (tel)
919.831.0017 (fax)
www.art.com
Reproductions of vintage travel posters and Tunisian-inspired paintings by Paul Klee.

Berber Trading Co.
9467 Main St.
Suite 120
Woodstock, GA 30188
877.277.7227 (toll free)
770.926.1900 (tel)
770.926.9009 (fax)
www.berbertrading.com
Couscousieres, and a lot more.

www.tagines.com (Berber's companion site)
North African clothing, tableware, cookware (like couscousieres and tagines), furniture, baskets.

Texas BBQ

A Party Brought to You by Pony Express!

A Party for 12

The Menu

Texas Sweet Iced Tea

Texican Pickled Vegetables

Slow-Cooked Mail-Order Texas Brisket

Homemade Tangy Texas BBQ Sauce

Jalapeño, Cumin, and Red Onion Coleslaw

Yellow Potato Salad with Pimientos

Texas Carrot Soufflé

Pepper Jack Cornbread

Long-Cooked Texas Beans with Beer

Spicy Peach Cobbler

Okay, I know that the Pony Express didn't gallop through Texas—but what better image is there for something great coming out of the West, right to your door? The secret behind this party is that you don't have to cook the main course yourself! One of our country's best little-known gastronomic secrets is that real Texas BBQ, made in Texas by Texans, ships and reheats wonderfully well. Scores of places in Texas are now shipping their BBQ. So order some, and build a big, no-fuss party around the great stuff that arrives via FedEx. The appetizer, side dishes, and dessert that follow are all easy work.

The Plan

You can run this party outside or inside. Normally, BBQ means outside, where the smokin' pit is. But your smokin' pit's in Waco, or Beaumont—and all you have to do is reheat the meat in the oven! This means that you can play "Texas" any time of the year. Of course, if you want to throw this party outside, you can either carry the meats from the oven to the patio, or wrap them in foil and reheat them outside in a covered grill. In either venue, a long buffet table laden with meats and side dishes is the perfect serving strategy.

You'll want to start cooking a bit ahead for this party, since the pickles will need to sit overnight and the beans will simmer for 8 hours.
Happy trails!

The Ingredient

Ain't no doubt about it, pardner— this party's all about the 'cue. Texas BBQ, as you'll discover, is a little different from other kinds that are prepared in the BBQ belt across the South. For one thing, the Texans are big-time into beef. Oh, you'll see some pork and other meats at a real Texas BBQ as well—but the undisputed centerpiece is a monster hunk of beef brisket, its tender, juicy, smoky meat ready for slicing.

The way the brisket is prepared is quite distinctive, too. Texas is not a place that emphasizes marinades, rubs, mops, or sauces. In Texas, with which you should not mess, you don't mess with the beef, either. Some BBQ specialists, particularly among the old German and Czech butchers in the Hill Country of central Texas, don't use anything on the beef except salt, pepper, and, as they say, "post oak." This type of minimal treatment—combined, of course, with 18 hours of very slow cooking, during which the meat is kept over indirect heat, and cooks only from its exposure to the not-very-hot smoke of the oak and/or hickory—ensures an amazing brisket, blackened on the outside, meltingly tender on the inside, dripping with juice, and intensely beefy in flavor.

And now the great news: you can have one of these babies on your doorstep tomorrow! I recently conducted a tasting of mail-order brisket from about 30 different BBQ meisters in Texas, and—while they were all pretty good—several really stood out.

My favorite was from Mikeska's Bar-B-Q in El Campo, Texas **(see Where to Find It, page 124)**. My notes say, "A huge, blackened, 5-pound slab...the smoke factor was on the light side...however, the greatest good in a Texas brisket, to me, is juiciness—and this gold-ribbon brisket was the most juicy, most shot-through-with-delicious-fat of any contender in the tasting. Great seasoning, too, just perfect, with salt and pepper—which served to bring out the key flavor, which was somewhat akin to the flavor of intense corned beef."

Almost as great was the brisket from Willy Ray's in Beaumont, Texas **(see Where to Find It)**. "A whole, untrimmed, 5-pound hunk o' beef," I noted, "that had a shiny, crusty, black-as-coal exterior. Perfect! It was purdy inside, too: a gorgeous layering of colors, including smoke-ring red, white fat, red fat, gray meat, tan meat, pink meat (like a medium roast beef), and red meat. There was no pot roast taste at all in this baby, but a heart-melting taste somewhere between corned beef and high-quality roast beef—with, of course, a huge smoke flavor laid on top of the beefy-tasting base, with no other distractions. The first-cut side of the brisket was just a touch dry, nothing seriously wrong—but the second-cut side was insanely juicy and flavorful."

A third possibility is the brisket from the famous Kreuz Market in Lockhart **(see Where to Find It)**. "A knockout," I said. "Ultra-Texas, with a crunchy black skin, subtle smoke and seasoning, gorgeous fat bands, and an ideal texture that's firm, even as it threatens to tenderly fall apart."

Beverage Time

Oh, you could get fancy with your choice of BBQ beverage; some effete Texans have even been known to serve wine at their BBQ parties! (Actually, joshing aside, rich red wine works kind of well with Texas brisket.) For me, however, a Texas BBQ party is a beer-all-the-way kind of thing.

What kind of beer? Well, if you can find it, Texas beer would add an amusing authenticity. However, Texas beer is not so easy to find in the other 49 states. And it's not that hard to find a substitute for Texas beer. Texas beer is made in two main styles (aside from scores of variations): your job is to find beers that simulate one style or the other—or both!

The first style is grounded in German culture. The same Germans who created the Central Texas style of BBQ also created a German style of beer in Texas, dating back to the 1840s, when a German brewery was established in Fredericksburg. One of the beers the Texas Germans brewed was "bock" beer, based on a beer first brewed in Germany's Bavaria, in the town of Einbeck, which is pronounced INE-bock. There is much confusion about bock beer; a myth exists (totally incorrect) that bock beer is made only in the spring when brewers clean out their barrels and extract a dark residue which becomes bock beer. In reality, traditional bock beer is dark and rich, but only because the brewers brew it that way. Traditional German bock is also quite malty, and it can be a little sweet. In Texas, the bock tradition soon morphed: Texas bock beers are less dark (as light as amber), less rich, less malty than traditional ones. If you can find Shiner Bock, brewed by the Spoetzl brewery in Shiner, Texas, that would be a coup for your party. But any amber-ish, slightly heavier lager would approximate the style, which goes very well with rich brisket. I particularly like Modelo Negro from Mexico to fill these Texan boots. Another possibility—and one with national distribution—is Michelob's Amber Bock.

The other style of Texas beer is exactly the style of beer that Americans everywhere favor: light lager, light color, light taste, and profound refreshment! This type of brewski—typified by San Antonio's Lone Star—actually goes terrifically well with BBQ; its sole purpose is to wash away the meat and heat of your last bite and prepare your mouth for the next bite. You might be able to find Lone Star long-neck bottles in some groceries around the country; but any light, commercial beer will play the role well. One of my favorite substitutes is widely available, even in a long-neck bottle: Corona, from Mexico. Another good substitute, though you'll find no long-necks, is Rolling Rock, from Pennsylvania.

The important thing with any beer you serve at this party is to keep it iced and keep it coming!

Teetotalers will be delighted to find that their beverage may be even more authentic than the alcoholic one. Texans all over love to drink iced tea with BBQ (as well as with everything else!). However, there is a huge difference between Southern iced tea and Northern iced tea: in the South, including Texas, sugar is added to the tea while it's still hot! You won't find Texans spooning sugar into their cold iced tea; it has already been sweetened by the tea-maker while the tea was being brewed. Hence its name: sweet tea. You'd be amazed at the difference in flavor: due to the "cooking" of the sugar, sweet tea takes on a subtle, delicious, molasses-like, caramel-like set of flavors.

The Recipes

Texas Sweet Iced Tea

· · • · · ·

Here's a great recipe for authentic sweet tea.

makes enough for at least 16 big glasses

**4 quarts cold water (bottled spring water is best, but good tap water
is fine)**
8 regular-sized tea bags
1 ³⁄₄ cups sugar
Lemon wedges, if desired
Sprigs of mint, if desired

1. Place 2 quarts of the water in a heavy-bottomed nonreactive saucepan with a capacity of 4 ¹⁄₂ quarts or more.

2. Using a pair of scissors, remove the tag from the string that is attached to each of the tea bags. Add the tea bags to the saucepan and place over very high heat. Once the water comes to a rolling boil, let it boil for 45 seconds more. Remove from the heat.

3. Using a slotted spoon, immediately remove the tea bags from the saucepan and reserve them in a small bowl. While the tea is piping hot add the sugar to the saucepan, and stir until the sugar has completely dissolved. Add the remaining 2 quarts of cold water to the saucepan, and stir. Taste the tea; if you want a stronger tea flavor, you can place the reserved tea bags back in the hot tea and let them steep for a few minutes longer, then remove them.

4. Pour the sweet tea slowly into a glass pitcher (don't use plastic). Let the tea cool completely at room temperature before serving.

5. When ready to serve, pour the tea into tall glasses filled with large ice cubes. Place lemon wedges and a few sprigs of mint on a small plate for your guests to add to their glasses of tea. Don't forget the long-handled iced-tea spoons!

Texican Pickled Vegetables

• • • • •

Spiced, pickled vegetables are very popular in Texas—both as a premeal munch at Tex-Mex restaurants and as an any-time-of-day snack (pickled okra is a particularly popular supermarket item). The quick, delicious pickles in this recipe should be prepared at least 1 day before the party—or up to a week before. With a cold, long-neck beer and a side of tortilla chips, they make a great, light starter before the heavy meat to come. And the flavor is so good, so addictive, that I've incorporated it into other recipes for this party.

makes about 2¹/₂ quarts

1 head cauliflower, stemmed, then broken into florets and floret–sized pieces

1 pound medium carrots, peeled and diagonally cut into ¹/₈–inch slices

10 ounces brussels sprouts, halved

1 pound whole okra

10 fresh jalapeños, halved and seeded

3 cups cider vinegar

2 cups white vinegar

2 cups water

7 tablespoons sugar

2 tablespoons kosher salt

1 teaspoon coriander seed

1 teaspoon celery seed

1 teaspoon yellow mustard seed

2 bay leaves, crushed

3 cloves garlic, thinly sliced

1 teaspoon honey

Tortilla chips, as an accompaniment

1. Place the cauliflower, carrots, brussels sprouts, and okra in separate pots of salted, boiling water, and simmer each vegetable until just tender. Drain. Stop the cooking process by placing the vegetables in an ice-water bath. Drain and reserve in a large bowl.

2. Cook the jalapeños for 30 seconds in boiling water. Stop the cooking by placing the jalapeños in an ice-water bath. Drain and add to the vegetables.

3. Place the vinegars, water, sugar, salt, spices, bay leaves, garlic, and honey in a nonreactive saucepan and bring to a boil. Lower the heat, and simmer for 5 minutes.

4. Pour the hot brine over the vegetables. Weigh the vegetables down with a plate so that none of the vegetables breaks the surface of the brine. Allow to cool to room temperature, and then refrigerate overnight.

5. Serve in brine, from a large serving bowl or vintage canning jars, with a basket of tortilla chips nearby.

Slow-Cooked Mail-Order Texas Brisket

• • • • •

Once you've received your mail-order Texas brisket (see recommendations on page 106), you're home free; reheating is a snap (especially if you order a whole brisket, as you should for a party of 12). Place foil all around and over the brisket, tenting the foil, so there's a little opening on top. Then place the tented brisket in a roasting pan in a preheated 250°F oven. A full brisket will take about 90 minutes to heat through (less time, of course, for smaller brisket pieces). To me, it's best to err on the side of underheating; you definitely don't want to "cook" your already-cooked brisket. Most producers recommend an internal temperature of 150°F, but I think that's too high; your meat will be juicier at about 120°F.

What do you do with the brisket when it's done? That's a controversial question, even in Texas. Everybody agrees that you cut the brisket into broad, thin slices—but the fun begins after that. Some like to eat their slices of brisket with a knife and fork—and no BBQ sauce! Others prefer to slather their slices with sauce, and then proceed with knife and fork. Many people—including me!—love brisket best of all when it's sauced and nestled on commercial white bread, creating an amazing Texas Brisket Sandwich.

I would highly recommend explaining all of these options to your guests, and letting each guest choose. Just make sure you've got plenty of white bread, the kind your mother used to pack in your lunch.

Other Texas BBQ Possibilities

You could throw a Texas BBQ party that features brisket alone; such a party would be utterly, authentically Texan. However, if you want to offer your guests more variety (and I'm all for that), there are a number of other typically Texan options to consider.

BBQ Chicken. Every BBQ joint in Texas makes a smoked chicken. They are usually velvety in texture, smoky in flavor, well seasoned, and with the occasional bonus of crisp skin. My favorite Texas BBQ chicken comes from Willy Ray's in Beaumont **(see Where to Find It, page 124)**.

Tent with aluminum foil; reheat for 30 minutes in a preheated 250°F oven.

BBQ Links. Smoked sausages are another very typical Texas BBQ item. They have the additional virtue of being very easy to reheat. My favorite Texas sausage, once again, comes from Willy Ray's in Beaumont **(see Where to Find It)**; it has a pink, coarse, chunky-fat look inside that's reminiscent of French garlic sausage. Crunchy skin, tender filling, amazing balance of flavors: pork fat, salt, spice (from red pepper flakes), and delicious smoke.

A few minutes over direct heat on a grill, or under the direct heat of a broiler, sizzles them up beautifully.

BBQ Pork Roast. Despite the Texas proclivity for beef, a lot of pork does get barbecued in the Lone Star state. You'll see many different cuts available—but my favorite of all is the insanely wonderful pork roast from Willy Ray's **(see Where to Find It)**. It has a black exterior like brisket, and wonderfully silky, smoky meat within; at roughly 4 pounds, it would give your party of 12 something wonderful on the side.

Reheat it just like a brisket.

BBQ Pork Ribs. Though pork ribs are much more frequently associated with Memphis, Kansas City, and St. Louis, endless slabs of pork ribs get cooked and consumed in Texas. My favorite purveyor is The Salt Lick **(see Where to Find It)**; their product features a crispy-peppery exterior, bands of meat and fat, and brilliant alternations of texture. They are porky and wonderful, especially with Salt Lick's unusual BBQ sauce.

Reheat in tented foil, or on a grill over medium-low heat; either way, slather with a bit of the BBQ sauce a few minutes before the ribs are warmed through.

Homemade Tangy Texas BBQ Sauce

· · • · ·

makes about 6 cups

3 cups ketchup

3 cups beef stock

¾ cup cider vinegar

½ cup Worcestershire sauce

1 ½ cups molasses

2 teaspoons garlic powder

¼ cup bacon fat

1 teaspoon cayenne

1 teaspoon kosher salt

1 teaspoon ground cumin

Mix all ingredients together in a large, heavy-bottomed pot. Simmer over low heat for 30 minutes, stirring occasionally. Cool to room temperature, and place on the buffet table near the meat.

Jalapeño, Cumin, and Red Onion Coleslaw

• • ● • • ·

makes approximately 10 cups

1 cup mayonnaise

½ cup buttermilk

5 tablespoons light corn syrup

2 ½ tablespoons white vinegar

½ teaspoon ground cumin

2 tablespoons finely minced red onion

1 large head cabbage, cored

8 pickled jalapeño halves (from Texican Pickled Vegetables, page 111)

Kosher salt

Freshly ground black pepper

1. Whisk the mayonnaise, buttermilk, corn syrup, vinegar, cumin, and onion in a large bowl. Reserve this dressing.

2. Shred the cabbage. Julienne the jalapeño halves. Toss the cabbage shreds and jalapeño strips together in a very large bowl. Season with salt and pepper.

3. Thirty minutes before serving, toss the cabbage and jalapeño with the dressing. Taste for seasoning just before serving, and add salt and pepper if necessary.

Yellow Potato Salad with Pimientos

· · ● · · ·

serves 12

6 pounds Yukon Gold potatoes, unpeeled

2/3 cup mayonnaise

1/4 cup prepared yellow mustard

1/4 cup cider vinegar

1 teaspoon freshly ground black pepper

1 teaspoon kosher salt

2 tablespoons sugar

1 (4-ounce) jar diced pimientos, drained

1 cup sliced scallions (about 1 bunch)

1/4 cup brine from Texican Pickled Vegetables (page 111)

1. Put the potatoes in a large pot and fill with cold water. Bring the water to a boil. Reduce the heat to medium-high, and simmer the potatoes until tender, approximately 30 minutes. Drain, and let the potatoes cool. Peel the potatoes and cut into large chunks.

2. Mix all the other ingredients together to make a dressing.

3. Toss the potatoes with the dressing. Chill, or serve immediately.

Texas Carrot Soufflé

• • ● • •

This sweet-and-wonderful side dish is based on the awesome carrot soufflé made at Willy Ray's in Beaumont. If you're ordering meats from them, you can order this soufflé as well! It is, however, easy to make yourself.

Double the recipe for a party of 12 and bake in two 8-inch cake pans.

makes enough for 6 side-dish servings

1 pound large carrots

8 tablespoons (1 stick) unsalted butter

1 cup sugar

3 large eggs

1 teaspoon vanilla extract

3 tablespoons all-purpose flour

1 teaspoon baking powder

⅛ teaspoon ground cinnamon

Pinch of freshly grated nutmeg

Kosher salt

1. Peel the carrots and trim off the ends. Cut the carrots into 1-inch chunks and put them into the work bowl of a food processor; add enough water to just cover the carrots. Pulse until the carrots are coarsely chopped. Drain the carrots in a sieve. Rinse out the work bowl of the food processor.

2. Melt the butter in a large skillet over medium-low heat. Add ½ cup of the sugar and the drained carrots. Cook, uncovered, until the carrots are candied and nearly translucent; this could take from 30 to 45 minutes. Stir occasionally, as the sugar mixture can scorch easily once the liquids from the carrots and butter evaporate. Remove from the heat and cool.

3. Heat the oven to 350°F. Lightly film an 8-inch round cake pan with cooking spray.

4. When the candied carrot mixture has cooled, transfer it to the work bowl of the food processor. Add the remaining ½ cup of sugar, the eggs, vanilla extract, flour, baking powder, cinnamon, nutmeg, and a pinch of salt. Pulse, scraping down the sides as needed, until the ingredients are just combined. (Don't purée; you still want to see discrete pieces of carrot.)

5. Transfer the batter to the cake pan. Bake on the middle shelf of the oven for approximately 60 minutes, or until the top just begins to brown. Place on the buffet table.

Pepper Jack Cornbread

· · • ● • · ·

This is a real Southern-style cornbread—made in a cast-iron skillet—austere, with no sugar added. Yankee that I am, however, I couldn't resist melting a little cheese on top. Delicious!

makes enough for 12

> ¼ **pound sliced bacon**
>
> **2 cups yellow cornmeal**
>
> ¼ **cup all-purpose flour**
>
> **1 teaspoon kosher salt**
>
> **2 ½ teaspoons baking powder**
>
> ½ **teaspoon baking soda**
>
> **1 ⅓ cups buttermilk**
>
> **2 large eggs**
>
> **1 cup creamed corn**
>
> **1 ½ cups grated pepper jack cheese**
>
> **1 ½ cups grated sharp cheddar cheese**

1. Heat the oven to 425°F.

2. Place the bacon slices in a cast-iron skillet that measures 9 or 10 inches across the bottom. Fry the bacon over medium heat until 3 tablespoons of bacon fat are rendered. Remove the bacon from the skillet and reserve for another use. Leave the fat in the skillet and place it in the oven.

3. Whisk the cornmeal, flour, salt, baking powder, and baking soda in a medium bowl to combine well.

4. Whisk the buttermilk, eggs, and creamed corn in a large bowl until well combined. Add the dry ingredients to the wet, and stir until just combined.

5. Remove the skillet from the oven and pour in the batter. Return to the oven and bake until the cornbread is golden brown and springs back after touching it, about 20 to 25 minutes.

6. Sprinkle the grated cheese evenly over the top of the cornbread. Place it under a hot broiler for a couple of minutes until the cheese browns and bubbles. Remove the cornbread from the broiler, let it rest for 10 minutes, and place it on the buffet table. Cut it into 12 wedges.

Long-Cooked Texas Beans with Beer

· · ● · ·

These beans simmer for 8 hours, so start very early in the day, or the day before.

serves 12

2 pounds dried pinto beans

1 ¾ cups small-diced onions (about 2 medium onions)

1 ½ cups small-diced salt pork

1 (12-ounce) bottle medium-bodied beer (preferably dark, like Shiner Bock or Modelo Negro)

4 ½ teaspoons chili powder

2 teaspoons freshly ground black pepper

½ teaspoon ground cumin

½ teaspoon dry mustard

14 cups water

Kosher salt

Freshly ground black pepper

1. Rinse the beans, and sort through to remove stones.

2. Place all the ingredients in a large, heavy-bottomed pot. Bring to a boil, and simmer vigorously for 30 minutes.

3. Turn the heat down to a gentle simmer, and cook, covered, for 8 hours, stirring occasionally. As the beans start to dry out, add more water as needed (you may need as much as 4 more cups over the course of the 8-hour simmer). The top layer of the beans should remain moist throughout the cooking time.

4. When done, the beans should be tender and swimming in a medium-thick sauce. Season with more salt and pepper as needed and place on the buffet table.

Spicy Peach Cobbler

. . ● . . .

For a fabulous Texas fillip, serve ice cream on top of the cobbler—in particular the ice cream you can order from the famous Blue Bell Creameries in Brenham, Texas **(see Where to Find It, page 124)**.

makes enough for 12 servings

Unsalted butter, for buttering the dish

8 pounds ripe peaches

2 ¼ cups sugar

¼ cup minute tapioca

¼ teaspoon cayenne

¼ teaspoon freshly ground nutmeg

2 cups all-purpose flour

2 large eggs, beaten

¾ pound (3 sticks) unsalted butter, melted

¼ teaspoon ground cinnamon

1. Fill a large saucepan two-thirds full with water and bring to a boil.

2. Heat the oven to 350°F. Butter a 9x13-inch baking dish.

3. Cut an "X" on the bottom of each peach with a paring knife. Slip the peaches into the boiling water for 30 seconds to loosen their skins. Remove with a slotted spoon to an ice-water bath to stop the cooking process. Peel the peaches, stone, and cut each into 12 slices.

4. Mix the peaches together with ¼ cup of sugar, the tapioca, cayenne, and nutmeg. Turn out into the baking dish.

5. Mix the flour, eggs, melted butter, cinnamon, and the remaining 2 cups of sugar together in a bowl. Pour over the peaches in the baking dish.

6. Bake for 45 minutes, or until the topping is golden brown and the filling is bubbling. Serve hot, warm, or at room temperature.

You've Got Options

If your guest list includes some macho types, don't forget to place an array of hot sauces, Texan and otherwise, on the buffet table. A few drops would be a great addition, for those so inclined, to a BBQ brisket sandwich.

Set Dressing

All right, let's get this straight: hundreds of thousands of Texans, every night, serve BBQ right in their Dallas, or Austin, or Houston apartments—which look very much like the apartments of most other Americans in most other American cities. To create an "authentic" Texan background for BBQ, you don't really have to do much at all.

On the other hand, the state of Texas has such a strong personality—backed up by its affiliation with the wild, wild West, its blurry culinary border with Mexico, its pugnacious proclamation that it's "The Lone Star State"—that the temptation is great, my friend, to do things big at your BBQ party! Push this danged thing over the top of the barbed wire fence!

Roy Rogers and Dale Evans. Armadillos. Cattle drives. LBJ's ranch. And don't forget the Alamo (is that how the saying goes?). Drawing on all of this too-good-to-ignore-ness, I settled on something middle-of-the trail for my party: haute chuck wagon!

Get as campy as you want. Both Roy and Dale are available as life-sized cut-outs from www.incrediblegifts.com.

Galvanized tubs filled with ice are a natural for chilling soda pop or beer, and you can tether church-keys to the handles of the tubs with generous lengths of rawhide, or rope, or twine. Oil-burning lanterns would be an authentic and practical touch. You could post a bouquet of stick horses in a barrel at the entrance to your house, flanked by bales of hay. When the grub's ready to go, don't forget to ring the dinner triangle.

For the host who has everything: you can even buy your own chuck wagon from www.texcowboy.com for just $7500 (plus delivery).

Table Dressing

Clearly, we're in oilcloth territory here, and oilcloth does come in a homey red-and-white check, as appropriate on the picnic table as on the dining room table. Even more appealing to me are the graphically beautiful wool saddle pads (usually 32 inches square) found at tack shops for reasonable prices. If your table is substantial, lay two or three of these at diagonals, and let their colors dictate your choice of dinnerware and serving pieces.

I like the enameled spatterware (variously called splatterware or speckled graniteware) that you can buy at camping equipment stores—or if you're lucky, in antique shops. New, it comes in red, blue, green, or yellow. Tie oversized denim napkins with braided lengths of rawhide cord; affix tiny charms of horses or horseshoes if you're so inclined. And please put flowers on the table! A soulful watering can or enamelware coffeepot filled with lupines (a relative of Texas's revered but protected bluebells) would be lovely. More playful vases, a friend suggested, would be vintage cowboy boots with waterproof containers nestled in them.

As for the food: by all means bring the cornbread to the table in the cast-iron skillet in which it was cooked. Consider a cast-iron Dutch oven for the beans. Your Texican pickles will look their colorful best in vintage canning jars. The salads (potato and coleslaw) beg for large pottery bowls in contrasting colors.

Spanish Ham (Jamon Serrano), page 14; Spanish Tortilla with Smoked Paprika, page 18; and Piquillo Peppers Stuffed with Salt Cod, page 20

Inset: Sangria, page 10

Gorgonzola and Caramelized
Onion Pizza, page 44

Pizza with Chicken Diavolo, Mozzarella, and Arugula, page 43

**Polenta Cookies with Chopped
Pistachio Nuts, page 47**

Light and Crispy Tempura with Shrimp and Assorted Vegetables, page 64

Tomato and Watercress Salad with
Deep-Fried Tofu, Miso Dressing, and
Black Sesame Seeds, page 71

Green Tea Ice Cream, page 74

Spicy Couscous with Homemade Lamb Sausages, Vegetables, Chick Peas, and Mint, page 90

Entertainment

If you wanted to turn this little BBQ party into a virtual state fair, it wouldn't be hard to do. For starters, to get everyone in the mood, the whole group could listen to the incredible CD called "Talkin' Cowboy," available from County Line in Austin **(see Where to Find It, page 124)**, which is an hysterical elocution lesson on the fine points of sounding like a Texan. Music could run the gamut from Reba McEntire to George Strait to Dave Matthews. If you could find a line-dancing expert, he or she could teach a few steps to everyone at the gathering (especially after a coupla three Lone Star beers). Games? Poker comes to mind, as well as checkers, but horseshoes would be excruciatingly perfect! And for closers, a demonstration, with guest participation of course, of hand-cranked ice cream to accompany the peach cobbler.

Where to Find It

Willy Ray's Bar-B-Q & Grill
145 I-10 North
Beaumont, TX 77707
409.832.7770 (tel)
409.832.4371 (fax)
www.willyraysbbq.com
Barbecued chicken, brisket, Texas sausage, BBQ pork roast.

Kreuz Market
619 N. Colorado St.
Lockhart, TX 78644
512.398.2361 (tel)
512.376.5576 (fax)
www.kreuzmarket.com
Barbecued brisket.

Mikeska's Bar-B-Q
4225 Hwy. 59
El Campo, TX 77437
800.388.2552 (toll free)
979.543.8252 (tel)
979.543.8296 (fax)
www.mikeskabbq.com
Barbecued brisket.

The Salt Lick
18001 FM 1826
Driftwood, TX 78619
800.725.8542 (toll free)
512.894.3117 (tel)
512.858.2038 (fax)
www.saltlickbbq.com
Barbecued pork ribs.

Blue Bell Creameries
1101 South Horton St.
Brenham, TX 77833
979.836.7977 (tel)
www.bluebell.com
Makers of Blue Bell ice cream, considered by some Texans to be an essential partner to dessert cobblers. There's limited distribution in the South, but Blue Bell will ship.

Spoetzl Brewery
603 East Brewery St.
Shiner, TX 77984
316.594.3383 (tel)
www.shiner.com
Brewers of Shiner Bock beer, which is available primarily in the South. Call for information on distribution in your area.

Pabst Brewing Company
P.O. Box 1661
San Antonio, TX 78296
800.935.BEER (toll free)
210.226.0231 (tel)
www.puretexanbeer.com
www.pabst.com
Brewers of Lone Star Beer. Call for information on availability in your state.

Anheuser-Busch, Inc.
One Busch Place
St. Louis, MO 63118
800.342.5283 (toll free)
www.anheuser-busch.com
Brewers of Ziegen Bock beer (available only in Texas), and the nationally distributed Michelob Amber Bock.

County Line (Air Ribs)
6500 West B Cave Rd.
Austin, TX 78746
800.247.7427 (toll free)
361.293.2254 (fax)
www.airribs.com
A pioneer in mail-order (and online) barbecue, this company also offers a riotous CD entitled "Talkin' Cowboy."

MyTexasStore.com
303.882.4531 (tel)
720.890.9567 (fax)
www.mytexasstore.com
Texas-themed apparel, flags, and wind socks as well as party supplies and gifts.

Lehman Hardware and Appliances, Inc.
One Lehman Circle
Kidron, OH 44636
888.438.5346 (toll free)
888.780.4975 (toll free fax)
www.lehmans.com
With a huge bricks-and-mortar store in the heart of Ohio's Amish country, as well as print and online catalogs, Lehman's carries enameled dinnerware and serving pieces, oil lamps, lanterns, and nearly everything else a pre- or non-electric household would require.

Party
Marseillaise
Celebrating a Mighty Pot of Fish

A Party for 12

The Menu

Pastis Cocktails

Iced Crudités with Assorted Olive Oils and Fleur de Sel

First Bouillabaisse Course
Fish Filets with Steamed Provençal Vegetables

Aïoli

Rouille

Pistou

Second Bouillabaisse Course
Sautéed Lobster, Mussels, and Shrimp with Concentrated Bouillabaisse Broth

Croûtes

Chilled Poached Peaches with Muscat Wine, Vanilla, and Mint

Picture this: we are somewhere along the Côte d'Azur, the French Riviera, returning to port at sunset with a group of particularly merry fishermen. At quayside, they sell all of their high-priced fish and save the rest for their big boil, in a big pot, right on the wave-splashed dock. There'll be garlic mayonnaise, Mediterranean vegetables, crusty bread, and iced anise drinks, and the wine will flow freely. The seagulls will cackle, the animals will mew, and the revelers will party long after the sun's gone down, gazing at the wine-dark sea. Can you reproduce this exactly? No. There will probably be no rascasse at your party (the junk-fish backbone of many a Marseillaise bouillabaisse), nor any wizened anglers (though it'd sure be nice if they came!). However, the festive spirit of that party-on-the-dock—and of an easygoing, southern European life—can certainly be transferred to your house.

What a party for the height of summer!

The Plan

The very best way, I think, to catch the flavor of the dockside moment is to make your bouillabaisse party an outdoor one, on a patio or terrace. But if it's easier for you to entertain inside, your living or dining room will also work beautifully.

The key to this party is alternation. Tastings, samplings, rhythm switches are all geared to create the feeling of a casual, impromptu event, bristling with energy. You start with a drinks-and-appetizer table, on which the grand bowl of crudités is placed, as well as the pastis station. Guests help themselves to the raw vegetables and to the tasting of Mediterranean olive oils that you've set up.

Next, you sit down to the first of two bouillabaisse courses. In the opening one, you serve platters of fish and vegetables; the guests help themselves, selecting fish and sampling the three sauces you've presented. In the second bouillabaisse course, things switch again: this time each guest is served an individual plate of shellfish, and an individual cup of concentrated bouillabaisse broth.

Hopefully, your seafood-sated guests will have just enough appetite reserved for muscat-poached peaches, which you've chilled in the refrigerator ahead of time.

●The Day Before the Party

Make the bouillabaisse stock

Poach the peaches

●The Day of the Party

Make the three sauces

Prep the crudités

Toast the croûtes

Cook the Fish Filets with Steamed Provençal Vegetables

Cook the Sautéed Lobster, Mussels, and Shrimp

The Ingredient

This party rises or falls with one item in particular: *seafood*. I don't believe that a great American bouillabaisse must have the same fish they use in Marseilles; you can't get most of those fish here, and those you can get don't come into this country incredibly fresh. No, I'm all for finding the highest-quality fish from our waters. There are many different fish in my bouillabaisse recipe, and one thing is clear: everything you buy for it must be spanking, sparkling fresh. Shop at fish stores, if possible, rather than supermarkets—or use the incredible services of two great online fish purveyors **(see Where to Find It, page 146)**.

In the first course of *l'affaire bouillabaisse*, you'll be serving an array of non-shellfish fish. Here's the breakdown, and some pointers on what to look for:

Fish Steaks. These are wonderful in the bouillabaisse, because your guests get to enjoy large, luminous flakes and chunks of fish—and the bone at the center of a steak adds a little gelatinous goodness to the broth. My top choices are **halibut,** with its lean, white meat, and **cod,** with its sliding, snow-white flakes. Ask the fishmonger to cut these steaks for you at the time of purchase.

Monkfish. This fish is much loved around the Mediterranean. Monkfish tail (the only part we eat) has a quite meaty and resilient texture. Buy the whole 2-pound portion, make sure the gauzy membrane that surrounds the filet is removed, then cut the fish into medallions yourself. There's no perfect substitute for monkfish.

Skin-on Fish Filet. This will be the most delicate fish in the pot; great filets will add a lovely sweetness to the mix. The type of fish you choose (and you need only one type) is not as important as the freshness. Freshness insures that the filets stay together. Some of my favorites for this role are **red snapper, lemon sole, grey sole, black bass, tilefish,** and **ocean perch.** Please make sure to handle these filets gently, both outside of the pot and in; do not overcook.

Small Whole Fish. This will be the most difficult ingredient to find; most American markets do not carry whole fish that are just 4 or 5 inches long. **Red mullet,** known as rouget in France, is as sweet and delicious as its red skin is pretty. It is often used in bouillabaisse in France; find fresh rouget and you've hit the jackpot. **Butterfish** and **sand dabs** are other possibilities. (Fresh sardines are too oily for this dish.)

Buying whole fish enables you to do a complete freshness inspection: make sure the gills are red, the eyes are clear, the skin's not clammy, and the smell is of the sea, not of fish.

Do you absolutely need whole fish in the pot? No. You could substitute 2 pounds of a second type of skin-on fish filet.

In the second course of the bouillabaisse, you'll be serving an array of shellfish. Here are some shopping tips.

Lobster. Look for lobsters that are very lively. The crustier they are on the outside, the more barnacled, the better.

Mussels. Freshness is the key consideration. The mussels you buy should be tightly closed; if some in the batch at the fish store have lazily opened, skip that batch. I happen to be a fan of mussels that are on the small side; larger ones tend to be mealy and mushy. Some of the tightest, crispest mussels I've tried on this side of the big pond have been the smallish ones from Penn Cove, Washington, available on the web from Farm-2-Market **(see Where to Find It, page 146)**.

Shrimp. Most shrimp sold at stores in the U.S. have been previously frozen but when you tangle with a fresh one, you can really taste the difference. The most breathtaking shrimp I've tasted in a long time—sweet, unbelievably crustacean-intense—have been the fresh head-on white shrimp from Louisiana, also available from Farm-2-Market **(see Where to Find It, page 146)**, though only sporadically.

Bones for the Stock. Have your fishmonger reserve the bones and heads from any of the fish you may be buying. Most fishmongers always have a supply of bones and heads. Any number of white-fleshed fish will yield carcasses suitable for this stock. Particularly good is the head from the monkfish, if you can find it. Avoid oily fish such as salmon or mackerel.

Beverage
Time

No flavor in a glass says South of France to me like the ancient flavor of licorice mixed with alcohol, ice, and water. Old-timers in Provence polish off untold numbers of pastis and Pernod bottles, sitting outside on eternal summer nights. I say, if you're making a party with a South of France theme, at any time of year, get to that scene-setting flavor right away. A pastis cocktail is powerfully evocative, and a quick way to dazzle your guests (or at least open up their receptors). I like to cut the cocktail with a good deal of water—as they cut ouzo in Greece—because not everyone can handle the full intensity of the licorice flavor.

Of course, there's bound to be a guest who doesn't like anise-based drinks. You can try to talk him or her into the Riviera-ness of it all, but you may well fail. Have ready for these palates a few bottles of chilled white wine. There are a number of whites produced along the southern French coast and in Provence—but your chances of finding a good one in the U.S. are not strong. I'd offer, instead, white wine from another place in France; a good village Chablis, or Premier Cru Chablis, should be just the thing to get that palate primed for seafood.

When the main course does arrive, I have no doubts about the dinner wine: a classic rosé from the South of France, which is somewhat more reliable in the U.S. than white wine from that region. Unfortunately, there is some French rosé in our stores that does not taste quite as fresh and vibrant here as it does there. Your first protection against that pitfall is vintage; do not serve a southern French rosé that was not made in the most recent vintage. The wines come into the U.S. in the spring following the vintage—so you want to drink a rosé that was made the year before the current year (for example, drink a 2005 in June 2006). The exception is January–May, when the last of the old vintage is still available; then, you'll be drinking a vintage that's two years before the current calendar year (for example, a 2005 in January 2007).

Here's one more protection: look for the very best brands. Year in and year out the rosé that tastes freshest to me comes from the Costières de Nîmes appellation, southwest of Avignon: the label I like is Chateau Grande Cassagne Rosé. Other southern French rosés I like a lot are Le Galantin from Bandol, Chateau de Roquefort, Corail from Côtes de Provence, and Chateau Calisse from Coteaux Varois.

The. Recipes

Pastis Cocktails

· ● ● ● ● ·

As your guests arrive, mix up this potion in pitchers— then pour into ice-filled cut-glass tumblers.

makes twelve 4-ounce cocktails

> **1 ⅓ cups pastis or Pernod**
> **4 cups club soda**
> **4 teaspoons sugar**
> **Lots of ice**
> **Fresh fennel stalks with lacy leaves**

Pour the pastis and club soda into a large pitcher. Add the sugar and stir well. Fill the pitcher with ice and stir again. Pour into individual glasses also filled with ice. Serve each glass with a fresh fennel stalk that has lacy leaves on top (save the fennel bulbs for the crudités bowl).

Iced Crudités with Assorted Olive Oils and Fleur de Sel

· ● ● ● ● ·

The bouillabaisse extravaganza features a lot of food in its two-part main course, so start your guests off with a light appetizer. Alain Ducasse recently began serving an elegant version of crudités at his hyper-elegant restaurant in Monte Carlo, with gorgeous, perfectly selected raw vegetables—and I think it's a good cue for hosts and hostesses with a big Mediterranean meal in the offing. Your guests' enjoyment of the crudités at this party will be bolstered by the accompanying drink I've recommended: iced Pastis is awesome with raw fennel, olive oil, and salt. Serve loaves of warm, crusty country French bread as well.

About 6 dozen pieces of raw vegetables
Crushed ice
Three kinds of extra-virgin olive oil
Fleur de sel (or other excellent, crunchy salt)

1. The choice of vegetables is entirely up to you, but I think you should offer at least six different kinds. Some of them may be whole—such as small radishes (particularly the long, cylindrical ones often called breakfast radishes), or scallions, attractively trimmed, or baby carrots, or sugar snap peas. Some may be cut into appealing shapes—such as fennel bulbs, or raw zucchini, or raw artichoke hearts, or cardoons (if you can find small, tender ones). Let your imagination and the market be your guides. Consider color as you choose; variety is good. Wash and trim your vegetables a few hours before party time; wrap them carefully in damp paper towels and refrigerate them.

2. At party time, fill the widest bowl you can find with crushed ice. Arrange the vegetables in the ice in the bowl, in a pretty pattern. Place the bowl on the drinks-and-appetizer table, alongside appetizer plates. (If you don't have one bowl that will accommodate all of the vegetables, you can use several bowls instead; see Cook's Note.)

3. Select three olive oils that are different from each other: Provençal, Tuscan, and Andalusian, for example, would be an exciting Mediterranean lineup. Pour the oils into three small cruets, and mark each cruet with a handwritten label, indicating which oil is in the cruet.

4. Provide several small salt cellars filled with an excellent salt (fleur de sel from the Guèrande in Brittany is good, as is Maldon salt from England, and Ravida salt from Sicily).

5. Service is simple: each guest selects crudités from the iced bowl, lays them on his or her plate, drizzles the vegetables with olive oil (sampling different oils), and sprinkles the vegetables with salt.

> COOK'S NOTE: *There is one other, even more spectacular way to present the crudités: on one or two of those three-tiered plateau de fruits de mer stands that French brasseries use to present raw shellfish. Fill each tier with crushed ice, then embed the raw vegetables in the ice. This presentation says three things simultaneously: seafood, French, and festive, all of which are perfect for this party. The stand can be purchased from Bridge Kitchenware in New York City* **(see Where to Find It, page 146)** *and used for shellfish at another party!*

Bouillabaisse in Two Courses

A night of letting the refrigerated stock sit on the shells and fish bones in the pot gives the stock an amazing concentration of flavor. Yes, you want your guests to love the fish—but it's awfully nice when they're loving the soup as well.

serves 12

Bouillabaisse Stock

· · · ● · ·

1 large orange

2 pounds medium-large shrimp (about 20 per pound)

6 live lobsters, 1 ¼ to 1 ½ pounds each

⅓ cup extra-virgin olive oil (preferably French)

2 medium leeks, split, cleaned, and coarsely chopped (white parts and an inch or so of green)

1 large onion, coarsely chopped

1 medium fennel bulb (including tops), coarsely chopped

2 medium carrots, peeled and coarsely chopped

3 medium celery stalks, coarsely chopped

1 clove of garlic, cut in half crosswise

1 bottle (750 ml) dry white wine

1 tablespoon tomato paste

1 (14-ounce) can tomatoes, drained and coarsely chopped

3 quarts water

4 pounds assorted fish bones and heads, cut into manageable pieces (see Bones for Stock, page 129)

1 tablespoon fennel seed

3 pods star anise

2 bay leaves

½ teaspoon saffron threads

1 ½ teaspoons sweet paprika

¼ teaspoon cayenne

2 sprigs fresh tarragon

6 sprigs fresh flat–leaf parsley

6 sprigs fresh thyme

1 teaspoon kosher salt

1. Heat the oven to 225°F.

2. Zest the orange with a vegetable peeler, making sure to leave the white pith behind. Reserve the orange fruit for another use. Place the pieces of orange zest on a small baking sheet and let them dry in the oven until just dehydrated, about 30 minutes. Don't let them brown. Reserve.

3. Peel and devein the shrimp, leaving the tails on. Wrap the shrimp tightly in plastic wrap and refrigerate. Reserve the shells.

4. Either cut up the lobsters yourself or ask your fishmonger to do it. Each lobster needs to be separated into two claws (with knuckles attached), the tail section (whole), and the chest/head section. Keep all lobster parts in the refrigerator until ready to use.

5. Heat the olive oil in a large stockpot over medium-high heat. Cut the 6 lobster chest/head sections down the middle, into 2 parts each (you will have 12 pieces of chest/head section all together). Working in batches if necessary, add the lobster chest/head sections and the shrimp shells to the oil; sear them, stirring regularly, until bright red all over. Remove them with a slotted spoon to a plate or bowl.

6. Add the leeks, onion, fennel, carrots, celery, and garlic; cook, stirring regularly, until the vegetables are a rich golden brown at their edges. Add the white wine, tomato paste, and tomatoes, bring to a brisk simmer, and reduce the liquid by half.

7. Add the water, fish bones, and the seared lobster and shrimp shells. Bring to a bare simmer, skimming any scum that rises to the surface. Add the fennel seed, star anise, bay leaves, saffron, paprika, cayenne, tarragon, parsley, thyme, salt, and the reserved dried orange peel. Cook at a bare simmer for 50 minutes.

8. While the broth is simmering, immerse the reserved lobster tails and claws in the broth, and poach for 2 minutes. Remove the tails. Continue cooking the claws for 3 minutes more, then remove. Let the lobster pieces cool a bit. Then cut the tails in half lengthwise (this will yield 12 tail pieces), crack the 12 claws in a few places, and snip 2 joints of each of the knuckles with kitchen shears. Wrap very tightly in plastic wrap and refrigerate the lobster overnight. If you wish, you may flatten out the lobster tail pieces by placing heavy weights on them.

9. When the stock has finished its 50-minute simmer, remove it from the heat, cool, and refrigerate overnight.

Fish Filets with Steamed Provençal Vegetables

• • ● • • •

You'll make a big splash with this first "sit-down" course: platters of poached fish, platters of bright, steamed vegetables, and three delicious Provençal sauces to mix and match. It is not traditional to serve all of these vegetables with bouillabaisse, but it is traditional to serve them with garlic mayonnaise as part of a classic local meal called the "Grand Aïoli." So I'm starting a new tradition, perfect for a party, of combining the two dishes. Let your guests help themselves to the multitude of options. When selecting fish for this course, see "The Ingredient" (page 128).

serves 12

for the fish:

Reserved, refrigerated Bouillabaisse Stock (page 134)

Kosher salt

2 fish steaks, each about 1 pound and 1 ¼ inches thick, pin bones removed

2 pounds monkfish (or other firm-fleshed fish), cut into 12 medallions

2 pounds of skin-on white fish filets, pin bones removed, cut into 12 portions

12 small whole fish, cleaned

Whole flat-leaf parsley leaves for garnish

for the vegetables:

6 large leeks, white and pale green parts only, cut on the bias into ⅜-inch slices, steamed until almost tender

5 large fennel bulbs, cut crosswise into ⅜-inch slices, steamed until almost tender and rubbed with lemon juice

3 pounds baby potatoes, cut in half and steamed until almost tender

2 small heads of cauliflower, cut into florets and steamed until almost tender

2 pounds string beans, trimmed and steamed until almost tender

Kosher salt

Fresh lemon juice

accompaniments:

Aïoli (page 140)

Rouille (page 140)

Pistou (page 141)

French extra-virgin olive oil, for drizzling

1. Gently bring the reserved stock to a simmer, and strain it through a colander placed over a large pot. Using a potato masher or sturdy spoon, mash the solids in batches in the colander over the stock, pressing firmly until each batch has given up all the flavorful moisture contained in the fish, shellfish, and vegetables. Return the broth to your largest pot and salt lightly.

2. Remove the seafood from the refrigerator; salt the fish filets on both sides, and the whole fish inside and out. Return the broth to a simmer. Add the fish to the broth, thickest pieces first, and let them poach until just cooked through, so that all of the fish is done at the same time. (Allow 8 to 10 minutes per inch of thickness.)

3. While the fish are poaching, finish steaming the pre-steamed vegetables in a separate steamer (this should just take a moment). When the vegetables are done, transfer to a platter, arranging them in vegetable groups. Salt well. Drizzle a little extra lemon juice on the fennel.

4. When the fish are done, carefully transfer them to a platter (leaving behind the stock in the pot over very low heat), and garnish the fish with a handful of parsley leaves scattered over the top. Serve the fish platter, the vegetable platter, the three sauces, and olive oil for drizzling.

Some Tips on Cooking Fish

Before your guests arrive, place your uncooked fish in a large glass dish or a sheet pan and give a bit of thought to cooking times of each shape and size. Typically, I arrange them flat (for easy salting) in the order that they will be added to the pot—thickest pieces first.

There may be no hard and fast rules for the cooking of fish, but there are a few simple guidelines. For most types of fish, when the flesh is just barely resistant to a knife point or a metal skewer inserted at its center, it is done (the residual heat performs the last bit of cooking before your guests sit down to eat). Undercooked flesh will not allow the knife to penetrate easily, and overcooked flesh allows the knife to slide through too easily. Another way to test for doneness is to insert your knife or skewer into the center of the fish and hold it there for 5 seconds. Now touch it to your lip. If the metal is cool, the fish is underdone. If it's hot, the fish is overcooked. If it's warm (125°F to 130°F), it's usually just right.

Whatever sort of fish you use, test for doneness early and often, and, if your timing estimates prove a bit wrong, remove the cooked pieces to a warm platter while the other fish finish cooking. Your bouillabaisse will be no less delicious.

Sautéed Lobster, Mussels, and Shrimp with Concentrated Bouillabaisse Broth

• • ● • •

Here the meal switches over to individual plating, which you will do in the kitchen.
Leave the three sauces from the first course on the table. Add a platter of croûtes to the table
and bring each guest a portion of mixed shellfish in a wide shallow soup bowl, and a cup
of the concentrated bouillabaisse broth on the side.

serves 12

Warm bouillabaisse stock (reserved from Fish Filets with Steamed Provençal Vegetables, page 136)

½ cup extra-virgin olive oil, preferably French

1 head of garlic, cloves peeled and coarsely crushed

12 pieces refrigerated lobster claws (reserved from Bouillabaisse Stock, page 134)

12 pieces refrigerated lobster tails (reserved from Bouillabaisse Stock, page 134)

4 pounds mussels, cleaned

Refrigerated shrimp (reserved from Bouillabaisse Stock, page 134)

Kosher salt

1. When you're ready to serve the second bouillabaisse course, return the stock to a gentle simmer. Heat the oven to 200°F.

2. Working with two very large frying pans, divide the ½ cup of olive oil and the crushed garlic between them; cook over medium heat until the garlic is fragrant, about 1 minute. Add the lobster claws and cook, shaking the pan and turning the pieces over regularly, for 1 minute. Add the tails and continue to cook the lobster until just cooked through, about 3 minutes more. Remove the lobster with a slotted spoon and place it on a platter and keep warm in the oven. Leave the oil and any garlic in the pans.

3. Now, working quickly, add the mussels to the reserved bouillabaisse stock and turn the heat to high. Cover the pot and cook until the mussels have opened, 4 to 6 minutes. Discard any mussels that remain closed.

4. As soon as you've added the mussels to the stock, add the shrimp to the frying pans with the garlic (in which you cooked the lobster) over medium-high heat. Sprinkle the shrimp with salt and cook until just opaque at the center, about 1 ½ minutes per side.

5. When the mussels have opened, turn the heat down, and add the lobster and shrimp to the pot; cook for 1 minute more, stirring well. Divide the shellfish among 12 dinner plates. Taste the broth for seasoning, and ladle about 1 cup of broth into each of 12 large cups. Serve each guest a plate of shellfish (moistened with a little broth), and a cup of the broth on the side.

Aïoli and Rouille

· · • · ·

makes 5 cups Aïoli; 1 ¹/₂ cups Rouille

mayonnaise base:

4 large egg yolks

2 large eggs

1 tablespoon fresh lemon juice

1 teaspoon kosher salt

2 cups good-quality extra-virgin olive oil (preferably French)

2 cups vegetable oil

for the two sauces:

8 large cloves garlic

1 ³/₄ teaspoons kosher salt

2 teaspoons sweet paprika

1 teaspoon cayenne

¹/₈ teaspoon ground star anise

1. Whisk together the egg yolks, whole eggs, lemon juice, and a teaspoon of salt in a large mixing bowl. Combine the oils in a large measuring cup. Whisking continuously, begin adding the oil, a drop at a time, until the mixture thickens considerably and a smooth emulsion forms (see Cook's Note). Whisk in the remaining oil in larger additions until each is incorporated and the mixture continues to thicken into a creamy and slightly fluffy mass, a bit looser than store-bought mayonnaise. You should have about 5 cups. Place 1 ¹/₂ cups of the mayonnaise in a small mixing bowl. Place the remainder in a larger mixing bowl and set both batches aside.

2. Smash the garlic cloves with the broad side of a knife on a cutting board and then mince them finely. Again, using the broad side of the knife, press down and firmly smear the garlic against the cutting board. Scrape it back together and repeat the smearing and scraping until a paste forms. Set the paste aside.

To make the Aïoli:

To the large batch of mayonnaise, add 1 tablespoon of the reserved garlic paste and 1 ¹/₄ teaspoons salt. Whisk to combine. Cover and refrigerate.

To make the Rouille:

To the small batch of mayonnaise add the remaining ½ teaspoon of salt, the paprika, cayenne, star anise, and ½ teaspoon of the reserved garlic paste. (Reserve ½ teaspoon more of the garlic paste for the Pistou, below.) Stir well or whisk to combine. Cover and refrigerate.

> COOK'S NOTE: *Whisking and simultaneously adding the oil is made much easier by wetting a large kitchen towel and forming a circular base on which to steady your mixing bowl. Mayonnaise can also be made in a stand-up mixer with a whisk attachment, but I really prefer the fluffier handmade versions.*

Pistou

This is the version of pesto that they make on the French side of the border.

makes 1 ¼ cups

2 cups tightly packed basil leaves

½ teaspoon garlic paste (reserved from Aïoli and Rouille, above)

4 tablespoons pine nuts, lightly toasted in a pan

3 tablespoons grated Parmigiano-Reggiano

½ teaspoon kosher salt

1 tablespoon fresh lemon juice

½ cup good-quality extra-virgin olive oil (preferably French)

Combine all of the ingredients in the bowl of a food processor and blend, pausing a few times to scrape down the sides of the bowl, until a loose paste forms. Cover and refrigerate.

Croûtes

· · ● ● ● ● ·

These bits of toasted bread are essential to the last bouillabaisse course. Topped with one of the sauces (or not), they can be placed in the shellfish bowl before you pour in a little of the broth. Or—and I particularly like doing this with an aïoli-smeared croûte—dunk them into the cup of broth.

These don't need to be hot, so make them earlier in the day.

serves 12

3 baguettes, cut on the bias into ⅜-inch slices

1. Heat the oven to 400°F.

2. Lay the slices of bread on the oven racks and toast them until just crisp, about 10 minutes.

Chilled Poached Peaches with Muscat Wine, Vanilla, and Mint

· ◦ ● ◦ ·

We came into this meal lightly, and we go out lightly—with this elegant and delectable fruit dessert. Find great peaches; if your local market does not have them, magnificent mail-order peaches are available at the height of summer from Frog Hollow Farm in Brentwood, California **(see Where to Find It, page 146)**. And if you can find Mexican vanilla beans—despite all the foodie buzz over Madagascar vanilla beans—I think you'll be happily surprised.

serves 12

12 large, ripe-but-firm yellow peaches

1 cup sugar

2 bottles (750 ml each) Muscat de Beaumes-de-Venise wine

Juice of 1 lemon

1 vanilla bean

12 sprigs fresh mint

1. To peel the peaches, bring a large pot of water to a boil and set up an ice and water bath nearby. Cut a small "X" in the bottom of each peach. Immerse the peaches in the boiling water for about 1 minute to loosen the skins, then transfer them to the ice bath. When they're cool enough to handle, slip the skins off the peaches.

2. Combine the sugar, wine, and lemon juice in a pot large enough to hold the peaches in a single layer (or in two pots, the ingredients divided equally). Split the vanilla bean lengthwise, scrape out its seeds, and add both pod and seeds to the pot. Add the peaches and just enough water to cover them. Place over medium-high heat, bring just to a simmer, and turn off the heat (simmer a few minutes longer if the peaches aren't very ripe). Let the peaches cool completely, occasionally spooning the poaching liquid over the fruit. Remove the fruit to a baking dish and set aside.

3. Return the poaching liquid to the stove over medium-high heat and reduce until lightly syrupy (you should have about 1 1/2 to 2 cups). Cool the syrup to room temperature and spoon it over the peaches. Place in the refrigerator and chill thoroughly (overnight is fine), occasionally spooning the syrup over the peaches to flavor them. When ready to serve, place the peaches on serving plates, spoon the syrup over each, and garnish with a sprig of mint.

Set Dressing

If you can stage this party outside, please do, and do take a hundred extra points for "somewhere outside near the sea." Failing that (as most of us will, including me), do your darnedest to evoke a seaside setting in France. Having two clichés to work with here—the seaside and France—gives you opportunities to avoid hokiness and suggest irony (a beret on a large conch shell is better than either the conch shell or the beret by itself, *non*?). Festoon the walls with watery-looking watercolors or maritime scenes. Set up a chalkboard on an easel (available from restaurant supply houses) with a list of the very fish you're serving in the bouillabaisse. No waves nearby? What the hell; set the aural stage by playing waves of ambient music, or ambient music of waves.

After all this frou-frou, bring bouillabaisse back down to earth, where it belongs. Distribute the most distressed-looking set of old pots and pans—tin wash basins, enameled dishpans, anything the local flea market will belch forth—all around the room. Americans have always "elevated" bouillabaisse, as you're doing at this party, by turning it into fancy restaurant food. Your lobsters, and shrimps, and multiple courses, are right in that vein. But you can stand up for all the fishermen of history who never heard of Le Creuset, and simply boiled their catch in whatever beat-up receptacles could take the fire. If that's just a little too…real…for your tastes, the irony of gorgeous flowers emerging from a stained and scratched aluminum coffeepot might be just the ticket.

Table Dressing

Riff on the beautiful colors evoked by the evening's main dish. On the dining table, lay down a huge white cloth, one that drops magnanimously to the floor, if you can manage it. Add top cloths (maybe set on a diagonal, if they're not sized to your table) in either royal blue or sea-foam green. Add saffron-colored napkins, if you can find them, or search for something in a tasteful orange/red that imitates the shells of cooked lobsters.

Put a long, narrow tray in the center of the table—the longer, the better. Zinc trays with narrow sides are widely available from plant-supply stores. Fill it with sand, and punctuate it with the most beautiful fishbowl you can find. Think creatively here. It could be an antique, such as the one I own—acanthus leaves cradling a voluptuous bowl—or something with a newer pedigree. Float flowers in it. (Think low. I hate to have an obstructed view of the person sitting across from me.) Fish in the fish bowl are optional. I can guarantee you that not everyone will want to eat fish while watching live ones in confinement—but I will also tell you that the live fish display animates the table like nobody's business. Surround the bowl with shells, antique fishermen's floats, netting, bits of driftwood, or salvaged sea-savaged glass.

For lighting, march squatty candles down either side of the centerpiece. I've seen candles poured into clamshells, and those would certainly serve the spirit of the party.

Here's a serving idea: get some seaweed from your fishmonger and sandwich it between two clear buffet plates; use this assembly as a theme-appropriate charger for the bouillabaisse part of the meal. (These plates can be rented. In fact, I would recommend it.) Place zinc pails on the table—the more they look like sand pails, the better to receive the discarded lobster shells.

For the dessert, a company called GemSugarUSA **(see Where to Find It, page 146)** makes an herbal sugar called "Jade," an edible, crystalline embodiment of sea glass. Serve the peaches in a stemmed glass on a wide plate—and scatter the "jade" on the plate.

True, the fishermen didn't do this. Their loss, I'm thinking.

Where to Find It

Browne Trading Co.
Merrill's Wharf
260 Commercial St.
800.944.7848 (toll free)
207.766.2404 (fax)
Portland, ME 04101
www.brownetrading.com
Seafood of all kinds.

Farm-2-Market
P.O. Box 124
Trout Town Rd.
Roscoe, NY 12776
800.663.4326 (toll free)
607.498.5275 (fax)
www.farm-2-market.com
Fish of all kinds.

GemSugarUSA
3202 W. Anderson Lane
Suite 203
Austin, TX 78757
800.678.8374 (toll free)
512.467.9008 (tel)
512.467.0347 (fax)
www.gemsugar.com
Source of large crystalline sugars in tasteful colors.

Sur La Table
(Multiple retail locations)
P.O. Box 34707
Seattle, WA 98124
866.328.5412 (toll free)
206.682.1026 (fax)
www.surlatable.com
Kitchenware and accessories with a French pedigree.

La Cafetière
160 Ninth Ave.
New York, NY 10016
866.486.0667 (toll free)
646.486.0667 (tel)
www.la-cafetiere.com
French tableware and housewares.

Bridge Kitchenware
214 E. 52nd St.
New York, NY 10022
212.688.4220 (tel)
212.758.5387 (fax)
www.bridgekitchenware.com
Professional-quality cookware and seafood *plateaux.* Not all their products are available online; you will need to request a paper catalog for the seafood stands.

Frog Hollow Farm
P.O. Box 872
Brentwood, CA 94513
888.779.4511 (toll free)
510.634.2845 (tel)
925.516.2332 (fax)
www.froghollow.com
The source of the best peaches I've ever tasted.

Mexican Street Party
The Joy of Real Tacos

A Party for 12

The Menu

Margaritas

Avocado and Romaine Salad with
Pomegranates, Pepitas, and
Orange–Sesame Vinaigrette

Chorizo and Red Pepper Tacos

Chicken, Chipotle, and Raisin Tacos

Tongue and White Onion Tacos

Beef Picadillo Tacos

Tomatillo Salsa

Salsa Mexicana

Roasted Poblano Rajas with
Marinated Onion

Mexican Soured Cream
(Crema)

Crumbled Cotija
(Mexican Hard Cheese)

Banana Bread Pudding with Cinnamon,
Cayenne, and Dulce de Leche

I love going to big-deal, fancy restaurants in Mexico. However, I usually eat lightly at these meals—saving some room for a midnight run to the local taco stand, when and where a boisterous street party, fueled by the great food, usually erupts. Frankly, I can't think of any food in Mexico that I truly love more than fresh, authentically made tacos—or any food in Mexico that forms a better foundation for a wild Mexican party back here in the States.

What is an authentic taco? Forget those crunchy shells used for what gringos call "tacos"; that's not what they use in Mexico. Typically, a Mexican taco is two small, moist, soft, lightly griddled, hot, fresh corn tortillas, placed on top of each other, to which a variety of fillings may be added. The fillings usually sit on a griddle near the tortillas, and only await your order before being scooped into the double tortilla. Then the pliable double tortilla is folded over, making a half-moon; the diner chooses from an array of salsas and toppings, and taco heaven is at hand.

Authentic taquerias are springing up in

major cities all across the U.S. these days—but I've seen no movement yet toward the very logical idea of a taco party at home. So, be the first gringo on your block to have one! With margaritas flowing, with colorful, upscale versions of taco stand food, and with your guests merrily taking control over what gets placed in their tortillas—you've got a mirthful, madly satisfying party on your hands.

The
Plan

The party kicks off, simply enough, with margaritas poured from the pitcher, and the Avocado and Romaine Salad, surrounded by tortilla chips, on the buffet table.

After that, things get interactive. This is a great party for you to serve off your stovetop and right on to people's plates. If your kitchen can accommodate this, ask your guests to congregate around your range, plates in hand. Or ask them to visit you one by one, forming a line, just like at a taco stand. At the range, where the four possible taco fillings are kept warm over low heat, you are warming tortillas, then asking each guest which filling he or she wants. You double up the warmed tortillas, and comply with the filling order. Off goes your guest, back to the buffet table arrayed with salsas, poblanos, crema, and crumbled cheese as well as the Avocado and Romaine Salad. A selection of bottled hot sauces, from Mexico and elsewhere, adds greatly to the fun. Guests top their tacos with any of the above. When that taco's done, they go back to see you in the kitchen for another.

The wonderful bread pudding can be served either from the buffet, or on individual plates which you pass around at dessert time.

One of the logistical joys of this party is that a good deal of it can be prepared in advance. The last-minute recipes are marked with an icon.

The Ingredient

There's no doubt about it: the star of a Mexican taco party is the corn tortilla. Since there are loads of tortilla possibilities out there, you have to know what you're doing when you set out to buy them. Happily, it's easy to get this right.

Ready-made corn tortillas are now available in many places (even supermarkets), and they're really very good—light-years better than the ones the supermarkets used to carry. All you have to do is get over to your nearest store likely to sell Mexican products—a Mexican grocery is best, a gourmet emporium is second best, but a supermarket should do the trick these days—and pick up a brand, or a few brands, of soft corn tortillas. Steam a few tortillas for a minute or so, and inspect them: if they're soft, tender, a little springy, with flaky layers, then you know you've got a winner.

One brand from my local supermarket that I've been liking is Mexican Original Corn Tortillas manufactured by Mexican Original in Springdale, Arizona. If you can't find good ones locally, you can always order tortillas on the internet. Look especially at the selection offered by www.mexgrocer.com.

Beverage
Time

There is little doubt as to the drink of choice at a Mexican taco party: margaritas! They work so well as cocktails, but as long as they're not too sweet, they work beautifully with dinner itself.

Making Margaritas

You can get fancy with margaritas, but I favor simplicity. Fill a pitcher with ice. Pour in tequila until it comes a third of the way up the side. Top that with another third of fresh-squeezed lime juice (it's gotta be fresh-squeezed!). Then fill up the last third of the pitcher with Cointreau. Add a small amount of sugar, according to your taste; for me, in an average-sized pitcher I wouldn't add more than a few teaspoons. Stir vigorously with a wooden spoon for at least 30 seconds. Taste for sweetness, adding more sugar if necessary. Pour margaritas from the pitcher into waiting glasses. If you'd like a salt rim on the glasses, simply prepare a flat plate of coarse salt. Rub a little lime juice around the rims of the glasses, then place them, one at a time, rim side down, in the salt. Rotate the glasses 360 degrees, and your rims are salted.

The big margarita question, of course, is: Which tequila? Tequila has become one of those endlessly upscaled commodities that used to be inexpensive, but now costs ungodly amounts of money at the high end. For me, those "finer" tequilas—usually carrying the designation añejo, or "aged"—are dandy, but they have more in common with some of the world's great brandies. When I'm in Mexico I observe that the real tequileros are drinking the simplest tequila category—blanco, or what's sometimes called "silver" in the U.S. So, for me, it's blanco or silver all the way for margaritas. I only insist on one thing: that the tequila you use be made from 100% blue agave (the bottle will indicate this).

One other drinking option that's great for this party is beer! Beer snobs pooh-pooh the light, easy-to-drink beer produced in Mexico—but it is *perfect* for washing down spicy food! With a party like this I would love bucketsful of iced Corona, or Tecate, or Pacifica Clara. If you can find tall, long-necked bottles (easy to do with Corona), slip a small piece of lime into the neck of the bottle.

The Recipes

Avocado and Romaine Salad with Pomegranates, Pepitas, and Orange-Sesame Vinaigrette

· ○ ● ○ ·

Here's a great salad, bright with some Mexican salad surprises—such as pomegranate seeds and pumpkin seeds. Best of all, it does double duty at your party. Place it on the buffet as the guests are arriving; guests help themselves to a portion of salad with chips on the side. Leave the salad out on the buffet when the taco action gets going, though, and encourage guests to pick out parts of the salad (a romaine strip here, a few pomegranate seeds there) to add to their tacos!

The dressing can be made 2 or 3 days ahead and stored in the refrigerator.

makes about 3 cups

the dressing:

5 cups orange juice, preferably fresh (from 20 to 24 medium oranges)

1 ½ teaspoons sugar

Finely grated zest of 2 oranges

⅔ cup fresh lime juice

1 generous tablespoon kosher salt

Generous pinch cayenne

2 cups extra-virgin olive oil

1 ¼ teaspoons dark sesame oil

makes enough for 12

the salad:

3 medium cucumbers, peeled, halved, seeded, and cut into ½-inch pieces

1 pound jicama, peeled and cut into ¼ x 1 ½-inch sticks

24 medium radishes, trimmed and quartered

6 ripe Haas avocados

2 tablespoons fresh lime juice

10 scallions, sliced very thinly on the bias

1 medium pomegranate, seeded (see Cook's Note)

1 cup roasted unsalted pepitas (Mexican-style pumpkin seeds)

4 to 5 medium heads of romaine lettuce

1. Make the dressing: Put the orange juice and the sugar in a medium saucepan and bring to a boil over high heat. Lower the heat and simmer the mixture until reduced to about 1 ¼ cups. Remove from the heat and let cool a few minutes. Whisk in the orange zest, ⅔ cup lime juice, salt, and cayenne. Transfer to a bowl and slowly pour in the olive oil in a thin stream, whisking continuously, so that an emulsion forms. Whisk in the sesame oil; taste for salt. Chill in the refrigerator before use. Whisk again just before dressing the salad.

2. Right before the guests arrive, make the salad: Toss the cucumbers, jicama, and radishes in a large salad bowl with half the dressing.

3. Peel the avocados, and cut the flesh into 1-inch chunks; toss the flesh with the 2 tablespoons of lime juice as you work. Add the avocado chunks to the salad bowl, along with the scallions, half the pomegranate seeds, and half the pepitas.

4. Cut the romaine crosswise, working from the leafy end to the root end, into strips that are about 1 inch wide (you need about 14 cups of strips). Add the lettuce to the salad bowl, along with half to two-thirds of the remaining dressing, tossing well to coat. Taste the salad, and add as much of the remaining dressing as suits your taste. Top the salad with the remaining pomegranate seeds and pepitas. Serve at once.

> Cook's Note: The simplest way to seed a pomegranate is to cut it into a few pieces and rap the skin side sharply with a spoon. Do this over a bowl of water and you can separate out any bits of membrane.

Tortillas for Tacos

· ∘ ● ∘ ·

96 (5 ¾-inch) corn tortillas

The most important thing you can do for your store-bought (or internet-bought)
tortillas is to make them soft and moist (no crispy shells!).

The easiest way to accomplish this, frankly, is to place the whole, unopened, plastic bag of tortillas
(with a tiny slit for a steam-hole) in the microwave for 40 seconds or so! Then remove them from
the bag and keep them warm under a dish towel. Another way to make them soft and moist is to
take them out of the bag and place them in a steamer over boiling water for a minute or so. Once
again, remove and keep tortillas warm under a kitchen towel. It is best to do the
microwaving/steaming not more than a few minutes before serving the tacos.

If you want to take it one little flavorful step further, dedicate a cast-iron pan or griddle for last-
minute tortilla prep. Grease the pan or griddle lightly with vegetable oil, or butter, or lard (my
choice), and keep it over medium-low heat. Before stuffing a taco for a guest, grab two warm
tortillas from under the towel, drizzle them on both sides with a few drops of water, and heat them
very briefly—about 20 seconds a side—in the pan or on the griddle. Place the two tortillas on top
of each other, and start filling 'em up. Remember: hot and soft, not hot and crisp, is what you want!

Chorizo and Red Pepper Filling for Tacos

. . • ● • .

You can make this filling ahead.

enough filling for approximately 24 tacos

3 medium red bell peppers, seeded and cut into ¼ x1 ½-inch strips

3 medium green bell peppers, seeded and cut into ¼ x1 ½-inch strips

½ cup vegetable oil

12 large cloves garlic, thinly sliced

1 ½ teaspoons dried oregano

Kosher salt

1 ½ pounds Spanish chorizo, cut on the bias into ⅛-inch slices (see Cook's Note)

1. Toss the red and green peppers together.

2. Place two large skillets over medium-high heat and divide the oil between them. Divide the garlic between the skillets and cook until pale golden at the edges, 1 to 2 minutes. Divide the peppers between the skillets and cook, stirring regularly, until they've softened, 8 to 10 minutes. Reduce the heat if the peppers threaten to burn.

3. Add the oregano, sprinkle with salt, and stir to combine. Divide the chorizo between the pans and mix well. Cook, stirring regularly, until the chorizo are heated through, but not browned. Combine in one pan for holding.

> COOK'S NOTE: *Chorizo is the great chile-inflected Spanish-style sausage now widely available in the U.S. You'll find long-cured ones in the market, which are quite hard and taste best thinly sliced at room temperature. Then there are the shorter-cured ones, which you want to use for this dish: they are much softer, more like fresh sausage, and are best when heated. If you see chorizo in your market, you can always tell which is which simply by squeezing. Two brands of soft chorizo that I find particularly good are Primera Chorizo from Los Galleguitos and Chorizos Ahumados from Ki Delicia Foods* (**see Where to Find It, page 172**).

Chicken, Chipotle, and Raisin Filling for Tacos

· ○ ● ○ ·

This filling can be made up to 2 days ahead and reheated on the stove top with a few tablespoons of water or, partially covered, in a microwave.

enough filling for approximately 24 tacos

2 (28-ounce) cans whole tomatoes, drained and halved lengthwise

Vegetable oil

8 medium dried chipotle chiles (about ¾ ounce), or more, stems removed

12 large cloves garlic, unpeeled

½ teaspoon ground cinnamon

¼ teaspoon ground cloves

1 teaspoon kosher salt, plus additional as needed

Freshly ground black pepper

12 medium chicken thighs, bone in, skin on

2 large white onions, thinly sliced (about 5 cups)

1 cup raisins, soaked in hot water for 30 minutes

2 cups chicken stock

1. Line two baking trays with foil, oil them lightly, and divide the tomato halves, cut side up, between the trays. Heat the broiler. Drizzle the tomatoes with a bit of oil and broil them, one tray at a time, until they're well charred in spots, but still moist, 10 to 20 minutes (timing depends on the strength of your broiler and its distance from the tomatoes).

2. Meanwhile, heat a large dry skillet over medium heat. Add the chiles a few at a time, pressing on them lightly with a spatula for 10 to 15 seconds per side to toast them. Take care to avoid burning them. Transfer to a bowl, cover with hot water, and soak until softened, about 30 minutes. Add the garlic cloves to the skillet and toast them on all sides, until the skins are a bit blackened and the garlic has softened slightly, about 15 minutes. Set aside to cool.

3. Transfer the tomatoes to a blender or food processor. Drain and seed the chiles and add to the blender. Peel the garlic and add it to the blender along with the cinnamon, cloves, 1 teaspoon of salt, and a few grindings of black pepper. Process, adding small amounts of tap water as needed, and pausing to scrape down the sides of the blender until a smooth purée forms. Reserve.

4. Generously salt the skin sides of the chicken and heat two large skillets over medium-high heat. Put 3 tablespoons of oil in each skillet and add the chicken, skin side down. Cook until deeply browned, about 10 minutes. Sprinkle with salt, flip the pieces over, and cook until browned on the second side, about 6 minutes more. Transfer the chicken to a plate.

5. Remove all but 3 tablespoons of the fat from each skillet. Reduce the heat to medium and divide the onion between the skillets. Cook, stirring regularly, until pale golden at the edges, 6 to 8 minutes. Divide the reserved chile purée between the skillets and cook for 2 minutes, stirring occasionally. Drain the raisins and divide them between the skillets. Stir 1 cup of chicken stock into each skillet, scraping the bottoms to loosen any browned bits. Return the chicken (and any juices) to the skillets, bring to a bare simmer, and partially cover each with a lid. Simmer gently, basting occasionally, until the chicken is tender and cooked through, 25 to 30 minutes.

6. Remove the chicken from the skillets with a slotted spoon, and when it is cool enough to handle, remove and discard the bones and skin. Shred the meat with your fingers into bite-sized pieces and return it to the skillets. Simmer for 10 minutes more, or until the chicken is coated in a thick, barely fluid sauce, thinning with water if needed. Combine in one pan for holding. Taste for salt and serve with warm corn tortillas.

Tongue and White Onion Filling for Tacos

· · · ● · · ·

Lengua, as they say in Mexico, is one of my very favorite taco fillings—and one of the most popular on the Mexican street.

The onions can be prepared a day ahead.

enough filling for approximately 24 tacos

4 tablespoons vegetable oil, plus additional as needed

3 medium white onions, sliced into 3/8-inch rounds (see Cook's Note #1)

Kosher salt

1 1/2 pounds cured, cooked beef tongue cut into irregular chunks about 3/8 inch thick and 1 1/2 inches long (see Cook's Note #2)

6 tablespoons finely chopped cilantro

4 1/2 teaspoons white wine vinegar

1. Put 4 tablespoons vegetable oil in a large skillet over medium-high heat. When the oil is hot, add the onion rounds in a single layer (you will need to do this in batches) and cook until browned, about 3 minutes. Flip the onions with a spatula and lightly brown the second side, about 2 1/2 minutes more. Sprinkle lightly with salt. Remove the onions to a bowl. Repeat until all the onions are browned, adding more oil as needed. Separate the onions into rings.

2. When ready to serve, add the tongue to the skillet and place over medium heat, stirring regularly. When it is heated through, add the onions and combine. When the onions are just heated through, add the cilantro and sprinkle the wine vinegar over the entire mixture. Stir well to combine, and serve with warm tortillas.

COOK'S NOTE #1: *Try to keep each slice "nested" within its concentric rings, forming one solid disc. When added to the pan in this way, the insides steam while the edges are browning, leaving them crisp and fresh tasting but still caramelized at the edges—just what you want for this dish.*

COOK'S NOTE #2: *You can usually buy whole, cured, cooked beef tongue at your supermarket, but you may have to order it ahead. It's delicious!*

Beef Picadillo Filling for Tacos

· · · ● · · ·

This filling can be made up to 2 days ahead and reheated on the stove top with a few tablespoons of water or, partially covered, in a microwave.

enough filling for approximately 24 tacos

6 tablespoons vegetable oil

3 pounds boneless beef chuck, trimmed of excess fat and cut into 1 1/2-inch cubes

8 cups water

2 medium white onions, each cut lengthwise into 8 wedges

12 large cloves garlic

4 bay leaves

4 teaspoons kosher salt

2 ounces ancho chiles (about 6 medium)

1 teaspoon ground cumin

1 teaspoon ground coriander

1. Heat two large skillets over medium-high heat and divide the oil between them. When the oil shimmers, divide the beef cubes between the skillets and brown very well on at least two sides. Add 4 cups of water to each skillet and scrape the bottom of each to loosen any browned bits. Divide the onions, garlic, bay leaves, and salt between the skillets and bring just to a simmer. Reduce the heat to medium-low and, stirring occasionally, gently simmer the mixture until very tender, 2 to 2 1/2 hours. Let the meat cool to room temperature in the liquid.

2. Meanwhile, heat another skillet over medium heat and briefly toast the chiles in it by pressing on them lightly with a spatula for 10 to 15 seconds per side. Transfer the chiles to a bowl, cover with hot water, and soak until softened, about 30 minutes. Stem and seed the chiles; chop coarsely and set aside.

3. Remove the cooled meat from the liquid and transfer it to a bowl. Shred the beef into small, bite-sized pieces with your fingers and set aside. Discard the bay leaves and transfer one skillet-full of the liquid—including all the onion and garlic pieces—to a blender jar. Add half of the reserved chiles and process until the mixture is smooth with no large bits of chile remaining. Repeat with the remaining liquid and chilies. Return each batch to its skillet and divide the shredded meat between the two. Add 1/2 of the cumin and coriander to each skillet. Simmer the mixture until the meat is coated in a thick sauce, about 20 minutes. Combine in one pan for holding. Taste for salt and serve with warm tortillas.

# Tomatillo Salsa

This is especially good with the chicken-chipotle-raisin taco and the tongue-white onion taco.

This salsa tastes best when freshly made. If you'd like to prepare it ahead of time, process the tomatillo mixture without the onion and cilantro. Chop and add them both just before serving.

makes about 2 cups

6 large garlic cloves, unpeeled

1 ½ pounds tomatillos (8 to 10 medium), husks removed, washed and dried

4 medium jalapeño peppers (about 2 ounces total)

1 teaspoon kosher salt

½ teaspoon sugar

6 tablespoons finely chopped white onion, soaked in cold water for 2 minutes and drained

4 tablespoons finely chopped cilantro

1. Heat a large skillet over medium heat. Add the garlic cloves to the skillet and toast them on all sides until the skins are a bit blackened and the garlic has softened slightly, about 15 minutes. When it's cool enough to handle, peel the garlic and add it to the bowl of a food processor.

2. Meanwhile, line a baking sheet with foil. Place the tomatillos (stem side down) and jalapeños on the foil. Broil them on both sides until they're charred and blackened in most places, 4 to 8 minutes per side depending on the strength of your broiler and its distance from the tomatillos and peppers. If necessary, rotate the tray to expose them evenly to the heat.

3. Transfer the tomatillos to the bowl of the food processor. Seed the peppers and add them to the bowl along with the salt and sugar. Pulse the mixture for 30 seconds and transfer to a mixing bowl. It will still have some chunks in it. Stir in the onions and cilantro; taste for salt, and serve.

Salsa Mexicana

· ∘ • ● • ∘ ·

This is especially good with the beef picadillo taco.

This salsa tastes best when served as fresh as possible.

makes about 6 cups

1 medium white onion, finely chopped (about 1 generous cup)

2 ½ pounds ripe tomatoes, cut into ½-inch pieces (about 6 cups)

6 to 8 medium serrano peppers (about 1 ½ ounces) or 3 to 4 medium jalapeños, finely chopped (seeds optional)

⅔ cup loosely packed chopped cilantro

2 teaspoons kosher salt

¾ teaspoon sugar

9 tablespoons fresh lime juice

3 tablespoons vegetable oil

1. Soak the onion in cold water for 2 minutes; drain and place in a mixing bowl. Add the tomatoes, peppers, and cilantro and combine.

2. Whisk the salt and sugar into the lime juice in a small bowl until dissolved. Whisk in the oil. Pour this dressing over the tomato-onion mixture and toss thoroughly to coat. Taste for salt, and serve.

Roasted Poblano Rajas with Marinated Onion

· · ● · ·

Rajas, or strips of roasted chile, are especially good with both the chorizo-red pepper taco and the tongue-white onion taco.

This dish can be made a few hours ahead.

makes about 3 cups

1 medium white onion, finely chopped (about 1 generous cup)
Distilled white vinegar
12 medium poblano peppers (about 2 pounds)
1 teaspoon kosher salt

1. Place the onions in a small bowl and cover with vinegar. Marinate for 1 hour.

2. Meanwhile, roast the peppers by setting them directly over a gas flame (resting on the grates), or under a broiler, until blackened and blistered all over, turning them as necessary. Do this as close to the flame as possible so that the peppers aren't given too much time to cook (their flesh is thinner than bell peppers'). Set the peppers aside until cool enough to handle, but don't cover or put them in a bag as you might for bell peppers—they'll overcook.

3. When the peppers are cool, remove most of the blackened skin from the peppers with your fingers, but don't rinse them. Remove the seeds and cut the peppers into ¼-inch strips. Place them in a mixing bowl. Drain the marinated onions and combine with the peppers. Toss well with the salt and serve at room temperature.

Mexican Soured Cream

. . . ● . . .

(Crema)

The sour cream that's ubiquitous at Tex-Mex restaurants and on Tex-Mex dishes is based on this thinner cream that's used in Mexico. To my taste, not only is *crema* thinner, but it's also much more delicious! By all means, use sour cream at your party if you're time-challenged; but once you prepare this easy *crema,* you'll never go back! It works well on all the tacos at this party.

Start this at least a day before the party.

makes 2¹/₂ cups

2 cups heavy cream

¹/₂ cup buttermilk, at room temperature

Pour the cream into a small saucepan and place over low heat. Stirring regularly, bring the cream just to 100°F (use a thermometer). Do not overheat. Immediately stir in the buttermilk and transfer the mixture to a glass jar with a lid. Let the cream rest at room temperature until thickened, about 15 to 20 hours. The *crema* will keep, refrigerated, for a week or two.

Crumbled Cotija

. . ● . .

(Mexican Hard Cheese)

Cotija is an aged, dry, hard, salty cheese originally made in Cotija, Mexico (Michoacán), and now made throughout central and southern Mexico, as well as in parts of the U.S. Traditionally, cotija was made from goat's milk, but modern producers usually use cow's milk. Some refer to it as the "Parmesan" of Mexico—and, indeed, it is usually used in Mexican cooking as an enlivening sprinkle on starchy foods. You can buy it pre-grated, which is fine, but I prefer to buy whole, irregularly shaped blocks in the market and crumble it (not grate it) myself. Serve crumbled cotija in a bowl as yet another possibility for your guests' orgy of taco-topping.

Banana Bread Pudding with Cinnamon, Cayenne, and Dulce dé Leche

· · • · ·

This is an out-and-out fabulous version of bread pudding. It is made even more exciting, and more Mexican, by the final soak in dulce de leche or cajeta, two different versions of reduced milk. They are not essential to the dish; you'll love it anyway without that final soak. But if you want to go all the way, purchase dulce de leche or cajeta—both are available at Latin markets—or make your own! It's not hard. Recipes follow.

serves 12

Unsalted butter for greasing the pan

1 ½ cups sweetened condensed milk

1 (16-ounce) store-bought loaf of unsliced white bread

1 ¼ pounds bananas (about 4 small or 3 large)

2 cups half-and-half

4 large eggs

½ teaspoon ground cinnamon (use Mexican canela if you can find it)

1 ½ teaspoons vanilla extract (preferably Mexican)

1 ½ teaspoons grated orange zest

Kosher salt

Cayenne

4 tablespoons unsalted butter, cut into small pieces

1 cup dulce de leche, or cajeta, at room temperature (see recipes below and on page 168)

1. Heat the oven to 350°F. Butter a 9x13-inch baking pan.

2. Heat the sweetened condensed milk in a medium, heavy-bottomed saucepan over medium heat, whisking continuously to prevent scorching. When it reaches a gentle boil, continue whisking and boiling until the condensed milk just begins to turn a very light butterscotch color, about 10 minutes in all. Remove from the heat and let cool.

3. Cut the bread into 1-inch cubes, leaving the crust on. Peel the bananas and cut into ¼-inch slices. Toss the bread cubes and bananas together in the buttered pan and spread them out evenly.

4. Add the half-and-half, eggs, cinnamon, vanilla, orange zest, a pinch of salt, and a big pinch of cayenne to the saucepan with the cooled sweetened condensed milk; whisk until thoroughly combined. Pour this custard over the bread and bananas. Press the bread down with your hands until all the bread pieces are slightly compressed and saturated in the mixture. Dot the top of the casserole with 4 tablespoons of butter.

5. Bake in the middle of the oven until the top is golden brown, about 40 minutes.

6. Warm the dulce de leche or cajeta in the microwave and pour over the top of the bread pudding while it is hot. Prick the top surface of the pudding with a fork to allow the topping to seep down. Let the pudding rest for 10 minutes, then serve immediately.

Dulce de Leche

· · ● · ·

Ever since Häagen-Dazs launched its dulce de leche ice cream a few years back, the item has had a near-cult following. But its history, of course, goes back very far, way before Häagen-Dazs. Dulce de leche is basically reduced milk; after you cook the milk in a pan for a long time, it turns thick, brown, and sweet. It has been beloved for ages in Latin America, where it is eaten as is, or spread on bread, or as the base for myriad dessert variations. You can easily find it in cans at Latin groceries, but nothing beats the taste of *dulce de leche casero,* or homemade dulce de leche.

makes 1 generous cup

1 (14–ounce) can sweetened condensed milk

1. Remove the label and wash and dry the can. Use a can opener or an ice pick to make two of the smallest possible openings, one on either side of the top of the can. Cover the top of the can loosely with plastic wrap and secure it with a rubber band.

2. Place the can in a 1½-quart saucepan. Pour boiling water into the saucepan until it reaches halfway up the can. Cover the saucepan and let the can cook over medium heat until the milk is a golden caramel color (you will see a little seeping out of the openings). This should take about 2 hours. During the cooking time, the water should just simmer gently. Check the water level from time to time, and replenish it to the halfway level as the water evaporates.

3. When the dulce de leche is ready, remove it from the saucepan. Carefully open the can, and transfer the dulce de leche to another container. Some will have seeped out onto the sides of the can, but it can be scraped off and mixed in with the rest. Use immediately, or refrigerate.

Cajeta

· · ● · ·

If you want to ratchet your dulce de leche up one more exotic notch, you can make cajeta, a treat that's very popular in Mexico. The principle is the same, but cajeta is usually made from goat's milk, which gives it an earthier flavor. Unfortunately, there are no readily available cans of goat's milk, so you'll have to stir continuously. The results are worth the trouble. Cajeta is eaten in Mexico just by itself, or as a topping for other sweets.

makes 1 1/2 to 2 cups

1 quart whole goat's milk

1 cup sugar

2 tablespoons light corn syrup

1/2 teaspoon baking soda dissolved in 1 tablespoon water

1. Bring the goat's milk, sugar, and corn syrup to a boil in a deep, heavy-bottomed 3-quart saucepan over medium-high heat, stirring constantly.

2. When the mixture comes to a boil, remove it from the heat and add the dissolved baking soda. The mixture will bubble up; stir for a minute or two off the heat until the bubbles subside.

3. Return the saucepan to medium-low to medium heat. Monitor the heat as this cooks, adjusting as necessary so that the mixture is boiling, but does not boil over. Let the mixture cook, stirring occasionally, for 45 minutes to an hour. You'll know it's ready when it looks like thin butterscotch pudding. As it's approaching that final stage, stir constantly to prevent scorching.

4. When the cajeta is ready, pour it into a metal bowl, cover, and refrigerate.

COOK'S NOTE: *If your cajeta's not perfectly smooth, you can strain it through a fine sieve.*

Set Dressing

The question here is not where to start, but where to stop!

Your guests will know they've arrived at the correct adobe when they see a strategically placed Mexican flag fluttering in the breeze. Or a wooden directional post, its haphazard arrows pointing the way not only to your party, but to Cozumel and Oaxaca. If the party begins at dusk, *luminaria* (candles set inside weighted paper bags) could mark the path to the entrance. Another option for overachievers is to post a donkey from Central Casting out front.

Once inside, shepherd your guests to a delightfully improvised bar, aglow with strands of white lights, festooned with the pierced-paper banners called *papel picado* **(see Where to Find It, page 172)**. Take advantage of the many ingenious props that can be bought, rented, or created out of what's at hand. Party and event rental centers are good places to start your search. I even found an oxcart and bales of fire-retardant hay at one! This party embraces all the clichéd symbols of Old Mexico: it celebrates piñatas, pottery, potted plants, painted barrels, posters, percussive castanets, Pancho Villa look-alikes, and preposterous jumping beans.

Table
Dressing

The color palette one associates with Mexico—those daring, impossibly saturated reds, blues, greens, yellows, oranges, and pinks—lends an intoxicating amount of freedom when you're selecting table linens. Whatever type of buffet table you have, you can cover it with a cloth, or cloths, that fit the eye-popping requirements. A Mexican blanket makes a fine stand-in for a tablecloth. Use a serape as a runner down the center of the table and allow its colors to cue the hue of your napkins (which you should cinch with jute twine, with, if you like, a fresh gerbera daisy in each one). If you're setting up smaller tables for guests to eat their tacos, go with smaller variations on the bright color/Mexican blanket/serape theme. By the way, clashing, mismatching colors are not possible at this riot of vividness.

Textural accents should be earthy, with a special reliance on tin, iron, copper, clay, or silver, but not the fancy stuff. I see unpretentious flatware with wooden handles, maybe even mismatched pieces from a flea market, a second-hand store, or a country antique shop. While the informality of this party could justify a drift toward paper plates (I did find some sturdy ones decorated with chile peppers), I recommend sticking to the real thing: colored plates if you have them, white if you don't.

Animate the buffet table, and the other tables, with diminutive potted cacti, tiny maracas, or miniature sombreros (all are available from online sources). Scatter colored corn kernels, available from Hispanic grocery stores, like confetti. Or mound an assortment of dried beans, gourds, and dried chile peppers in *molcajetes* (the lava rock mortars used for making guacamole).

Flowers? Keep the arrangements low and humble. Consider using empty tin cans with interesting labels (such as the especially beguiling chipotle chiles in adobo made by La Morena) as vases. Or sheath watertight containers with small brown paper bags, roll down the collars, and embellish with ties of raffia or jute. Tight little bouquets of bright red carnations or black-eyed Susans would hit just the right floral note. Of course, the large tissue-paper flowers that are ubiquitous in Mexico would also be right at home here.

Lighting should be dim, with most of it coming from candlelight. I would deploy an army of votive candles, but would also endorse trios of pillar candles of varying heights, bound together with several turns of jute twine and standing on platforms of tile or terra-cotta. If you're a Mexican food freak and own a *metate*—a flat slab of volcanic rock traditionally used to grind corn—it would make an emblematic and clever base for your candles.

Entertainment

Music will knit the elements of the party together. It can be as simple as a few well-chosen CDs, or as elaborate as a strolling mariachi band. But be sensitive to your guests and the shifting moods of the party; if it's conversation they want, keep the music in the background.

To help create the atmosphere of a Mexican street fair, offer games such as Bingo (using dried kidney beans or dried corn kernels as tokens), or improvise a ring toss with cerveza or tequila bottles.

Where to Find It

Melissa's/World Variety Produce, Inc.
P.O. Box 21127
Los Angeles, CA 90021
800.588.0151 (toll free)
www.melissas.com
Online source of fresh fruit, vegetables, and exotic produce including tomatillos and avocados.

Los Galleguitos
147 48th St.
Union City, NJ 07087
201.865.7232 (tel)
A source for Spanish-style soft-cure chorizo.

Ki Delicia Foods
8012 Grand Ave.
North Bergen, NJ 07047
800.777.3146 (toll free)
www.kidelicia.com
This website carries one of my favorite Spanish-style soft-cure chorizos.

www.MexGrocer.com
An online purveyor of nonperishable food and ingredients from Mexico.

The CMC Company
P.O. Drawer 322
Avalon, NJ 08202
800.262.2780 (toll free)
609.861.3065 (fax)
www.thecmccompany.com
Large selection of common and uncommon ingredients essential to Mexican cooking including dried, powdered, and canned chiles; Mexican oregano; and kitchenware such as molcajetes, tortilla presses, and comals.

CheeseSupply, Inc.
P.O. Box 515
Vashon, WA 98070
866.7.CHEESE (toll free)
206.463.1992 (tel)
www.cheesesupply.com
Mexican-style cheeses, including cotija.

www.gourmetsleuth.com
Traditional and modern Mexican cookware (including a ceramic molcajete, which doesn't require seasoning like those made of lava rock), Mexican ingredients.

www.latinworks.com
Clothing and textiles including serapes, peasant blouses, and Baja pullovers; party supplies; maracas; pottery; folk art; Frida Kahlo memorabilia.

www.melissaguerra.com
877.875.2665 (toll free)
Select Mexican ingredients, kitchenware, and vitroleros.

www.partymaster.com
One-stop online shopping for your Mexican-themed party decorations including Mexican flags, bunting, hats, paper products.

www.nationalguild.com /HiPlainsTradingPost
If you're looking for a "Clint Eastwood Poncho," this is the site for you. Also features kiva ladders, sombreros, serapes, Mexican blankets, and other southwestern merchandise.

Sunland Home, LLC
P.O. Box 17053
Tucson, AZ 85731
888.786.8876 (toll free)
520.844.1116 (fax)
www.sunlandhome.com
An online source for southwestern-inspired home furnishings and accessories; self-proclaimed "Chili Pepper Central," a line that includes chili lights, ceramics, posters, candles, and paper products.

Reign Trading Co.
3838 Walnut Grove
Rosemead, CA 91770
626.307.7744 (fax)
www.mexicansugarskull.com
Papel picado, Mexican oilcloth tablecloths, Day-of-the-Dead party supplies.

A Totally Frank Party

Hot Dogs, in Dazzling Variations

A Party for 12

The Menu

Homemade Lemonade

The Chicago Dog
(Tomatoes, Onions, Pickles, Cucumbers, Peppers, Relish, and Bright Yellow Mustard on a Poppy-Seed Bun)

The Southern Slaw Dog
(Foot-Long Hot Dogs with Chili, Raw Onions, and Coleslaw)

The Kansas City Dog
(Sauerkraut and Melted Swiss on a Sesame-Seed Bun)

The Reykjavik Dog
(Rémoulade Sauce and Crunchy, Deep-Fried Onions)

The Mexican Dog
(Bacon, Tomatoes, Green Salsa, and Hot Sauce)

The Swedish Dog
(Mashed Potatoes, Green Relish, and Dill on Flatbread)

The Do-It-Yourself Banana Split Bar

If you're expecting a big crowd, but not relishing the idea of a lot of preparation and cooking, *this* is the party to choose! Everyone lights up at the idea of hot dogs, and your guests will be especially gleeful when you've laid out a universe of possible wiener permutations that will enable your guests to re-create the hottest hot dog hits from around the country and around the world. Everyone has a good time at this party—the eats are great and everyone learns something about a simple food that is too often taken for granted. This is a perfect party for kids—or for kid-hearted adults.

The Plan

There are multiple ways to think about your party venue for this fete—the chief consideration being the way in which you wish to cook your hot dogs!

If a hot dog is nothing to you if it's not grilled, well, you're headed toward a back-yard, outside party. If, on the other hand, you prefer to coddle your dogs in the moist surroundings of a pot of simmering water, then I'd say you have a classic indoor party on your hands. Some hosts, of course, will want to offer their guests both options—which can be done, as long as you figure out a way to add a boiling pot arrangement to your smoky grill arrangement.

Either way, this is a do-it-yourself party. Set up the various hot dog "stations"—all the Chicago dog fixin's grouped together, all the Southern slaw dog fixin's grouped together, and so on—on a huge buffet table. Your job is to produce *hot* hot dogs by whatever cooking method you choose. You need to familiarize yourself with the wiener options, so a guest can say "I want a Chicago dog" and get a dog from you that has been placed in the proper poppy seed roll, which you will have at your station. The guest then proceeds to the buffet, for all the Chicago garnishes. You may, of course, give a guest more than one hot dog at a time, so he or she can go make one or more types of hot dogs at the buffet table. To facilitate this multi-tasking, you might want to acquire some sturdy paper cartons for hot dogs, available from Dean Supply Company in Cleveland **(see Where to Find It, page 191)**.

Back at your cooking station, you will also need to keep four other things hot: chili, mashed potatoes, sauerkraut, and pourable melted cheese. You serve these items to your guests, right on their hot dogs, if they've chosen the dogs that characteristically include 'em.

When the last hot dog has hit the last bun, it's time to clear the buffet table and replace the hot dog fixin's with another simple pleasure that makes people happy—ice cream and sundae fixin's!

The Ingredient

You can put anything you want on a lousy hot dog, and it'll still taste like a lousy hot dog. But serve a fabulous hot dog plain, and you've got something special. Serve a fabulous hot dog with fabulous toppings, and you've got a very special, very fabulous party! The hot dog is the key.

I'm sad to report that the vast preponderance of hot dogs consumed in America are pretty lousy. They're what you're likely to run into at the supermarket, and are, therefore, what most people buy. What characterizes a lousy hot dog? Inferior dogs often have filler in them, such as cereal or dried milk or soy protein; these ingredients cheapen, soften, trivialize, and compromise the chew. Inferior dogs taste processed. Inferior dogs may have artificial flavorings and too much of them; sometimes a bad dog cloys with artificial smoke or rancid garlic powder. And inferior dogs are sometimes wrapped in artificial casings—which offer artificial chew—or no casings—which offer no chew at all!

Great dogs taste like great meat. They are subtly seasoned and harmonious, usually with no flavor predominating. The essential alchemy of hot dog–making is emulsification: meat is ground into a paste and mixed with ice chips at high speed, which creates the fine interior of a hot dog. When a wienermeister has done this, the result is a work of art, with fascinating texture and chew; when a schlockmeister has done this, the result is soft or spongy. To gild the lily, the true hot dog artisan wraps his mighty mousse in a natural casing—usually sheep's intestine—which helps create the awesome "snap," or crunch, that to me is the highest good a hot dog can attain on this earth. With just a little diligence, dogs like these can easily be found, so that you may dazzle your guests.

However, before you set out on your quest, I must make you aware of the great dichotomy in the world of available hot dogs: "Bologna" dogs vs. "New York" dogs. You will never see these words on the packages of hot dogs, though; the terms are terms that I made up to make things clearer for myself.

Most of those supermarket dogs I referred to are in what I call the "Bologna" style (pronounced "baloney"), as opposed to the "New York" style. Bologna dogs are pale in color, pink rather than red. They are usually dominated by pork and veal, whereas the classic New York dog is usually dominated by beef. The meat of a Bologna dog has minimal spicing, little or no garlic, and not too much fat; the meat of a New York dog is garlicky, with much more spice and much more fat. The Bologna dog is usually softer to chew than a New York dog. The only category in which the Bologna dog has "more" of something is smoke; many a supermarket dog has the flavor of liquid smoke.

My preference? The New York dog by several lengths. Oh, yes, there can be great Bologna dogs; there are still some Old World artisans (like Liehs & Stiegerwald in Syracuse, New York) who turn out elegant, fluffy, subtle dogs in the Austro-German tradition. But there are many more producers of great New York dogs out there—and, to me, the pleasures of a great New York dog are higher than the pleasures of a great Bologna dog. Plus, New York dogs stand up better to toppings.

My recommendation: acquire New York dogs for your party; just one well-selected brand will be just fine. (Several brands are sold through supermarkets.)

I've got a caveat. Many producers of New York dogs have given in to the American preference for less chewing and are turning out skinless franks. Yikes! This removes the crunchy, "snap" potential from those dogs! The dogs can still be excellent, but, to me, they have something missing. Maybe not to you. So I am going to give you two lists to consider in your hot dog quest: producers of great New York dogs with natural casings, and producers of great New York dogs with no casings (see Where to **Find It, page 191**).

Producers of Great New York–Style Hot Dogs with Natural Casings: (some of these producers also make skinless dogs, so make sure the package says "Natural Casing"):

Boar's Head Frankfurters

Katz's Frankfurters

Sabrett Beef Frankfurters

Usinger's Beef Frankfurters

Alexander & Hornung Beef Franks

Miller's Beef Frankfurters

Nathan's Famous Beef Franks

Producers of Great New York–Style Hot Dogs with No Casings:

Hebrew National Kosher Beef Frankfurters

Omaha Steaks Kosher Beef Franks

Fluky's Chicago-Style Hot Dogs

New West Foods Buffalo and Beef Hot Dogs

Beverage
Time

I think the main potable contenders are obvious: lots of cold beer, lots of cold soda. For an extra kick with these items, gather the most retro examples of these drinks that you can find. Some beer brands from the 1950s—like Rheingold, in the New York City area—are enjoying renewed popularity these days. Great! And of course, nothing says "good old times" like old-fashioned Coca-Cola bottles.

But one other beverage strikes me as perfectly in key with this party: lemonade, particularly if it's homemade, particularly if it's summertime, particularly if the party's outdoors.

The Recipes

Homemade Lemonade

· ○ ● ○ ·

This large pitcher of lemonade is enough for six or seven people to get a
good drink. If you expect more of your guests to be lemonade-drinkers—and if the day is
hot!—prepare two, or even three pitchers.

makes 1 large pitcher

5 large lemons, washed
¾ to 1 cup sugar, according to taste
3 cups water
4 cups ice cubes

1. Roll the lemons with your palm on the countertop to soften them. Cut off their stems. Cut each lemon in half at the equator, and juice with a juicer or reamer. Each lemon should yield about ¼ cup of fresh lemon juice.

2. Place the squeezed lemon halves and the lemon juice in a large pitcher (one that holds 9 to 10 cups is perfect). Sprinkle the lemons with ¾ cup of sugar, and stir the sugar in well with a wooden spoon. Bruise and muddle the lemon halves just a bit as you stir.

3. Add the water and stir vigorously to dissolve the sugar. Taste for sweetness; add a little more sugar if you think it's necessary. Refrigerate for at least 1 to 2 hours.

4. When ready to serve, stir the lemonade, and fill the pitcher up with ice cubes (4 cups should be just about right). Stir again, and serve.

Cooking Hot Dogs

All hot dogs are precooked, so when you "cook" a hot dog, what you are actually doing is "reheating" a hot dog. That said, some people swear by hot dogs "cooked" in water, and some people swear by hot dogs "cooked" on the grill. Me, I like 'em both, and for different reasons.

When I prepare very high-quality hot dogs, with great meat inside and the quintessential "snap" or "crunch" on the exterior that comes from a great natural casing, I prefer boiling. This less intrusive cooking method enables you to experience more of the good taste and texture factors crafted into that dog. To boil hot dogs, don't really boil them; just slip them (at room temperature, ideally) into a large pot of simmering unsalted water. Maintain a slow simmer. Cooking time depends on the girth of the hot dog, but anywhere from 4 to 8 minutes should suffice.

The grill comes in very handy when the hot dogs are not the greatest. I would never boil one of those mass-marketed dogs from the supermarket, for example. But if you grill that dog, the browning on the outside adds flavor to what is essentially a bland product. And since most of these dogs are skinless, boiling would lead to no external texture at all—whereas grilling, due to the browning and toughening of the exterior, supplies at least some "crunch" to these dogs.

Grill the hot dogs over a medium-hot fire until browned on the outside and heated through on the inside—normally about 4 to 6 minutes depending on the girth of the hot dog and its temperature when it hit the grill. (If you are hosting this party indoors, a grill pan on the stove top will suffice.)

Steaming Buns

Improvise a bun steamer by using Oriental bamboo steamers or a lidded Dutch oven outfitted with a rack. Or put a rack in a big roasting pan, pour in hot water to a level beneath the rack, place buns on rack, and cover. You can keep these on the heat source (very low heat) for the duration of the party as long as you replenish the water. Use caution when you reach for a bun: escaping steam can burn!

The Chicago Dog

· ● ● ● ● ● ·

*(Tomatoes, Onions, Pickles, Cucumbers, Peppers, Relish,
and Bright Yellow Mustard on a Poppy-Seed Bun)*

I'm serious about this: the Chicago dog is one of America's all-time greatest gastronomic contributions! Lots of people think they don't like the idea of a "salad" on a hot dog, but when they taste it, they understand the compelling gustatory logic.

To make a proper Chicago dog, you should start with a poppy-seed hot dog bun. They're not easy to find. As an alternative, lightly steam hot dog buns before the party, then roll them in a tray of poppy seeds; the seeds will stick. Give your guest a hot dog in a poppy-seed bun, and send him or her to the Big Table.

Here's what you will need to supply in the Chicago section of the buffet, along with suggested methods of application and a suggested order of architecture:

- **bright yellow mustard on the dog**
- **green relish on the dog**
- **chopped raw onions on the dog**
- **thin tomato slices alongside the dog**
- **short pickled green peppers alongside the dog (in Chicago, they call them "sport peppers," but feel free to substitute sliced pepperoncini)**
- **a long, thin slice of cucumber alongside the dog**
- **a long, thin slice of dill pickle alongside the dog**
- **a sprinkle of celery salt over all**

The Southern Slaw Dog

· · • ● • · ·

(Foot-Long Hot Dogs with Chili, Raw Onions, and Coleslaw)

To make a superlative Southern Slaw dog, it would be wonderful to stock some super-long hot dogs and super-long buns for your party. If you can't find them, however, simply give your guest a regular hot dog in a regular bun. Pour a few tablespoons of hot chili—preferably your favorite spicy chili without beans (the canned grocery-store brand often used in the South is Bunker Hill)—over the hot dog, and send your guest off to the Big Table.

Here's what you will need to supply in the Southern Slaw section of the buffet, along with suggested methods of application and a suggested order of architecture:

- **bright yellow mustard over the chili on the dog**
- **ketchup over the mustard on the dog**
- **mayonnaise over the ketchup on the dog**
- **chopped raw onions over all**
- **coleslaw over all (best if you make your own coleslaw with mayonnaise, a little buttermilk, sugar, and cider vinegar, but store-bought will work)**

The Kansas City Dog

(Sauerkraut and Melted Swiss on a Sesame-Seed Bun)

This dog has two warm elements: sauerkraut and melted cheese. You serve all this at the cooking station; no trip to the buffet table is necessary unless a guest wishes to improvise on top of the classic Kansas City dog.

The preparation of the sauerkraut is simple: just empty a refrigerated pouch of sauerkraut (available in any supermarket) into a saucepan and warm it up.

The preparation of the melted cheese is trickier. In Kansas City, they just melt Swiss cheese over the dog. For this party, especially if you're holding it outside, it's easier to just pour melted cheese over the dog. And the best way to accomplish a pot of melted cheese is to make a version of a fondue. You could prepare it several hours before the party and hold it at room temperature. Keep it warm during the party, so it's pourable.

You'll also need a sesame-seed bun. The method is the same as for the Chicago poppy-seed bun: before the party starts, lightly steam hot dog buns, then roll them in a tray of sesame seeds. The seeds will stick.

So, to serve a K.C. dog, start with a sesame-seed hot dog bun. Place a cooked dog in the bun, and top it with ¼ cup of sauerkraut. Then pour on a few tablespoons of melted cheese.

Quick Fondue

Toss 4 cups grated Swiss cheese (about 14 ounces) and 3 cups grated Gruyère (about 10 ounces) together in a large bowl with ¼ cup all-purpose flour.

Pour 1 ½ cups dry white wine and 4 teaspoons fresh lemon juice into a medium, heavy-bottomed saucepan. Bring to a boil over high heat. Then lower the heat so the liquid simmers, and start stirring in the cheese mix, little by little, making sure each addition has melted before adding the next. You'll end up with a smooth sauce. Season with a pinch of grated nutmeg and some salt and pepper.

The Reykjavik Dog

. ◦ ● ◦ .

(Rémoulade Sauce and Crunchy, Deep-Fried Onions)

There is a small hot dog stand by the sea in downtown Reykjavik, Iceland's capital. At 3 in the morning, in an otherwise deserted city, there are lines practically around the corner. Their version of the Reykjavik dog is known to be the best. And that's saying something, because—though it's little-known internationally—the Reykjavik dog is one of the world's major hot dog treats.

The question is: How authentic do you want to be? If you want to go all the way and use the ingredients that the Icelanders use, you can actually purchase all the fixin's, including the lamb-based hot dogs, from the online Icelandic Store **(see Where to Find It, page 191)**. But you can also make a great Reykjavik dog with ingredients that are more widely available.

When you're ready to serve, place a warmed hot dog (either the usual one you're using for the rest of the party, or the specialty Icelandic one) in a regular hot dog bun, and send your guest off to the Big Table.

Here's what you will need to supply in the Reykjavik section of the buffet, along with suggested methods of application and a suggested order of architecture:

- **a red sauce on the dog (mix together equal portions of BBQ sauce and ketchup)**
- **a sprinkle of canned, deep-fried onions on top (French's or Durkee brands work just fine)**
- **a yellow mustard squeeze on one side of the dog**
- **a "rémoulade sauce" squeeze on the other side (you can reproduce this by stirring a little green pickle relish into mayonnaise)**

The Mexican Dog

· · ● · ·

(Bacon, Tomatoes, Green Salsa, and Hot Sauce)

They serve a great hot dog along the side of the roads in Mexico. The Mexican dog is wrapped in bacon and grilled. If you are holding an indoor party and boiling away in your kitchen, simply put a sauté pan on the stove top to griddle these dogs, or one ridged grilled pan to indoor-grill them. You also need two kinds of salsa to make these babies. The red kind is available anywhere. The green kind may be a little trickier to find. A good one is available by mail order from the Desert Pepper Trading Co. **(see Where to Find It, page 191)**. It is called the Salsa del Rio, Medium. Or make your own.

To proceed: wrap each hot dog in one slice of bacon, spiraling the bacon around so that most of the dog is covered. Cook the dog on the grill in a grill pan, or in a sauté pan until the bacon is crisp and the dog is heated through. Place it on a bun. In Mexico, the bun is kind of yellowish, so a "potato" hot dog bun from the supermarket would be great if you can get it—and send your lucky guest off to that buffet table.

Here's what you will need to supply in the Mexican section of the buffet, along with suggested methods of application and a suggested order of architecture:

- **yellow mustard on the dog**
- **ketchup on the dog**
- **mayonnaise on the dog**
- **diced raw sweet onions on the dog**
- **diced raw tomatoes on the dog**

- **tomatillo or green salsa on the dog**
- **red salsa on the dog**
- **a few squirts of hot sauce on top of everything**

Tomatillo Salsa

makes about 2 1/2 cups

Husk 6 medium tomatillos, chop into 1/4-inch pieces, and place in a bowl. Add 3/4 cup chopped roasted poblano (see page 164) or green bell pepper, 4 finely chopped jalapeño peppers (veins and seeds removed before chopping), 2 minced cloves of garlic, and 1/2 cup chopped white onion. Stir in 1 teaspoon fresh lime juice and 2 tablespoons olive oil. Season with salt.

If the salsa seems too wet, drain off the excess liquid using a colander. This tastes best when you make it right before you serve it.

Deep-Fried Brik with Tuna, Capers, and Egg, page 88

Slow-Cooked Mail-Order Texas Brisket, page 112, with Homemade Tangy Texas BBQ Sauce, page 114; Jalapeño, Cumin, and Red Onion Coleslaw, page 115; Pepper Jack Cornbread, page 118; Long-Cooked Texas Beans with Beer, page 119

Spicy Peach Cobbler, page 120

Sautéed Lobster, Mussels, and Shrimp with
Concentrated Bouillabaisse Broth, page 138,
with Croûtes, page 142

Gascon Prune Tart with Orange Zest, Fresh Thyme, and Armagnac, page 304

Chorizo and Red Pepper Tacos, page 157; Chicken, Chipotle, and Raisin Tacos, page 158; Roasted Poblano Rajas with Marinated Onion, page 164

Banana Bread Pudding with Cinnamon, Cayenne, and Dulce de Leche, page 166

Avocado and Romaine Salad with Pomegranates, Pepitas, and Orange–Sesame Vinaigrette, page 154

The Swedish Dog

· · ● ● ● ● ·

(Mashed Potatoes, Green Relish, and Dill on Flatbread)

The *varmkorv,* in Sweden, is a beautiful thing; the Swedes need a "warm" sausage to help fight the chill! Unlike Americans—who tend to think of the hot dog as a great warm-weather, 'round-the-grill kind of treat—Swedes make their dogs as winter-heavy and comfort-foody as possible! To make this treat, you're gonna need a pot of mashed potatoes, kept warm in a double boiler.

The bun's unusual, too: they roll their dog up in a large, round, thin, pliant bread called *tunnbröd.* This may be hard to find, but a big, floppy flour tortilla or lavosh (say, 9 inches in diameter) would be a great substitute.

When ready to serve, grab a tortilla, or *tunnbröd,* and smear it heavily all over with hot mashed potatoes, leaving just a thin unsmeared margin on the edges. Place a warm dog on the potatoes at one end of the bread—plate it, and hand it off to your guest!

Here's what you will need to supply in the Swedish section of the buffet, along with suggested methods of application and a suggested order of architecture:

- **coarse brown mustard to squirt on the still-exposed dog**
- **ketchup to squirt on the still-exposed dog**
- **green relish to spoon on the still-exposed dog**
- **dried dill to shake on the still-exposed dog**

Once the dill goes on, the exposure ends! Each guest rolls up the dog in the round bread, and gets to work.

The Do-It-Yourself Banana Split Bar

. . ● . .

A recent book celebrating the banana split notes that it is "a primal culinary exercise and an opportunity for spectacle." The author, Michael Turback, goes on to say that the banana split "is at once highbrow, lowbrow, flashy and trashy, foolish, fancy, and unapologetically eccentric."

So as soon as those hot dog stations are cleared, use a big space right at the center of the buffet table, and start assembling your constellation of banana split star ingredients:

Lay out bananas, unpeeled, on a big cutting board. The guests should peel and split the bananas themselves, so the bananas don't turn brown. Advise each guest to split a peeled banana lengthwise, and to lay the two halves on one of the long banana split plates. Let the topping begin!

You'll need ice cream in various flavors, each container with an ice cream scoop in it. Vanilla, chocolate, and strawberry ice creams are traditional, but let your imagination be your guide as to what you supply.

Next, sauces and syrups are expected. If you can manage heat at this station, lay out hot fudge sauce and hot caramel syrup with ladles. If not, chocolate sauce, caramel sauce, strawberry syrup, and maple syrup are some of the most popular pours.

Fruit is required for the next layer—either fresh or crushed (fresh strawberry pieces or crushed strawberries, fresh pineapple pieces or canned crushed pineapple, and so on).

Then, chopped nuts are required. Pecans, walnuts, peanuts, and chopped mixed nuts are among the most popular. I like macadamia.

Whipped cream is the topper. I think it's perfectly in key here to set out ready-to-go spray cans of Reddi-wip.

Then there's always the topper's topper. Sprinkles, chocolate chips, and crushed cookies can bring the banana split building to a festive conclusion.

Oh, and don't forget the maraschino cherries.

You've Got Options

You certainly have enough condiments on your buffet table to keep your guests happy. However, for the more conventionally minded—those who don't want to deal with any of your dog-specific set-ups—you might want to arrange a "nondenominational" section that simply includes an array of all-purpose mustards, relishes, and, for the young and young at heart, ketchups.

Anything else? A few enormous bowls of potato chips would be appropriate. Go for the supermarket brands, by all means, or seek out some of the best potato chips in the country, such as Cape Cod, Dark Russet Potato Chips; Tim's Cascade Style Potato Chips; Zapp's Potato Chips; Rusty's Chips; Balboa Island Style Handmade Potato Chips; Kettle Chips; Natural Gourmet Potato Chips.

There is an obsessed chip purveyor who stocks 'em all—and would love to have you as a regular premium-chip-receiving member—and that's Anchor O'Reilly's Chip of the Month Club **(see Where to Find It, page 191)**.

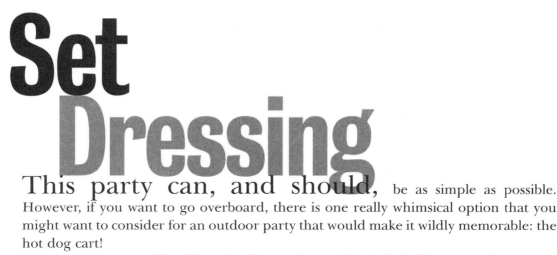

Set Dressing

This party can, and should, be as simple as possible. However, if you want to go overboard, there is one really whimsical option that you might want to consider for an outdoor party that would make it wildly memorable: the hot dog cart!

If you rent one with a big umbrella over it—making it look like one of those push-carts on the streets of New York—you add festivity but you also get a tremendous serving stand. Position it next to your grill, and keep steamed hot dogs in its warming tray, which allows you to offer your guests the option of either grilled or boiled dogs. Use that tray to keep the chili, mashed potatoes, sauerkraut, and pourable melted cheese warm, too. And it's also where you can park the dozens of hot dog buns you'll need for serving.

Hot dog cart rental is a local business, for the most part. I do know one company—Big Louie's Hot Dog Carts in Miami, Florida—that supplies hot dog sellers in Chicago, New York, and other cities with pushcarts; Big Louie's also carries "teeny weenie hot dog carts" for home and party use. I also know a New York-area company called Pushcart Parties that can set you up in New York and New Jersey **(see Where to Find It, page 191)**. Check the Yellow Pages for "party rentals." Or, if you're searching online, log onto www.google.com. Go to Advanced Search, and in the first line, the one that reads "with all of the words," type: *hot dog rentals* (followed by the name of your city), i.e., hot dog rentals nyc; or hot dog rentals des moines. And then prompt the Google search.

One other possibility is the Tabletop Hot Dog Service Cart you can buy from Hammacher Schlemmer in New York City **(see Where to Find It, page 191)**. The good news: it will keep up to 50 hot dogs at the perfect serving temperature. The bad news: it's expensive, and you must allow 4 to 6 weeks for delivery.

Where to Find It

Anchor O'Reilly's Chip of the Month Club
3300 N. Summit St.
Toledo, OH 43611
800.313.2332 (toll free)
www.chipofthemonth.com
Carries many brands of potato chips.

Desert Pepper Trading Company
909 Texas Ave.
El Paso, TX 79901
888.4.SALSAS (toll free)
www.desertpepper.com
Carries Salsa del Rio.

Dean Supply Company
3500 Woodland Ave.
Cleveland, OH 44115
800.ASK.DEAN (toll free)
216.361.5587 (tel)
www.deansupplyco.com
This large restaurant supply house carries approximately 30,000 items on their website.

Big Louie's Hot Dog Carts
5411 Northwest Third Ave.
Miami, FL 33127
800.265.9757 (toll free)
www.hotdogcarts.net
A hot dog cart manufacturer and purveyor with a Dun and Bradstreet rating!

Pushcart Parties
631.588.3348 (tel)
www.pushcartparties.com
For hot dog cart rentals in the New York metropolitan area.

Hammacher Schlemmer
147 East 57th St.
New York, NY 10022
800.321.1484 (catalog toll free)
212.421.9000 (tel)
www.hammacher.com
This venerable catalog and online retailer with a flagship store in New York City carries an electric Tabletop Hot Dog Service Cart.

Hot Dog Purveyors

Boar's Head
400 Sarasota Quay
Sarasota, FL 34236
800.352.6277 (toll free)
www.boarshead.com

Katz's Delicatessen
205 East Houston St.
New York, NY 10002
212.254.2246 (tel)
212.674.3270 (fax)

Usinger's Famous Sausage
1030 N. Old World Third St.
Milwaukee, WI 53203
800.558.9998 (toll free)
414.291.5277 (fax)
www.usingers.com

Alexander & Hornung
10023 Gratiot Ave.
Detroit, MI 48213
800.499.HAMS (toll free)
313.921.6041 (fax)
www.alexander-hornung.com

Miller's Hot Dogs
P.O. Box 986
Oakland, CA 94604
800.624.2328 (toll free)
510.465.1812 (fax)
www.millerhotdogs.com

Hebrew National
Two Jericho Plaza, 3rd Floor
Jericho, NY 11753
800.275.5454 (toll free)
www.hebrewnational.com

Omaha Steaks
10909 John Galt Blvd.
Omaha, NE 68103
800.960.8400 (toll free)
877.329.6328 (fax)
www.omahasteaks.com

Fluky's Chicago–Style Hot Dogs
5225 W. Touhy Ave.
Suite 103
Skokie, IL 60077-3266
877.876.3663 (toll free)
847.329.1454 (fax)
www.thebestofchicago.com
In addition to hot dogs, Fluky's sells poppy-seed buns, bright green relish, and sport peppers.

The Icelandic Store
800.997.7614 (toll free)
www.icelandicstore.com
Your best bet in the United States for obtaining an Icelandic-style hot dog and the necessary accoutrements. But contact for availability. The dogs are not always in stock.

Love Me Tandoor
A Spicy Indian Feast

A Party for 12

The Menu

The Frosty Plymouth Gin & Tonic

Assorted Indian Snacks

Spicy Ginger-Garlic Shrimp with Coconut Milk and Cilantro Leaves

Chicken, Tandoori-Style

Naan

Okra in Buttermilk with Black Mustard and Fresh Curry Leaves

Deep-Fried Cauliflower with Chile and Tomatoes

Cilantro Relish

Raita with Cumin and Tomato

Gulab Jamun
(Deep-Fried Milk Balls in Spiced Syrup)

Americans, despite decades of relative indifference, are finally waking up to the fabulous cuisines of the Indian subcontinent. Big-time. I have lots of friends who enjoy going to Chinese, Italian, and French restaurants, but they get truly revved up when the destination is Indian! As host, you can do something special for these converts—and likely create a whole new group of devotees as well.

The one dish that always seems to grab the neophytes is Chicken Tandoori—skinless, marinated chicken parts, rubbed with spices that turn them red-orange, seared in an intensely hot clay oven known as a "tandoor," and brought to the table on sizzling platters. An adaptation of that classic will be the culinary centerpiece of your party. Overreaching hosts take note: you can now buy your own tandoor for home use by logging on to www.claytandoor.com! But even without it, you can still make amazing chicken, tandoori-style (I prefer to call it that if it hasn't cooked in a tandoor). Team that spicy bird up with Indian snacks, condiments, sides, bread, and dessert—and you've got a party anyone with a live palate will savor.

The Plan

A chicken tandoori party is not hard to make or to serve. Everything but the spiced syrup can be done on the day of the party, as long as you start in the morning, but I've given you a timetable if you want to work over two days. Last-minute dishes are marked with an icon. When your guests arrive, Indian snacks (which you've purchased) are set in bowls around the party room; gin and tonic is the cocktail of the evening. Some last-minute cooking brings everything to the proper temperature. When you're ready for the main event, line up all of the many dishes and condiments for the meal on your buffet table. This enormously colorful array of foods is one that guests will be happy to visit, over and over again.

● The day before the party

Freeze tonic water for the Frosty Plymouth Gin and Tonics.

Make the spiced syrup for Gulab Jamun.

Make ghee (optional).

Prepare Deep-Fried Cauliflower with Chile and Tomatoes.

● Early in the day of the party

Prepare the marinades for the chicken; marinate for 1 hour in the oil-vinegar marinade; marinate for 6 hours in the yogurt marinade.

Prepare Okra in Buttermilk with Black Mustard and Fresh Curry Leaves.

Prepare Raita with Cumin and Tomato; chill.

● Up to 2 hours before guests arrive

Prepare the Spicy Ginger-Garlic Shrimp with Coconut Milk and Cilantro Leaves through Step 1 (1 hour required).

Make the Cilantro Relish.

Prepare the Gulab Jamun; warm the spiced syrup, and drop the Gulab Jamun into the syrup (reheat later in microwave).

Set out the Indian snacks.

Set up the beverage center.

● During the party

Make naan and keep warm.

Bake and broil the chicken (20 to 25 minutes).

Gently reheat the okra and cauliflower dishes.

Finish the shrimp (15 to 20 minutes).

The Ingredient

The heart and soul of Indian cooking is in the spices; Indian chefs, I'm convinced, are the spicing masters of the known universe. Unfortunately, many of us who'd like to cook great Indian food often make the mistake of not respecting the spices.

One manifestation of this mistake is the belief that Indian food derives its spicy character from the use of "curry powder." Nothing could be further from the truth! Curry powder—the development of which was encouraged by the English—is a blend of many Indian spices, and can be quite tasty; unfortunately, any curry powder you regularly use will make any dish in which it appears taste similar to all the other dishes. The genius of Indian spice cookery is that the chefs make new blends of spices, treated in different ways, for each dish. Imagine cooking Italian food by reaching into your spice cabinet and pulling out "Italian powder" to be used, over and over again.

So your first directive in finding the great, party-making ingredient: avoid curry powder! Use lots of individual spices to achieve flavor!

Now comes an even thornier issue. The very best way to make vivid-tasting Indian food is to work with *fresh* spices. How do you find fresh spices? None of us has any idea how long a container of spices has been sitting on the supermarket shelf. The answer is simple: buy your spices from Indian food specialists who have rapid turnover in their spice inventories. In the sources section **(Where to Find It, page 217)** you'll find an array of great Indian purveyors who will ship fresh spices directly to your door. You really can taste the difference in the food!

When you get your spices, try to use them as quickly as possible. Wrapped in airtight bags and kept away from heat and sunlight, the spices will be potent for months, but they'll never taste livelier than when they arrived. If at all possible, buy spices that are whole and grind them yourself, either with a mortar and pestle or with a spice grinder (I use a coffee mill dedicated to spice grinding). And when you buy whole seeds, you have the happy option of toasting them before you grind them, which adds even more flavor to the spice.

Beverage Time

If there were an Indian margarita—a knockout signature cocktail—I'm sure you'd see a boom in Indian restaurants. That's why I decided, some time ago, to appoint my own official Indian preprandial cocktail: the gin and tonic. It seems just right: an English distillate, touched with spices, served over ice in the hot Indian climate, stirred up with a quinine-bearing soda that protects you from disease in the tropics. Moreover, gin and tonics taste great with Indian food—from appetizers right through the meal! A designated mixologist at your party's bar is all it takes to keep those frosty G&Ts coming.

I do have a preferred gin for gin and tonics: it's the venerable Plymouth Original Dry Gin, one of the lightest, most refreshing, yet most complex gins on the market. I also have a preferred tonic: Schweppes, which has a livelier quinine taste than any other I've tried. And I even have a gin and tonic secret: use ice cubes that are actually frozen tonic water! (They won't dilute the drinks like conventional ice cubes.)

Another logical beverage option for your Indian party is beer; it makes a wonderfully refreshing accompaniment to spicy food. A number of Indian beers are available in the U.S. now, Kingfisher and Taj Mahal being the two most popular; my favorite, Flying Horse, is just a little harder to find. What sets it apart for me is the fact that it's a little drier than the others and sometimes shows a subtle, intriguing, smoky flavor.

Lastly, don't assume that wine can't go with Indian food. I would avoid serving wine with the most fiery of Indian dishes, but none of the recipes in this particular party is wine-averse.

I like sparkling wine with moderately spiced Indian food; it scrapes spicy oils off of your palate nicely. You wouldn't want to spend a great deal of money for subtle sparkling wine, like Champagne. But a good Spanish cava, costing between $6 and $10, will be great with all the foods at this party. Full-bodied but dry whites also work well; I particularly enjoy Sauvignon Blanc–based wines from New Zealand and South Africa with Indian food. Lastly, red wine can also work—if you avoid subtlety in the wine, and if the food's not too spicy. A great wine to serve with the Chicken, Tandoori-Style, would be young California Zinfandel, as long as it's not too tannic.

The Recipes

The Frosty Plymouth Gin & Tonic

· · ● · ·

Here's a recipe that your bartender can easily make for your guests
as each gin and tonic is ordered.

makes 1 gin and tonic

4 Schweppes tonic-water ice cubes (see Cook's Note)

3 ounces Plymouth Original Dry Gin (see Where to Find It, page 217)

4 ounces Schweppes tonic water

1 tablespoon fresh lime juice

Lime wedge, for garnish

Place the ice cubes in a tall, narrow, chilled glass (the cubes should come near the top). Add the gin, then the tonic water, then the lime juice; stir well. Garnish with a lime wedge and serve immediately.

> COOK'S NOTE: *To make the ice cubes, simply fill an empty ice cube tray with Schweppes tonic water and let the cubes freeze. It takes just a few hours.*

Assorted Indian Snacks

You'll be amazed how delicious Indian crispy snacks are—right out of the bag! Think potato chips, or peanuts, or Japanese rice crackers, but with a huge surge in excitement and exotica. They get an Indian party off to a colorful, flavorful, authentic lift—with no effort at all on the part of the host or hostess.

Indian people love to snack on these things with drinks just before a meal. The category as a whole is known as *mathari*, and *mathari* come in a bewildering profusion of forms. The forms vary in size from fine shreds to big logs; they vary in heat from mild to very spicy; they vary in ingredients from legumes, to nuts, to raisins, to noodles, to the most common ingredient of all, crisps made from chickpea flour. Convenient bags of *mathari* usually carry a variety of types mixed together into a special blend.

My favorite company for Indian snacks is Shamiana, a division of House of Spices **(see Where to Find It, page 217)**. I love their Punjabi Mix, their Hot Mix, and especially their Navrang Cheda—the lightest, flakiest, frilliest snack of all, with startling flavors from all over the subcontinent. Medium-hot, with a great salty-sweet balance.

I also like the Regal Kashmiri Mix, available through the impressive Kalustyan's store in New York City **(see Where to Find It, page 217)**. If you live near an Indian grocery, the best way to find a mix you like is to pick up half a dozen kinds (they're relatively inexpensive), and start tasting.

Don't eat all of the snacks while you taste, though! Start your party by setting out bowls of four, five, or six different snacks all around the party room, as you begin serving your gin and tonics.

Spicy Ginger–Garlic Shrimp with Coconut Milk and Cilantro Leaves

· · ● · ·

Indian meals normally don't follow the Western practice of dividing dishes into "courses." At an Indian feast, everything goes on the table at once. So place this great spicy-sour shrimp dish, inspired by southern Indian cooking, on the buffet table along with all of the other dishes.

serves 12

About 1 cup vegetable oil

4 pounds jumbo shrimp, peeled, shells reserved

1/2 cup unsweetened coconut milk

4 tablespoons grated fresh ginger

4 generous tablespoons minced garlic

1 1/2 tablespoons tamarind paste (also called tamarind concentrate)

2 tablespoons ground coriander seed

1 teaspoon ground turmeric

1/2 teaspoon hot Indian chile powder or cayenne, or more

2 tablespoons kosher salt

1 cup chopped cilantro leaves

2 tablespoons amchoor powder (or substitute 1 more tablespoon of tamarind paste)

8 small green chiles, such as Thai bird chiles, seeded and very finely minced

1. Heat 2 tablespoons of vegetable oil in a large pot over medium-high heat until smoking. Add the shrimp shells and cook, stirring regularly, for 4 minutes. Add water to just cover the shells and bring to a boil. Reduce the heat to a brisk simmer and cook until the liquid is reduced to 1 cup, about 35 to 45 minutes. Strain into a bowl through a sieve, pushing hard on the solids with a wooden spoon to release their flavor. Add the coconut milk to the shrimp broth and set aside.

2. Combine 4 tablespoons of vegetable oil with 2 tablespoons of ginger, all of the minced garlic, the tamarind paste, ground coriander, ground turmeric, chile powder, salt, and ½ cup of cilantro in a large bowl. Add the shrimp and toss well to coat. Set aside for 10 minutes to marinate.

3. Place 3 tablespoons of vegetable oil in each of two large skillets set over medium-high heat. When the oil just begins to smoke, add one-quarter of the shrimp to each skillet; sear the shrimp on one side until lightly browned at the edges, no more than 1 ½ minutes. Quickly turn the shrimp over and sear the second side until lightly browned, about 1 ½ minutes more; remove the shrimp to a bowl and reserve. Repeat with the remaining shrimp, adding more oil if necessary. When this batch has browned on both sides, leave it in the skillet. Reduce the heat to medium-low and divide the first batch of browned shrimp between the two skillets (along with any liquid).

4. If there's any remaining shrimp marinade, whisk it into the reserved shrimp-coconut broth.

5. Working quickly over medium heat, divide the reserved shrimp-coconut broth, the amchoor powder, green chilies, and the remaining 2 tablespoons of ginger between the skillets, stirring well to coat the shrimp. Bring to a simmer and let the mixture thicken slightly, no more than 2 minutes. Taste for salt and serve immediately, garnished with the remaining cilantro leaves.

Chicken, Tandoori-Style

· · • · ·

I adapted this dish from a recipe in a cookbook I bought in India, and using only oven and broiler, it brings my kitchen insanely close to an Indian restaurant. Since I'm this close, in fact, I've decided to go with the food coloring that Indian restaurants always use; the red-orange tones bring a Hindu kind of festivity to the dish that I think, despite the artificiality of "food color," is well worth including.

Start this dish the morning of the day you plan to serve it; it needs 7 hours of marination.

serves 12

3 whole chickens, 3 ½ to 4 pounds each

12 tablespoons vegetable oil

6 tablespoons malt vinegar

1 ½ tablespoons mild chili powder

1 tablespoon kosher salt

6 whole cloves

Seeds from 15 green cardamom pods

4 dried red chiles, each torn into a few pieces

2 tablespoons black peppercorns

1 tablespoon caraway seeds

1 ½ teaspoons freshly ground mace

¾ teaspoon freshly grated nutmeg

6 tablespoons grated fresh ginger

6 tablespoons finely minced garlic

3 cups plain yogurt

2 tablespoons orange food color powder (see page 204)

Sizzled onions for garnish (see Serving Note), optional

Lemon quarters for garnish

1. Cut the chickens (or ask the butcher to cut the chickens) into 4 pieces each: 2 breasts without wings (save wings for another use), and 2 legs (drumsticks and thighs must remain attached to each other). You will have 12 pieces altogether. Remove and discard all skin. Slash the flesh, not too deeply, with a small, sharp knife (about a dozen small slashes, evenly spaced, on each piece).

2. Whisk 9 tablespoons vegetable oil, the vinegar, chili powder, and salt together in a small bowl. Place the chicken pieces in a pan large enough to just contain them in one layer, rub the oil-vinegar mixture all over the chicken, and marinate for 1 hour at room temperature.

3. In the meantime, prepare the yogurt marinade. Place the following ingredients in a spice grinder: cloves, cardamom seeds, chiles, peppercorns, caraway seeds, mace, and nutmeg. Grind to a fine powder.

4. Place the spice powder in the work bowl of a food processor. Add the ginger, garlic, yogurt, and the remaining 3 tablespoons of vegetable oil. Process until smooth. Add the food color and process until blended.

5. When the chicken has finished its initial marinade, transfer it to a large bowl. Cover the chicken with the orange-colored yogurt marinade, stirring to make sure the marinade covers all parts. Refrigerate, covered, for 6 hours.

6. When you're ready to cook, heat the oven to 500°F. Place the chicken pieces on a rack or a grooved broiler pan. Place in the oven and cook for 15 minutes.

7. Remove the chicken pieces from the oven and place them under a hot broiler. Broil until both sides of the pieces are sizzling and a little brown, turning once, about 5 to 10 minutes of broiling in all. Serve immediately.

SERVING NOTE: To serve chicken tandoori the restaurant way, sizzle some thick onion slices under the broiler along with the chicken. Serve the chicken pieces with sizzled onion and lemon wedges.

To really do it up, buy a sizzle platter at a restaurant supply store, heat it in the 500°F oven while the chicken is broiling, and place the finished chicken, onions, and lemon wedges on the hot sizzle platter for service. As you deliver the platter to the buffet table, the sound and the steam are amazing!

Special Ingredients for Your Chicken, Tandoori-Style

Here are some specific products that will make your chicken taste especially authentic; they are all available by mail **(see Where to Find It, page 217)**.

Chili Powder. There are many Indian chili powders available at many levels of spicy heat. There is a good amount in the first marinade—for flavor and to set the color—but the dish should not be blazing hot. Use one of the milder chili powders, like Kalustyan's Mild Kashmiri Red Chili Powder, which is full of paprika-like flavor.

Green Cardamom Pods. Cardamom pods encase cardamom seeds, the part of the cardamom you use in cooking. I've cracked many a green pod and found a real favorite: Nirav Green Cardamom, available from Namaste **(see Where to Find It, page 217)**. After I got to the seeds, I found them to be the sweetest, least medicinal of all the seeds I tasted. Big surprise here: they come from Guatemala!

Mace. Oh, you can use powdered mace if you wish. But it is so worth the trouble to acquire Kalustyan's Blades of Mace (Myristica Fragrans), Joyatri-India, and to grind them yourself in a spice grinder.

Orange Food Color Powder. If you wish to arrive at the precise color that you find in Indian-restaurant Chicken Tandoori, you must buy a food color specifically designed for Indian cooking. I use Preema Orange Food Color, a powder made in England and available through Kalustyan's.

Naan

· • ● • · ·

The starch orientation at this chicken tandoori party is from northern India—where chefs typically stick wads of risen dough on the inner walls of the tandoor to create naan, a bread that tastes remarkably like good puffy pizza crust.

There's so much good news about naan for your party. First of all, you can go to your local pizza shop and ask the owner if you can buy about 5 pounds of his already-made, uncooked pizza dough! (I've never been told "no.") It cooks up into "naan" that is remarkably reminiscent of the real thing. Second, you don't need a tandoor to pull off this trick; any heavy skillet will do the job on your stove top. Of course, the larger the skillet, the better, because size enables you to make more naan simultaneously. And that's why I recommend using a large cast-iron griddle for this job, the type that fits right over two burners on your range.

makes 24 naan

5 pounds premade pizza dough

All-purpose flour

2 to 3 cups melted ghee or clarified butter, as needed (see Cook's Note on page 209)

1. Heat a large, heavy griddle or several skillets over medium-high heat. Heat the oven to 175°F and put a large platter in to warm.

2. Tear off a 3-ounce piece of dough and form it into a ball. Roll it out on a lightly floured surface to a diameter of 7 to 8 inches, between 1/8 and 1/4 inch thick. Brush both sides generously with ghee and place on the hot griddle. Do the same with another piece or two, as many as your griddle will hold. Cook the pieces on the first side until nicely browned in spots, 1 to 2 minutes. Turn and cook until just cooked through, 30 seconds to 1 minute more. Adjust the heat if the bread seems to burn before cooking through. Transfer the bread to the warm platter and cover with foil or a towel. Repeat with the remaining dough. Serve hot.

Okra in Buttermilk with Black Mustard and Fresh Curry Leaves

. . • . .

This wonderful side dish is absolutely *made* by the inclusion of curry leaf—a fresh ingredient that has nothing whatsoever to do with curries or curry powder. The flavor of curry leaves is inimitable—geranium-like with a hint of iron—and adds remarkable depth to Indian dishes.

The dish can be made earlier in the day and reheated. When reheating, just let the mixture warm through, stirring regularly. Don't let it simmer or boil, or the yogurt will separate.

½ cup vegetable oil

½ cup Indian mustard oil (see Cook's Note #1)

3 tablespoons black mustard seeds

40 fresh curry leaves (see Cook's Note #2)

3 tablespoons ground turmeric

2 teaspoons grated ginger

6 to 8 small dried red chiles, coarsely chopped, or 1 teaspoon crushed red pepper

4 pounds fresh okra, trimmed and cut into ½-inch pieces (frozen okra works well, too)

8 cups buttermilk

Kosher salt

1 cup whole milk yogurt

1. Pour ¼ cup vegetable oil and ¼ cup mustard oil into each of two large skillets. Place the skillets over medium heat, and divide the mustard seeds between them. When the mustard seeds begin to pop, divide the curry leaves, turmeric, ginger, and chiles between the skillets, stirring to combine. Cook 30 seconds more.

2. Increase the heat to medium-high, and divide the okra between the skillets. Stir well for 1 to 2 minutes to coat the okra with the spices.

3. Reduce the heat to medium-low. Divide the buttermilk between the skillets; bring to a gentle simmer. Stir about a tablespoon of salt into each skillet, and continue to simmer until slightly thickened, 2 to 3 minutes. Reduce the heat to low; stir half of the yogurt into each skillet and heat until just warmed through. Remove from the heat, taste for salt, and serve.

*Cook's Note #1: Mustard oil is a very pungent oil that is a specialty of Bengal; make sure to buy one that is manufactured in India. My favorite is the Laxmi Mustard Oil, available through House of Spices (see **Where to Find It, page 217**).*

*Cook's Note #2: Fresh curry leaves may be found at Indian groceries or ordered from Kalustyan's (see **Where to Find It, page 217**).*

Deep-Fried Cauliflower with Chile and Tomatoes

. . ● . .

Though we tend to associate cauliflower more with Europe than with Asia, cauliflower
is one of the most widely planted, most beloved vegetables in India. And it combines fabulously
well with Indian spices.

Serve this hot or at room temperature.

serves 12

½ cup ghee or clarified butter (see Cook's Note)

3 tablespoons grated ginger

6 large cloves garlic, minced

1 tablespoon mild Indian chili powder (or 2 ¾ teaspoons sweet paprika
  mixed with ¼ teaspoon cayenne)

1 tablespoon ground coriander

1 teaspoon ground cumin seed

¾ teaspoon ground cinnamon

3 (28-ounce) cans tomatoes

1 tablespoon kosher salt

1 ½ teaspoons sugar

Vegetable oil for frying

4 to 5 pounds cauliflower (about 3 heads), broken into
  1- to 1 ½-inch florets

2 to 3 teaspoons fresh lime juice (optional)

1. Heat two large skillets over medium heat and divide the ghee or clarified butter between them. Divide the ginger, garlic, chili powder, coriander, cumin, and cinnamon between the skillets and cook, stirring, for 2 minutes. With your hands, crush the tomatoes, divide between the skillets, and stir them in along with the juices from their cans. Divide the salt and sugar between the skillets and bring to a boil. Reduce to a simmer and cook, stirring occasionally, until thickened slightly but still quite "saucy," about 10 to 12 minutes. Remove from the heat and set aside.

2. Fill a heavy, high-sided pot with vegetable oil to a depth of 2 inches. Heat the oil to 360°F. Fry the cauliflower in batches until pale golden in color but still crisp-tender inside, between 4 and 8 minutes, depending on the size of your batches and cauliflower pieces. As the pieces finish cooking, drain on paper towels, then toss them in a bowl. Sprinkle with salt. Transfer the cauliflower to the tomato sauce, dividing it equally between the skillets.

3. Bring the tomato sauce and cauliflower to a gentle simmer and cook, stirring regularly, until the cauliflower is very tender and the sauce has thickened considerably, about 20 minutes. Stir in the lime juice to taste, if you care to, and taste for salt. Serve hot or at room temperature.

> COOK'S NOTE: *Ghee, or clarified butter, has a high smoking point and does not easily burn, but, more important, it adds a festive lift to Indian dishes (hosts, frankly, sometimes use it just to show off!). It is very easy to make: just melt some butter in a small saucepan over very gentle heat. After 10 minutes or so, carefully skim off the white foam at the top of the saucepan and discard. Then pour the butter out of the saucepan into a clean container, making sure to leave the milky sediment in the bottom of the saucepan behind. You can also buy ghee—which I prefer to do, since it sometimes has a little "funk" that adds flavor. My favorite brand is Vrindavan 100% Pure Cow Ghee—made in West Virginia—available through Kalustyan's* (**see Where to Find It, page 217**).

Cilantro Relish

. . . ● . . .

Very popular in Indian restaurants now (where they often call it "coriander chutney"),
this green purée is a very tasty condiment for the chicken.

makes about 2 cups

> 6 cups loosely packed cilantro leaves (thin stems are OK)
>
> 4 large cloves garlic, sliced
>
> 1 ½ teaspoons kosher salt
>
> 1 ½ teaspoons sugar
>
> 1 teaspoon mild Indian chili powder (or 1 teaspoon sweet paprika and a
> generous pinch of cayenne)
>
> ¼ teaspoon ground cumin
>
> ¼ cup fresh lime juice
>
> ¼ cup cold water
>
> 2 teaspoons malt vinegar (or white wine vinegar)

Process all of the ingredients in the work bowl of a food processor, pausing to scrape down the
sides, until the ingredients are finely chopped and the relish is the consistency of a very loose
paste. Thin with more water as necessary. The relish tastes best when made and served as soon
as possible. But if you like, it can be made earlier in the day, covered tightly, and held in the
refrigerator.

Raita with Cumin and Tomato

· · • · ·

Here's another good condiment for an Indian meal. The yogurt helps douse chile fires.

makes about 4 cups

2 teaspoons cumin seeds

3 cups plain whole-milk yogurt

1 ½ cups diced fresh tomato

1 teaspoon kosher salt

1. Toast the cumin seeds in a small skillet over medium heat until fragrant, 1 to 2 minutes. Let cool, transfer to a mortar, and coarsely crush (or crush with the underside of a small skillet).

2. Combine the cumin with the remaining ingredients in a bowl and mix thoroughly. Serve cool.

Gulab Jamun

· · ● · ·

(Deep-Fried Milk Balls in Spiced Syrup)

These deep-fried balls of milk solids, soaked in a spiced syrup, oozing buttery goodness, are among my very favorite Indian desserts, especially when they're served warm. Unfortunately, they are quite a bit of trouble to make from scratch. But if you find a good gulab jamun mix—and I have! **(see Where to Find It, page 217)**—the keys to the gulab jamun kingdom are yours. *Important:* do not follow the directions on the package of my favorite mix, the MTR brand; follow my directions.

Start the spiced syrup the day before. I would advise you to make the balls themselves just before your guests arrive, and drop them in the warmed syrup before the doorbell rings. If they are not warm at dessert time, a quick visit to the microwave will remedy that.

serves 12

> **3 cups water**
>
> **2 cups sugar**
>
> **1 tablespoon coarsely broken cinnamon sticks**
>
> **6 whole cloves**
>
> **36 smashed green cardamom pods**
>
> **3 (3.52–ounce) boxes MTR Instant Gulab Jamun Mix (see headnote)**
>
> **2/3 cup whole milk**
>
> **3 cups ghee (see Cook's Note on page 209)**

1. The day before the party, place the water, sugar, cinnamon, cloves, and cardamom (smashed pods and seeds) in a saucepan. Bring to a boil, and boil for 5 minutes. Turn off the heat, and let stand, covered, overnight.

2. When you're ready to prepare the dessert, combine 3 cups of gulab jamun mix with the milk in a mixing bowl. Moisten your hands with a little ghee, then roll out 36 evenly sized balls from the MTR dough. Heat the reserved syrup.

3. Heat the remaining ghee in a saucepan to 265°F. Fry the balls in batches until they are a rich brown and cooked through, 10 minutes or so. As soon as the balls are done, drain them on paper towels, then drop them into the hot syrup. Repeat with the remaining balls. The gulab jamun are just fine to eat with only 10 to 15 minutes in the syrup, but they hold beautifully for several hours in a warm place. Serve 3 warm balls to each guest in a small bowl along with some of the syrup.

You've Got Options

Serving such condiments as Indian chutneys and pickles has become an absolutely essential part of my Indian-party strategy. The strong, vivid flavors of these products add amazing accents to Indian foods. You simply use them as you would salsas, or relish, or even ketchup or mustard! And to enrich your party in this way, all you have to do is open jars! But first you have to find the *good* jars.

There's massive confusion about "chutney." The term is apparently based on the Indian word *chaat-na,* "to lick," and was applied originally to fresh uncooked preparations, made daily from fruits and spices. Enter the English—who starting cooking mangoes "like jam," according to food writer Linda Bladholm, "adding raisins, candied peel, and dried apricots." And thanks to the success the English had with Major Grey's Mango Chutney on the world market, this sticky-jammy stuff is now what most think of as "chutney."

But Indians recognize many types of chutney, from the English type to the fresh type (coconut chutney is popular). Things get particularly confusing because not all chutneys are thick and sticky-sweet; sometimes a "chutney" can be more like a savory, thinnish sauce.

Now, the issue of Indian pickles is of a different order: not confusion but strangeness. This is one Indian condiment for which Americans have a tough time developing a taste; I know intrepid foodies who have tried many a jar of Indian pickles and have still come away with the impression that they all taste like furniture polish. I, too, had this prejudice once—until I traveled through India and discovered how amazing pickles can be. Now I know what to look for and wouldn't consider eating an Indian meal without them.

Citrus fruits and mangoes are the most popular candidates in India for "pickling," but the way an Indian chef pickles is far, far different from the way a guy pickles on Manhattan's Lower East Side. In India, the ingredient is typically preserved in oil (mustard oil is popular), with lots of spices and salt, so when you finally eat it, it's not a brine pickle at all but a thick, rich, oily, hot, and salty thing. Strangest of all, to the neophyte, is the taste. It's highly exotic and, I'm afraid, very difficult to describe; if you're familiar with the taste of Moroccan preserved lemons, you're in the right universe—except that Indian pickles are much, much more intense. The problem is that many jars of this already strange stuff are made stranger still by long storage, developing musty tastes on top of the pickle taste.

Do you want a simple solution for your party? Buy your pickles and chutneys from Kalustyan's **(see Where to Find It, page 217)**, makers of the freshest-tasting Indian condiments in the American marketplace. All of their chutneys and pickles come in 10-ounce jars. I'm particularly fond of Kalustyan's Home-Made Lime Pickle: absolutely dead-on, high-quality Indian pickle. Perfect preserved citrus taste, sour and salty and hot, with no off-flavors whatsoever. Just enough texture in the chew. I also love Kalustyan's Hot Mango Chutney, which has big chunks, a dark reddish color, and a deep taste reminiscent of dried fruits or cooked tomato. It is fairly spicy.

Whichever pickles and chutneys you buy, serving them is a breeze. Scoop them out of their jars with a spoon into colorful serving bowls, and place the bowls, with serving spoons, right on the buffet table. I would recommend at least one pickle and one chutney for your party, but it sure wouldn't suppress the fun to offer your guests several kinds of each.

Set Dressing

So many options. You could go with anything from a timeless religious celebration on the banks of the Ganges to a cool urban party in a contemporary Mumbai apartment, from 19th-century raj to a modern "Bollywood" musical extravaganza.

Frankly, I quake at the myriad possibilities; Indian food is so colorful, so vivid in every way by itself, that you need not make the venue compete with the food. Your guests, through their sense of smell alone—not to mention what their eyes will make of the bright orange-red of the chicken tandoori and the colorful satellite side dishes—will be immediately transported into a rich fantasy environment.

I advise the subtlest selection of "props" for your set, just as tasteful background to the food—a Kashmiri rug, a dancing Shiva, a poster, perhaps, splashed with the almost painfully lurid colors of a Hindu temple. You could, of course, consider tents and canopies (available from rental centers) to hang over it all; but, to me, this is one party where the food makes a fashion statement on its own that's as impressive as the gastronomic one.

Table Dressing

For me, the table's where the real action is, principally in the amazing food. But it would be great to reinforce the drama of the fare with a well-appointed table. Should the ruling aesthetic be Indian or British? One option is to strive for dining and decorative détente by combining elements from both cultures on the buffet. Banana leaves (see Note), used as chargers, might keep company with English transferware plates, platters, and bowls. Fearlessly mix metals like copper, brass, silver, and tin—either with the patina of rustic English pewter or with the gleaming metallic look of the very authentic compartmentalized platters that the Indians call "thali platters."

It would be dynamic to crown the buffet table with a tent of mosquito netting (found at import stores), draw back the side panels like drapes, and secure them with tasseled cords. The same idea could be adapted to a beverage station. Table linens, under the netting, could run the gamut from colorful batiks or paisleys to rich solids.

Because the genius of Indian cuisine is in its spicing, I like the idea of incorporating spices into the tableau. Buy colorful ground spices like turmeric and paprika in bulk. Partially fill clear glass votive holders with them, and add candles. Or pour spices on a tray or platter and set pillar candles in their drifts. Punctuate with whole spices: nutmeg, green cardamom, star anise.

Finally, the elephant, camel, tiger, and ox are revered in India; their images could be used liberally on your table in whatever iconic form you find them.

NOTE: In the U.S., banana leaves are sold frozen at ethnic markets. Do not allow food to come into direct contact with fresh leaves, as they may have been chemically treated for the floral industry.

Entertainment

One way or another, there must be Indian music! Indian recordings can easily be acquired from music stores or online sources like www.amazon.com. To put your party dizzyingly over the top, hire a sitar-tabla duo to provide live Indian music! It's not as expensive as you might imagine. The trick is in finding a pair of Indian musicians, because you can't look up "sitar player" in the Yellow Pages. However, you *can* look up "musicians," "musical instruments-rental," "music instruction," and other "musical" categories. By telephoning places that have Indian-sounding names, even Indian restaurants, you may well be able to track down your own local version of Ravi Shankar. Calling the Indian consulate in your city, or an Indian cultural center, is another strategy that could pay off.

Another live-artist idea is to engage the services of a henna artist to circulate among your guests! Some of them will go home with a little something extra to admire in the morning.

Where to Find It

Kalustyan's

123 Lexington Ave.
New York, NY 10016
800.352.3451 (toll free)
212.685.3451 (tel)
www.kalustyans.com
This store carries more than 500 spices and herbs, as well as Middle Eastern and European food products. *The* source for Indian chutneys and pickles.

Todhunter Imports, Ltd.

West Palm Beach, FL
561.837.6300 (tel)
Importers of Plymouth Original Dry Gin; ask for retailers in your area.

House of Spices

127-40 Willets Point Blvd.
Flushing, NY 11368
718.507.4600 (tel)
www.hosindia.com
A great source for Indian snacks in the Shamiana line, as well as many terrific food items in the Laxmi line.

IndianFoodsCo.com

8305 Franklin Ave.
Minneapolis, MN 55426
952.593.3000 (tel)
www.indianfoodsco.com
One of my favorite online purveyors of Indian food products (including the Ajika line).

Namaste

695 Lunt Ave.
Elk Grove Village, IL 60007
847.640.1105 (tel)
847.640.9571 (fax)
www.namaste.com
Carries a large assortment of Indian foods, kitchen equipment, and tableware (including stainless steel plates and glasses), movies, music, bindis and other fashion accessories, and games such as cricket and carrom.

Coosemans–Denver, Inc.

5135 Peoria St.
Denver, CO 80239
303.371.3130 (tel)
www.coosemansdenver.com
Supplier of specialty produce; stocks frozen banana leaves.

IndiaPlaza.com

960 Saratoga Ave.,
Suite 207
San Jose, CA 95129
877.924.6342 (toll free)
408.345.3900 (tel)
408.345.3963 (fax)
www.indiaplaza.com
A virtual online department store of things Indian including food (like MTR Gulab Jamun mix), kitchenware, music, movies, gifts, clothing, and jewelry.

iShopIndian.com

10633 North Ave.
Wauwatosa, WI 53226
877.786.8876 (toll free)
www.ishopindian.com
An affiliate of Indian Groceries & Spices, Inc. An easy-to-negotiate website with a diverse line of shelf-stable groceries as well as fresh foodstuffs like curry leaves and chapatis, utensils, gifts, music, and movies.

Steak on the Grill

South American Style

A Party for 12

The Menu

Caipirinhas

Salt Cod and Red Pepper Fritters with Brazilian Black Beer Batter

Buenos Aires Parrillada with Chimichurri Variations:
Seared Filet, Skirt Steak, Rib Steak

Classic Chimichurri and Chimichurri Red

Gratin of Black Beans and Corn with Crusty Cheese

South American Salad, with Tomatoes, Potatoes, Avocados, Purple Onions,
Hard-Boiled Eggs, and Green Vinaigrette

Coconut-Mascarpone Roulades with Mangoes

South America is tremendously diverse, with many cultures and many cuisines. One strand of the big weave, however, is rapidly making its way into North American consciousness: the South American love of beef and beef barbecue parties. The Brazilians, the Uruguayans, and particularly the Argentineans all seem to have been on the Atkins Diet for about 500 years.

Who—other than a commited vegetarian—would not want to emulate this terrific tradition? At an Argentine *asado,* or grilled meat party, huge quantities of salt-rubbed beef—as well as sausages, innards, lamb, and chicken—are grilled over glowing hardwood embers. *Asado* participants go back and forth from the grill to their tables, taking a few bites, then returning for more. The Argentine expression for this constant motion is *asado es un viaje de ida y vuelta*—meaning "*asado* is a journey of going and coming."

Don't you think it's time to get your guests coming and going? For this party, I've eliminated the exotica; most Americans aren't too keen on sweetbreads, kidneys, or blood sausage. The focus is on the meat that brings the two Americas together. Steak! But I've included enough steaky variety, not to mention an array of drinks and side dishes, to mimic the intoxicating heterogeneity of a South American meat party.

The Plan

This is an outdoor grill party, to be sure, with smoke-scented air and sizzling food served from a buffet table. As you'll see from the recipes, though, you've got some work to do in the kitchen a few days ahead.

To get the party started, serve caipirinhas. You'll need a bartender—you, or a willing conscript—and you'll need a caipirinha station, which could be one end of the buffet table.

Circulate among your guests with platters of salt cod fritters, which you have just deep-fried in the kitchen. (Of course, if you have an electric deep-fryer and an outdoor electrical outlet, you could set up a frying station right outside at the party!)

The fun accelerates with the lighting of the fire. You will cook the steaks in three groups: filet cutlets, skirt steaks, and rib steaks—and bring them to the buffet table, one by one, to which your guests will be coming and from which they'll be going. Time your service so that when the filet cutlets appear on the buffet table, the side dishes appear at the same time. Immediately begin grilling the skirt steaks, which will become "the second steak course." After you've plattered those and placed them on the buffet, fire up the rib steaks. When you at last serve those from the buffet table, as "the third steak course," the savory part of the party comes to an end.

Clear the buffet table, and bring the roulades out, along with a cutting board, a knife, dessert plates, and dessert forks. Slice the roulades on the cutting board and plate the slices. Ask your guests to come to the buffet table one more time before they leave.

The Ingredient

Steak, unless it's great steak, is just steak. Ultra-quality steak is one of the world's finest eating experiences. So the key to making your discriminating guests swoon is finding some amazing steak that will raise the bar of the party.

Alas, great steak is often reserved for the country's best steakhouses. Even the most well-connected butcher in your area may not have the very best steak there is. But don't be frustrated. For this party, you can get away with lesser-quality steak in the beef tenderloin, which gets flattened by pounding and then seriously marinated with garlic. Outrageously good tenderloin won't be too different, in this context, from merely good tenderloin. Buy a hunk of this at your supermarket.

The party is constructed so that the importance of steak quality rises as the night goes on. The skirt steak can be one of the world's wonderful steak experiences, or it can be chewy and gristly. Those differences will come through, despite the chimichurri marinade. So buy your skirt steak at a top-quality butcher shop, not at the supermarket. We all know that USDA "Prime" steak—a category that includes only about 2 percent of all steak—is the best, and we all think "Prime" when buying shell steaks and porterhouses. But did you know that there is Prime skirt steak as well? It's amazingly buttery and velvety, as well as deeply beefy in flavor. Ask your butcher if he can get you some.

The thick rib steak, which gets the plainest cooking treatment of all at this party, is the crowning glory of the meal—so it had better be great! Prime, of course—with wonderful marbling throughout the meat. Once again, get your butcher on the case.

Now, in case you don't have a local butcher who is able to dazzle you with Prime steak, take heart. These days, the blue ribbon products of butchers all over the country are just a phone call or log-on away. See **Where to Find It, page 240** for a list of great mail-order steak purveyors whose products have pleased me mightily. But pay special attention, if you can, to the butcher shop that has most consistently delighted me with their Prime steaks (including skirt!): Lobel's, in New York City, a quality-obsessed operation. You will pay dearly for what they send you, but you will reorder, nonetheless, once you taste what they send.

Beverage Time

Your guests have a real treat in store for them at this steak party: the caipirinha (pronounced ky-per-EEN-ya), a Brazilian cocktail that has zoomed to the tippy-top of my global cocktail chart. It is made from cachaça (pronounced ka-SHA-sa), a clear sugar-cane distillate made in Brazil, with the remarkable ability to make you feel every bit as silly as tequila does. But forget the wacky high. It's the taste of the caipirinha that has me hooked! Think of a caipirinha as a Brazilian margarita, without the tequila taste, to be sure, but with a wild taste of lime rind that marries beautifully with the cachaça.

The key to that taste is muddling the lime. Pounding it with a small mallet (called a muddler, of course) forces the essential lime oils out of the zest and into the drink. If you don't have an official muddler, you can substitute a pestle, a wooden spoon, the handle of a screwdriver, whatever works. After that, making the drink's a breeze.

The Art of the Caipirinha

Just before the party starts, have the bartender start muddling away. Into each of 12 glasses, he or she should place half a lime, cut into small cubes, and start muddling. During the muddling (which should go on for a minute or so), a teaspoon of superfine sugar (sometimes sold as bar sugar) is added to the glass and pounded in (use more or less sugar, depending on taste). Line up the glasses, and wait for the victims.

When the first guest asks "What are you pouring?" the barkeep springs into action. Add a handful of cracked ice to one of the glasses with the pre-muddled lime. Pour in 1 1/2 ounces of cachaça. Top the glass with a cocktail shaker and shake like you're possessed for about 30 seconds. Put the glass back down on the table, remove the shaker, and garnish the glass with a slice of lime. Then start making another guest happy.

Make sure to have a supply of cut limes on hand. When the guests come back for more caipirinhas, and they will, the muddling begins all over again, this time on the spot, in the guest's used caipirinha glass.

You'll need to acquire at least 12 glasses—ideally low, wide tumblers, like old-fashioned glasses. My favorite brand of cachaça, Pitu, and actual caipirinha glasses are both available from EFCO Importers **(see Where to Find It, page 240)**.

One more caipirinha note: key limes make the delicious caipirinha even more delicious. Look for them at your local market; or, if you think it's worth the trouble (I do!), you can always mail-order from Melissa's/World Variety Produce, in Los Angeles **(see Where to Find It, page 240)**.

Now, I have been known to simply stick with caipirinhas throughout a South American meal, even a grilled steak party. I think your guests should have that option, too (teach them to make their own). But some guests are going to want to drink wine. They're lucky, too, since wonderful wine is coming from South America these days.

I must confess: despite all the attention that Chile gets for its wine, I think the general level of Argentinean wine is higher. I love starting a meal with Argentinean white made from a grape variety, Torrontes, that you won't find elsewhere in the world. The wine should be dry, with a teasing taste somewhere between peachy Riesling and spicy Muscat. The most famous spot in Argentina for Torrontes production is Cafayate, in the province of Salta, but I prefer the Torrontes made by the Santa Julia winery in the great Argentinean wine region of Mendoza, to the south of Salta. Santa Julia Torrontes is widely available; look for a young vintage, no more than 2 years old.

Mendoza is renowned for its excellent red wines, which would go perfectly with the grilled steak at this party. The grape variety that has become a Mendoza specialty is Malbec, one of the five red-wine grapes that used to go religiously into the basic red Bordeaux blend in France. These days, you'd have to say that Argentina is the world's epicenter of Malbec production. The wines are big, purple, glossy, with tons of rich fruit and, usually, a rather sophisticated balance. I like 'em young, for the fruit rush; but if you can find a good aged example (say, 10 years old), from a winery like Cavas Weinert, you've got one of the world's complex reds on your hands. At the other end of the Malbec spectrum is a fruit-gusher called Viña Hormigas, from the Altos de Medrano winery, that vintage-in, vintage-out, is one of the best values in the international red-wine marketplace. Other Mendoza Malbec producers I like are Terrazas, Finca La Anita, La Garde, Bodegas Norton, and Catena.

The Recipes

Salt Cod and Red Pepper Fritters with Brazilian Black Beer Batter

• ◦ • ● ◦ •

There's plenty of meat ahead. So start it all off, as Brazilians do, with a bit of deep-fried seafood.

You need to start soaking the cod 2 days ahead.

makes about 48 fritters

½ pound boneless, skinless salt cod

About 3 cups milk (enough milk to cover the salt cod twice)

Vegetable oil for deep-frying

2 ¾ cups all-purpose flour

2 cups Brazilian dark beer (or substitute another dark, sweetish beer)

2 large red bell peppers, roasted, peeled, seeded, and puréed in a food processor

2 teaspoons hot sauce

2 teaspoons kosher salt, plus additional for sprinkling

½ teaspoon freshly ground black pepper

Lime wedges, if desired

1. Two days prior to serving the fritters, place the cod pieces (keeping them as whole as possible) in a large bowl. Cover the cod with milk. Keep in the refrigerator, covered. After 24 hours, drain the milk, discard, and cover the cod again with fresh milk.

2. When you're ready to prepare the fritters, drain the milk and discard. Dry the soaked cod with paper towels, and using a very sharp knife, cut it into pieces that are about 1 1/2 inches long, 1 inch wide, and 1/4 inch thick. Don't cut the cod straight down; use a slanting cut to expose more of the surface.

3. Pour the vegetable oil into a deep-fat fryer or deep pot and heat it to 360°F.

4. Put 2 cups of flour into a medium bowl. Add the beer gradually, mixing with a fork to just blend with the flour. Don't overmix; lumps are okay.

5. Blend the red pepper purée with the hot sauce in a bowl. In another bowl, combine the remaining 3/4 cup of flour with the salt and pepper.

6. When the oil is hot, spread 1/2 teaspoon of red pepper purée onto each side of the cod pieces. Dust the pieces with the seasoned dredging flour, then dip them into the batter, making sure to apply only a light coating. Add the fritters to the oil in batches, taking care not to crowd the fryer (which would make the temperature drop). Fry the fritters for about a minute on each side. Drain on paper towels. Serve immediately, sprinkled with salt if desired. Garnish with lime wedges.

Buenos Aires Parrillada with Chimichurri Variations: Seared Filet, Skirt Steak, Rib Steak

· · • · ·

The famous meat restaurants in Rio de Janeiro—*churrascarias, rodizio*-style—place long skewers of meat over fires in their kitchens, then parade the skewers out to you in the dining room. But in the Buenos Aires restaurant tradition, meat—including various cuts of steak—is cooked on a grill right in front of the diner, ensuring a type of meat experience that is very close to rural Argentine *asados* and to our own American backyard grilling.

A grilled meat assortment in Argentina is called a *parrillada* (pronounced par-ree-JAH-da), and that is exactly what you'll be serving your guests in this great South American party, with pounded cutlets of filet mignon, marinated skirt steak, and a thick rib steak all taking a turn on the grill. Of course, there are differences between here and there. You won't find A-1 steak sauce or ketchup with steak in Argentina. Argentines serve the bright-green sauce called chimichurri with their grilled steaks. And with the profusion of Argentine steak houses in America now, chimichurri has become quite famous here; some have called it the pesto of the new century! I don't think it'll get that far in the American culinary pantheon, but it sure is a delicious accompaniment to steak. So delicious, in fact, that I have found a way to incorporate it into all three steak portions of this steak party, in three different ways.

Start the skirt steaks early in the day.

serves 12

for the seared filet:

9 garlic cloves, finely minced
6 tablespoons olive oil, plus extra for oiling the grate
a 1 to 1 ½-pound beef tenderloin (even thickness, if possible)
Kosher salt
3 cups Classic Chimichurri (page 230)

1. Combine the garlic with 6 tablespoons of olive oil in a bowl.

2. Cut the tenderloin into 12 round, even slices. Smear the slices on one side with the garlic-oil mixture, dividing the mixture evenly. Place plastic wrap on top of the garlicky sides, and pound the filets with a mallet (or the back of a heavy pan) until they are wide and thin. Let rest at room temperature for 1 hour.

3. When you're ready to cook, prepare a very hot charcoal or gas fire. Oil the grate with olive oil. Knock the garlic off the filets, salt them well on both sides, and place them on the grill. Cook very quickly, turning once, about 30 to 60 seconds a side, depending on the fire. You want the filets to be crunchy-seared outside, rare to medium-rare inside.

4. Place the filets on a platter and serve immediately on the buffet table with Classic Chimichurri on the side.

for the skirt steak:

4 ½ pounds skirt steak (see Cook's Note)
1 ½ cups Classic Chimichurri (page 230)
Olive oil

1. Cut the skirt steaks into 12 pieces, each about 5 x 3 x ¾ inches. Smear the steaks evenly with the chimichurri sauce and let them marinate for 6 hours in the refrigerator. Turn while marinating to ensure that each side is coated with chimichurri.

2. When you're ready to cook, oil the grate with olive oil. Cook the steaks about 3 minutes per side for rare to medium-rare. Serve immediately—without sauce or condiments.

> COOK'S NOTE: *Skirt steaks are usually the same width, but can vary widely in thickness and length. Length doesn't matter here; you'll be cutting the steaks into smaller pieces. What does matter is thickness: try to buy skirt steaks that are all about ¾ inch thick, so they'll cook evenly.*

for the rib steak:

Olive oil
Kosher salt
Freshly ground black pepper
3 boneless rib steaks, each 1 ½ inches thick, at room temperature
3 cups Chimichurri Red (page 231)

1. When you're ready to cook, oil the grate with olive oil. Season the steaks with plenty of kosher salt and freshly ground black pepper.

2. Grill the steaks, turning once, about 4 to 6 minutes per side for rare to medium-rare meat. Let them rest for 10 minutes, then carve on the diagonal. Place the slices on a platter and serve immediately, with Chimichurri Red on the side.

Classic Chimichurri

· · ● · ·

Make this sauce 2 to 3 days before using it to give the flavors time to meld.

makes approximately 8 cups

4 cups loosely packed flat-leaf parsley leaves

4 cups loosely packed cilantro leaves

4 tablespoons dried oregano

4 bunches scallions, cut into 1 1/4-inch slices, including 1 inch of the green part

8 cloves garlic, roughly chopped

2 hot green chiles, such as jalapeño, seeded and roughly chopped

1 cup white wine vinegar

1 cup rice wine vinegar

4 cups extra-virgin olive oil

Kosher salt

Freshly ground black pepper

4 red bell peppers, roasted, peeled, seeded, and cut into 1 1/8-inch dice

1. Working in batches, place the parsley, cilantro, oregano, scallions, garlic, and chiles in the work bowl of a food processor. Combine the vinegars and oil in a pitcher. With the motor running, add the liquid in a thin, steady stream, stopping occasionally to scrape down the sides of the bowl. After all of the oil-vinegar mixture is added, continue blending until the mixture is only slightly chunky; it should look and feel like a not-quite-smooth purée. Add salt and pepper.

2. Pour into a storage container and stir in the diced red pepper. Keep covered in the refrigerator.

Chimichurri Red

· • ● • ·

The chimichurri takes on a whole different character when you blend it with tomato;
it is wonderful slathered on rib steak.

makes about 3 cups

1 cup good-quality tomato paste
2 cups Classic Chimichurri (opposite)
About ¼ cup hot sauce

Place the tomato paste in a mixing bowl. Beat in the Classic Chimichurri, blending well. Add hot sauce to taste. Adjust salt and vinegar, if necessary.

Gratin of Black Beans and Corn with Crusty Cheese

· · ● · ·

This oozing casserole of indigenous American starches simultaneously tastes historic and contemporary. Above all, it tastes delicious alongside grilled steak.

Start soaking the beans the night before. You can make the dish a day ahead, but don't top with cheese until you're ready to reheat the gratin.

serves 12

2 cups dried black beans

1 onion, about 4 ounces, peeled, kept whole, plus 1 cup ¼-inch diced onion

4 cloves garlic, peeled

2 bay leaves

Kosher salt

4 cups fresh corn kernels (cut from approximately 8 ears of corn)

¾ cup (1 ½ sticks) unsalted butter

1 cup ¼-inch diced green bell pepper

6 tablespoons all-purpose flour

4 cups whole milk, heated

Freshly ground black pepper

1 pound sharp cheddar, coarsely grated

2 tablespoons butter for greasing the casserole (or use nonstick spray)

1. The night before making the casserole, pick over the beans, discarding any stones. Rinse the beans briefly, then cover with water and let sit overnight.

2. The next day, place the beans in a 4-quart pot along with their soaking liquid. Add the whole onion, the garlic, and the bay leaves. Add fresh water to cover the beans by 2 inches. Bring to a boil, then lower to a simmer. Cover and cook until the beans are tender but not mushy, about 1 1/2 hours. Check during cooking, and add hot water when necessary. When the beans are almost done, add salt. Drain the beans, discarding the water. Discard the onion, garlic, and bay leaves; reserve the beans.

3. Meanwhile, while the beans are cooking, blanch the corn kernels in a large pot of boiling salted water for 1 minute. Drain the corn, cool, and refrigerate.

4. Heat the oven to 375°F.

5. Melt the butter in a 4-quart pot over medium-low heat. Add the diced onion and green pepper. Cook until soft, but not brown, about 20 minutes.

6. Stir in the flour and cook for 2 minutes, stirring constantly. Add the hot milk all at once, stirring vigorously with a whisk. Increase the heat to medium, and cook, stirring occasionally, until thickened, about 6 minutes. Add salt and pepper.

7. Reserve 1 1/2 cups grated cheese; stir the remaining cheese into the milk mixture. When the cheese has melted, fold in the corn and the beans.

8. Grease a 3-quart casserole with butter or film with nonstick spray. Place the bean-and-corn mixture in the casserole. Sprinkle the reserved cheese over the top. Bake until the cheese is melted, about 10 to 15 minutes. Just before serving, pass under a hot broiler to lightly brown the cheese.

South American Salad, with Tomatoes, Potatoes, Avocados, Purple Onions, Hard-Boiled Eggs, and Green Vinaigrette

· · ● · ·

serves 12

1 pound small, waxy potatoes, peeled

4 firm, ripe Haas avocados

Fresh lime juice

Kosher salt

2 cups loosely packed flat-leaf parsley leaves, large leaves torn in half

1 medium purple onion (about 6 ounces), cut into 1/2-inch dice

8 firm, ripe medium tomatoes, cored and cut into 1/2-inch dice

Freshly ground black pepper

Green Vinaigrette (opposite)

8 large hard-boiled eggs, peeled

1. Boil the potatoes in salted water until cooked but still firm, 30 to 50 minutes, depending on the size of the potatoes. Drain and cool. Quarter, and cut quarters into 1/2-inch slices. Place in a large serving bowl.

2. Cut the avocados in half and remove the pits. Scoop out the flesh in one motion using a large spoon, then cut into 1/2-inch dice. Drizzle with fresh lime juice over all surfaces, toss with salt, then add the avocados to the bowl with the potatoes.

3. Add the parsley to the potatoes and avocados.

4. Add the onion and tomatoes. Season with salt and pepper, then add Green Vinaigrette to taste, tossing gently but well.

5. Cut the eggs into quarters lengthwise, then cut each quarter in half. Work carefully so that the whites and yolks stay together. Add the eggs to the salad, and toss just enough to combine the eggs with the other ingredients. Taste for seasoning, add more dressing if needed, and serve.

Green Vinaigrette

· · · ● · ·

makes 2 cups

> 2 to 3 shallots, roughly chopped (about ½ cup)
>
> 4 cloves garlic, roughly chopped
>
> 1 cup flat-leaf parsley leaves
>
> 1 teaspoon kosher salt
>
> ½ teaspoon freshly ground black pepper
>
> ½ cup red wine vinegar
>
> 4 teaspoons Dijon-style mustard
>
> 1 ½ cups extra-virgin olive oil

1. Place the shallots, garlic, parsley, salt, pepper, vinegar, and mustard into a blender jar. Blend until smooth, scraping down the sides of the jar as needed.

2. Remove the cap, and with the motor running, slowly add the oil in a steady stream. Taste for seasoning.

Coconut–Mascarpone Roulades with Mangoes

· ● ○ · ·

Brazilian and Argentine restaurants often feature fluffy, creamy, fruit-studded pastries such as this one.

Serve the roulades, of course, with two great South American beverage options: Colombian coffee or yerba maté tea from Argentina. Use cups or mugs for the coffee, but the maté could be served out of *cuia,* or South American gourds. The tea and gourds are available online **(see Where to Find It, page 240)**.

makes 2 cakes, each serving 6

for the cakes:

½ cup canned, unsweetened coconut milk

4 tablespoons unsalted butter

1½ cups plus 2 tablespoons superfine sugar

6 large eggs

4 large egg yolks

1 teaspoon liquid coconut flavoring

2 cups sifted cake flour

Kosher salt

2 teaspoons baking powder

for the syrup:

¼ cup water

¼ cup sugar

¼ cup dark rum

for the mascarpone filling:

1 cup sweetened flaked coconut

1 pound mascarpone

6 tablespoons confectioners' sugar

for the final assembly:

2 ripe mangoes, peeled and sliced

Confectioners' sugar for dusting

1. Heat the oven to 400°F. Coat two 9 1/2 -x 13-inch jelly-roll pans with nonstick spray. Line the bottom of the pans with parchment paper and spray again.

2. For the cakes, heat the coconut milk and butter in a small saucepan over medium heat until the butter melts. Keep warm.

3. Combine 1 1/2 cups superfine sugar, the whole eggs, egg yolks, and coconut flavoring in the bowl of a standing mixer. Beat at medium-high speed until tripled in volume, about 10 minutes.

4. Combine the flour with a pinch of salt and the baking powder. Fold the flour mixture into the beaten eggs one-third at a time, taking care not to lose any volume in the eggs.

5. Fold 1/4 cup of the batter into the warm coconut milk in the saucepan. Then gently fold the coconut milk mixture back into the batter.

6. Divide the cake batter between the jelly-roll pans and spread it evenly to the edges. Bake until the cakes shrink from the sides of the pans and spring back when touched, 10 to 12 minutes. They should be lightly golden in color.

7. Let the cakes cool in the pans on cake racks for about 10 minutes.

8. Sprinkle 2 clean tea towels (at least 9 1/2 x 13 inches each) with the remaining superfine sugar, 1 tablespoon sprinkled evenly over each towel (this helps to prevent sticking).

9. Carefully turn the jelly-roll pans over onto the tea towels, spilling the cakes onto the towels so they're centered on each one. Peel off and discard the parchment. With the short end of each towel facing you, roll the cakes up in the towels, until you reach the other short end of the towel. Set the cakes aside, still rolled up in their towels, while you prepare the syrup and filling.

10. For the syrup, combine the water and sugar in a small saucepan over medium-high heat. Cook until the sugar is dissolved, about 2 minutes. Remove from the heat and stir in the rum.

11. For the filling, spread out the flaked coconut in a large nonstick skillet. Place the skillet over medium heat, and toast the coconut, tossing, until it's light brown, about 3 minutes. Remove from the skillet and reserve.

12. Whip the mascarpone with an electric beater on medium speed for 1 minute. Add the sugar and coconut, and beat until combined, 10 seconds more. Set aside.

13. To assemble, unroll the cakes and remove them from their towels.

14. Brush with syrup, dividing the syrup evenly between the cakes.

15. Spread each cake evenly with half of the mascarpone filling, then arrange the mango slices on top. Re-roll the roulades and transfer to a serving plate and refrigerate. Remove from the refrigerator at least half an hour before serving. Dust with confectioners' sugar, slice, and serve.

Set Dressing

This is a steak party, so why don't we imagine that we're out on the pampa with the gauchos, grilling up dinner?

Of course, we don't have to reach back too far into history; I think the idea of the "modern" gaucho, who's probably wearing blue jeans, will be easier to live up to. Let's give that modern gaucho some money and lots of taste. Perhaps he has an "outdoor living room"—an ultra-comfy space, open to the elements but with interior motifs, decorated with large-scale, manly furniture, cowhides, leather, impossibly cushy cushions, and a branding iron or two for decoration. Obviously, this is not realistic for most of us. But hold onto the "outdoor living room" concept, and do what you can to create an inviting atmosphere for your guests with what you have on hand, or can acquire, within reason.

Table Dressing

This is going to be a masculine-looking table, beautiful, but mucho macho. Have a seamstress (or a gifted friend) sew a tablecloth with what are called box pleats at the corners; this means the cloth will go over your table with the tailored kind of fit normally reserved for toaster covers. A rough weave in a dark color—chocolate, perhaps?—would be a great choice; burlap even comes in some wonderful hues these days. For color contrast, you could use a runner in a complementary color (green? orange?) right down the center.

Materials to focus on would be leather, wood, clay pottery, and metal (especially silver). I'd use hefty plates, to be sure (maybe terra-cotta), and I'd keep the cutlery on the chunky side. Belt your napkins with leather or silver. *Bombillas*—the unique metal filtered straws—would make great party favors.

Table centerpiece? A generous display of unusual tropical fruits (most people have never seen cashew fruit), vegetables (a multicolored array of chiles is always a kick), or flowers, such as the ultra-dramatic anthurium. Candles should be kept on the squatty side. Large clear-glass cylinders could be partially filled with whole coffee beans. Hit the olfactory high notes by occasionally throwing fragrant wood or herbs on the fire.

Entertainment

But here's another idea that's not so obvious: miniature hot-air ballons. There is a festive tradition in South America of floating these things, powered by candles, at parties. They are known as *globo*, Spanish for "balloon." **See Where to Find It, page 240** for places that actually sell these things, then ask your guests to help get them in motion!

Where to Find It

Lobel's
1096 Madison Ave.
New York, NY 10028
877.783.4512 (toll free)
www.lobels.com
One of the country's greatest butchers, with a huge mail-order business. Best skirt steak I've ever tasted.

Palm Restaurant
Palm Pak
1730 Rhode Island Ave. NW
Suite 900
Washington, DC 20036
800.388.PALM (toll free)
202.775.8292 (fax)
www.thepalm.com
Great steaks from a great chain of steakhouses.

Main Street Steaks
4417 Main St.
Manayunk, PA 19127
215.487.1700 (tel)
www.kansascityprime.com
A mail-order butcher connected to the best steakhouse in Philadelphia.

Peter Luger
185–195 Broadway
Brooklyn, NY 11211
718.387.0500 (tel)
718.387.3523 (fax)
www.peterluger.com
This is probably the world's greatest steakhouse, and they ship!

Allen Brothers
3737 S. Halsted Rd.
Chicago, IL 60609-1689
800.957.0111 (toll free)
773.890.9146 (fax)
www.allenbrothers.com
Chicago-based supplier of meat to many top restaurants since 1893.

Melissa's/World Variety Produce, Inc.
P.O. Box 21127
Los Angeles, CA 90021
800.588.0151 (toll free)
www.melissas.com
Key limes, as well as exotic fruits and vegetables.

El Mercado Grande
862 E. 7th Place
Mesa, AZ 85203
480.862.2964 (tel)
www.elmercadogrande.com
An online purveyor of South American foodstuffs.

EFCO Importers
P.O Box 741
Jenkintown, PA 19046
88.234.9210 (toll free)
215.885.8597 (tel)
215.885.4584 (fax)
Pitu cachaça and caipirinha glasses.

Guayaki Sustainable Rainforest Products
P.O. Box 14730
San Luis Obispo, CA 93406
888.482.9254 (toll free)
www.guayaki.com
Artisan-made *bombillas*, natural gourd drinking vessels, and a large selection of yerba maté teas.

Ma-tea.com
1783 Ridgewood Dr. NE
Atlanta, GA 30307
404.849.2240 (tel)
www.ma-tea.net
A source for yerba maté as well as gourd drinking vessels and *bombillas*.

Hawaiitropicals.com
175 East Kawailani St.
Hilo, HI 96720
877.961.4774 (toll free)
www.hawaiitropicals.com
An online source for tropical flowers such as anthurium.

Overflite
Thomas Taylor
222 East Pearson St.,
Suite 1206
Chicago, IL 60611
www.overflite.com
Ready to fly (but tethered) unmanned hot air balloons.

Otherland Toys, LTD
Lee Valley Technopark
Block 1A, Unit 103
Ashley Road, Tottenham
London, N17 9NL
United Kingdom
44.0.208.880.4919 (tel)
www.otherlandtoys.co.uk
Miniature hot air balloons. International shipments via FedEx.

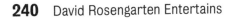

Bollito Misto

The Winter Party Your Italian Mama Would Have Thrown

A Party for 12

The Menu

Celery Stuffed with Gorgonzola-Mascarpone Cream

Bollito Misto, with Chicken, Veal, Tongue, Beef Brisket,
Garlic Sausage, and Vegetables

Salsa Verde

Salsa Rossa

Apple Mostardo

Warm and Creamy Rice Pudding with Dried Fruits and Campari Syrup

Fabulous entertaining need not be elegant entertaining! Across northern Italy—but particularly in and around Modena in the food-rich, rich-food region of Emilia-Romagna—Italians come together in cold weather to partake of a massive stockpot, out of which emerges profound broth, a mountain of juicy, long-boiled meats (*bollito misto* means "mixed boil"), and heartwarming side dishes of tender winter vegetables. Traditional condiments on the buffet table lend color, vivacity, and flavor counterpoints. The party that swirls around this simple meal inevitably reminds party-goers of one very important thing: winter, too, is a wonderful gastronomic season.

The Plan

There are restaurants in Emilia-Romagna devoted to bollito misto. A rolling cart appears at your table, and you inform the server which pieces of meat (all held at a perfect serving temperature) you'd like to have. Broth and condiments are served on the side.

Now, I'm not suggesting that you go out and buy a bollito misto cart for your party. But the spirit of individual choice is a great one here; it's like choosing the cheeses you want from a cheese cart. You might want to set up a side table, right next to the dining table, on which you place the steaming platter of meats, a cutting board, a stack of 12 dinner plates, and an array of condiments. Then, after the pass-around of stuffed celery, you ask each guest to come and select meats. You carve them to order, place meats on a single plate, comply with the condiment order (adding them right to the meat plate), drizzle a tiny bit of broth over the meat, and serve. You'll have plates ready for everyone in no time. Place the remaining bowls of condiments on the table, along with good balsamic vinegar, and an individual cup of hot broth for each diner. Simplicity itself—and a great deal of gustatory excitement.

The Ingredient

Of all the terrific meats in this carnivore's treasure trove, the one that always has the potential to score highest with me is the garlicky sausage. And that's why I usually pay the most attention to it as I shop for the party. The other meats will all cook down to velvety tenderness during their long cooking, so there's no need, for example, to seek out the perfect chicken. But the sausage gets added late. It will be the tastiest bite in the pot—if you get a great one.

It's not that difficult these days to obtain one of northern Italy's most popular "cooking" sausages, cotechino. This beauty goes back a long way—to 1511, they say, when the troops of Pope Julius II laid siege to the town of Mirandola. The townspeople, in retreat, needed a way to easily transport their food—and began encasing pork in pigskin, creating cotechino. With time, the pigskin casing was dropped; but the sausage today, which you usually buy precooked, still has a great spicy-garlicky flavor.

I know of three terrific sources for cotechino. The first is Fratelli Beretta, a fine New Jersey *salumi* specialist that makes very authentic-tasting products; you can order their cotechino through igourmet.com. Another top producer, P. G. Molinari & Sons in San Francisco, makes an excellent product (which they call "coteghino") that is shipped all over the country by A.G. Ferrari Foods. My favorite of all, however, is the "cotechini sausage" made by the Alps Provision Co. in Astoria, New York (available from Todaro Bros.). Their sausage is 9 inches long, almost 3 inches in diameter, and weighs close to 2 pounds. It is uncooked when you buy it, so you'll need to simmer it gently for about an hour. Stuffed in its own natural pork casing, this coarse, pinkish sausage has a phenomenal pork flavor—helped along by perfect seasoning, a wild array of spicy-garlicky notes, and a perfect tender-resilient chew. (**See Where to Find It, page 258,** for all those suppliers.)

Now, should you *really* get motivated to make a splash, you can order garlic sausage that is still stuffed in pigskin! And sublimely delicious, to boot. It is called zampone, and textbooks tell us that it evolved from cotechino; apparently, the sausage-makers of Modena, in less threatened, less ambulatory times, started stuffing whole forelegs of pigs with the garlicky sausage stuffing. And that's what zampone is today: a sausage stuffed inside a small pig's leg. A very talented sausage-maker in New York—at the Salumeria Biellese, from which chefs all over the country order products—makes an uncooked zampone year-round and is willing to ship it to you (**see Where to Find It, page 258**). It's a good idea, especially at holiday time, when zampone is popular, to order 3 days in advance. Your zampone will be larger than the amount you'll need for this dish, but leftovers will be glorious later on (you can even freeze it) with lentils, with stewed cabbage, with beans, with garlic mashed potatoes. As with the Alps-brand cotechini sausage, simmer gently for about an hour.

If you don't want to bother with ordering a special sausage (oh, go on! order one!), you can always go to your supermarket and pick up the coarsest, most garlicky kielbasa you can find. The results won't be quite as grand, but your bollito misto will still be loved by everyone.

Beverage Time

Wintertime celebrations often commence with sparkling wine. It's not the elegance of French Champagne you're seeking here, though. No, northern Italy's favorite sparkling aperitif, Prosecco—produced not far from Venice and now wildly fashionable around the world—would be the perfect starter here; it is a little fruitier than Champagne, a little less dry, a little lower in acid, a little simpler in flavor. Ideal! If you wish, let those Italian bubbles flow with the main course. The fruitiness of Prosecco gives this wine the credentials to stand up to the delicious mustard apples that accompany the bollito misto.

You may prefer to switch to red wine with all that meat. I heartily endorse this policy, as long as the wine is resolutely downscale (no expensive old Barolo here!), and once again, suitable for the mustard apples. It's not easy to find off-dry red wines, unfortunately—but Italy offers a terrific possibility: Novello, or the Italian equivalent of Beaujolais Nouveau. Unlike Beaujolais Nouveau (which is made only in France's Beaujolais region), Novello is made all over Italy. Another difference is that Beaujolais Nouveau is made only from the Gamay grape, while Novello is made from whichever grape the local Italian winemaker wants to use. Generally speaking, Italian Novello wines are as fruity, ebullient, and as party-friendly as Beaujolais Nouveau—but often a little richer, and a little less dry. Perfect! One of my favorites is made in the Veneto, by the house of Mionetto (who also produce excellent Prosecco); Mionetto Novello is made for the bollito and mustard apples because it is squarely on the off-dry side. Another festive Novello I always look for is Terra di Luna, made in the Friuli region.

The. Recipes

Celery Stuffed with Gorgonzola-Mascarpone Cream

· ◦ ● ◦ ·

This is a magical combination of elements—especially if you include the optional anchovies listed below. However, if you know some of your guests to be anti-anchovy, the anchovy-less stalks will still be delicious.

serves 12

12 ounces Gorgonzola dolce

¼ cup mascarpone

1 ½ teaspoons grappa

24 stalks celery, each cut 4 inches long (see Cook's Note)

24 flat anchovy fillets (optional)

½ cup grated Parmigiano-Reggiano or Grana Padano

Radicchio for garnish

1. Using a fork, thoroughly beat together the gorgonzola, mascarpone, and grappa in a small bowl until a creamy paste is formed. Stuff a sturdy sealable plastic bag with the cheese and cut a very small hole in one corner.

2. Stuff each celery stalk with 1 anchovy, slipping the fillet in the long way on its thinnest edge. Cover the anchovy by piping some gorgonzola-mascarpone cream onto it from the plastic bag. Sprinkle each stuffed stalk liberally with grated cheese. Arrange the stalks decoratively on a bed of radicchio leaves, and pass.

> COOK'S NOTE: *You could use stalks for this recipe from any part of the celery head as long as you cut them down to 4 inches long (so an anchovy fillet fits in neatly). However, the dish is at its best if you can extract 24 celery stalks from the hearts of several celery heads. For maximum effect, leave on some of the frilly light-green leaves at the bottom of each stalk drawn from the heart (the leaves should extend an inch or so beyond the 4 inches). Those outer stalks of celery that are left over? It's time for cream of celery soup!*

Bollito Misto, with Chicken, Veal, Tongue, Beef Brisket, Garlic Sausage, and Vegetables

· · · ● · ·

I love the particular combo of meats and vegetables in this recipe, but please remember that any improvisational substitutions you wish to make will work out perfectly—as long as you remember "Italy" and "winter." Recipes for the classic accompaniments follow the main recipe, but I suggest that you place something else on the table, too: a good bottle of aged balsamic vinegar (native to the bollito misto region!), which makes a lovely, enlivening splash on the long-cooked meats.

If you had a restaurant kitchen, you might have a stockpot large enough to accommodate the entire bollito misto that follows. But most home cooks have nothing of the sort—so, for their benefit, and mine, I've divided the dish among three large pots, all of which finish cooking at the same time.

Start early in the day.

serves 12

6 quarts chicken broth

3 quarts water

3 medium white onions, cut in half lengthwise

6 bay leaves

2 stalks celery, cut in half crosswise

2 carrots, peeled and cut in half crosswise, plus 8 carrots, peeled and cut into ½-inch chunks

6 large cloves garlic

1 (1-pound) piece prosciutto, cut in half (see Cook's Note #1)

3 pounds beef brisket, cut into two equal pieces

Kosher salt

2 fresh veal tongues, 1 to 1¼ pounds each

1 (3-pound) veal shoulder roast, cut into two equal pieces, each one tied

3 (2½-pound) chickens, giblets removed

24 very small potatoes (about 2 pounds), peeled and cut in half

24 very small turnips, peeled

6 medium red onions, cut lengthwise into quarters, stem attached

3 pounds precooked garlicky pork sausage, like cotechino or kielbasa, divided in half (or Alps uncooked cotechini, or zampone; see Cook's Note #2)

⅓ cup chopped curly parsley

Aged balsamic vinegar

1. Pour 2 quarts of chicken broth and 1 quart of water into a large pot. Pour another 2 quarts of chicken broth and another quart of water into a second large pot. Add 2 white onion halves and 2 bay leaves to each pot. Divide the celery, the halved carrots, garlic, and the prosciutto between the pots, and bring both to a simmer over medium-high heat. While the broths are coming to a simmer, rub the brisket generously with kosher salt. Once the pots are simmering, divide the brisket between the pots and slowly return to a bare simmer. Reduce the heat slightly and cover the pots, checking within a few minutes—and again throughout the entire cooking process—to ensure that the broths are at the laziest possible simmer.

2. Meanwhile, place the veal tongues, 2 onion halves, 2 bay leaves, and a generous pinch of salt in a third large pot with water to cover. Bring to a boil, reduce the heat, and simmer, uncovered, for 45 minutes. Remove from the heat and leave the tongues immersed. When they are cool enough to handle, peel the membranes from each tongue and return the tongues to the liquid until needed.

3. After the brisket has simmered for 3 hours, generously rub the veal shoulder pieces with kosher salt and let them sit for 5 minutes. Add them to the brisket pots, one piece per pot. Cover and return to a lazy simmer for 1 hour. Add a veal tongue to each pot and continue to simmer, covered, for another hour—a total of 5 hours so far. Clean the pot you poached the tongue in.

4. After the meats have cooked for 5 hours, salt the chickens generously, inside and out. Bring the remaining 2 quarts of chicken broth and 1 quart of water to a simmer in the clean stockpot and add the chickens. Cover and gently simmer for 25 minutes.

5. Add the 8 chunked carrots, the potatoes, turnips, and red onions to the chicken pot. Divide the sausage between the pots of beef and veal. Cover all three pots, and continue simmering until the chicken is cooked, the vegetables are tender, and the cotechino is warmed through, about 25 to 30 minutes more.

6. To serve, slice the brisket *against* the grain into ½-inch slices. Cut the veal into ¾-inch slices. Cut the tongue and cotechino on the bias into ⅜-inch slices. Cut each chicken into 8 pieces. Place the meats on warmed serving platters. Lay the vegetables attractively in and around the meats. Discard the prosciutto ends. Strain the brisket broth. Skim and discard any surface fat. (Reserve the chicken broth for another use.) Moisten the meats and vegetables with a few ladles of broth. Sprinkle the vegetables with parsley. Prepare a cup of brisket broth for each guest, and serve. The aged balsamic vinegar, served in a cruet, goes on the table for drizzling, along with the salsas and the mostardo.

COOK'S NOTE #1: *When a deli gets to the end of a prosciutto ham, they usually discard the hard, un-fatty pieces. With any persuasive skill, you can easily talk the deli man into discarding them into your shopping bag. Even paying a small per-pound price is a good strategy for procuring this wonderful flavor enhancer.*

COOK'S NOTE #2: *If you're using my favorite cotechino—the cotechini sausage from The Alps Provision Co.—it is uncooked; you will have to simmer it longer. Buy two of these cotechini sausages and place one in each of the beef and veal pots when you start to cook the chicken; the sausages will take 1 hour to cook.*

If you're using the zampone from Salumeria Biellese, you will also need to simmer it for about an hour. Cut off two chunks that are about 1 ½ pounds each, and immerse each one in one of the beef and veal pots an hour before serving the bollito misto. Reserve leftover zampone for future use.

Re-Bollito?

If you have a significant quantity of meat left over from your bollito misto party—and you might!—there are wonderful things to do with it. Some Italian chefs like to re-warm the meats gently in a tomato sauce the next day, giving the dish a whole different character. Some grind the meats and use that mixture as a basis for meatballs or meat loaf. My favorite bollito misto leftover dish, however, is a salad of shredded meats, tossed with a good vinaigrette that includes capers, anchovies, cornichons, and herbs. By the way, leftover broth makes great cooking stock. Or a good dish just by itself with some stuffed pasta (like tortellini) floating in it.

Spicy Ginger–Garlic Shrimp with Coconut Milk and Cilantro Leaves, page 200

Chicken, Tandoori-Style, page 202; Naan, page 205; Cilantro Relish, page 210; Deep-Fried Cauliflower with Chile and Tomatoes, page 208; Raita with Cumin and Tomato, page 211

Inset: Assorted Spices

Raw Gulf Oysters with Green Tabasco
Sauce, page 269; Cajun Crab Boil,
page 270; Cajun Bloody Mary with
Pickled Vegetables, page 267

Cassoulet with Home-Cured Duck,
Home-Cured Pork, and Garlic
Sausage, page 300; Leafy Green Salad
with Walnuts, Walnut Vinaigrette,
and Crumbled Roquefort, page 298

English Tea Cake with Dates, Walnuts, and Apricots, page 379; Miniature Scones with Clotted Cream and Strawberry Jam, page 377

Cucumber and Cream Cheese
Sandwiches with Fresh Mint, page
372; Egg and Watercress Sandwiches,
page 373; Rolled Smoked Salmon
Sandwiches with Dill, page 374

Salsa Verde

· ▪ ● ▪ ·

Serve with the Bollito Misto

makes about 1 ¾ cups

2 cups loosely packed flat-leaf parsley leaves

½ cup loosely packed mint leaves

4 anchovy fillets, chopped

2 heaping tablespoons capers

3 hard-boiled egg yolks

1 large garlic clove, sliced

1 ½ tablespoons white wine vinegar

½ teaspoon kosher salt

¼ teaspoon freshly ground black pepper

Generous pinch cayenne

1 cup extra-virgin olive oil, plus additional as needed

Combine all the ingredients except the olive oil in the bowl of a food processor. Pulse the mixture to chop, pausing to scrape down the sides. With the motor running, add the olive oil through the feed tube in a steady stream until a fluid, slightly thickened sauce forms and the ingredients are finely chopped. Process with additional oil as needed. Taste for salt and pepper.

Salsa Rossa

· ◦ ● ◦ ·

Serve with the Bollito Misto

makes about 3 cups

¼ cup extra-virgin olive oil

1 medium onion, diced

4 large cloves garlic, sliced

1 medium carrot, peeled and diced

1 stalk celery, diced

1 tablespoon tomato paste

1 (28-ounce) can tomatoes, drained

2 teaspoons kosher salt

Generous pinch cayenne

⅛ teaspoon ground cinnamon

1 tablespoon red wine vinegar

1. Heat the olive oil in a medium skillet over high heat until it just begins to smoke. Add the onion, garlic, carrot, and celery. Reduce the heat to medium and cook, stirring regularly, until the vegetables are soft and pale golden at the edges, about 4 to 6 minutes. Stir in the tomato paste and cook 1 minute more. Crush the tomatoes with your hands and add them to the skillet along with the salt and cayenne. Gently simmer the mixture, stirring occasionally, until well thickened, about 25 minutes.

2. Remove from the heat, transfer to the jar of a blender, and add the cinnamon and vinegar. Purée the mixture until smooth, adjusting the seasoning with additional salt, cinnamon, and vinegar.

Apple Mostardo

· · · ● · ·

A side dish of mustard-scented fruits is one of the things that makes bollito misto so memorable; the pungent mustard does for the meat what horseradish does for boiled beef, with the additional surprise of a little fruity sweetness. The most famous version of the condiment is Mostardo di Cremona, a specialty of one northern Italian town. But towns all over the bollito misto belt have their own versions—such as the following one, which I found not far from Modena, made with apples.

makes about 3 cups

1 ½ cups sugar

3 cups water

2 tablespoons Coleman's dry mustard, whisked to a slurry with ½ cup water

2 tablespoons yellow mustard seed

1 ½ teaspoons grated ginger

1 teaspoon freshly ground black pepper

Pinch of kosher salt

3 tart apples (such as Granny Smith), peeled, cored, and sliced into ¼-inch wedges

3 sweet apples (such as Red Delicious), peeled, cored, and sliced into ¼-inch wedges

3 tablespoons apple cider vinegar

3 tablespoons Indian mustard oil

Combine the sugar and water in a large skillet and bring to a boil. Reduce the heat so the syrup simmers and stir in the mustard slurry, mustard seed, ginger, pepper, salt, and the apples. Simmer, stirring occasionally, until the water has evaporated and the apple preserve is thick and syrupy, 20 to 25 minutes. Remove from the heat, let cool slightly, and stir in the vinegar and mustard oil. Serve at room temperature.

Warm and Creamy Rice Pudding with Dried Fruits and Campari Syrup

· · ● · ·

You may substitute 2¼ cups of any small chopped dried fruits you like for the combination I've given below. Think of this as a dessert risotto!

serves 12

¾ cup raisins

¾ cup dried cranberries

¾ cup dried apricots, diced

2 cups water

½ cup Campari

1½ cups sugar

1 gallon whole milk

Finely grated zest of 1 lemon

1½ teaspoons vanilla extract

Pinch of kosher salt

1½ cups Italian short grain rice, such as arborio or carnaroli

4 tablespoons unsalted butter

Mascarpone, for garnish

¾ cup roasted almonds, chopped, for garnish

1. Soak the raisins, cranberries, and apricots in warm water to cover for 15 minutes. Drain and discard the water.

2. Combine the 2 cups water, Campari, and 3/4 cup sugar in a medium skillet. Bring to a boil. Reduce the heat, stir in the drained, dried fruit, and simmer the mixture, stirring occasionally, until the fruit is submerged in a light, still-runny syrup. Remove from the heat and cool to room temperature.

3. Combine the milk, lemon zest, vanilla, and salt in a large, heavy casserole or stockpot. Bring just to a simmer, taking care to avoid a milk boilover. Whisk in the rice and the remaining 3/4 cup sugar. Return to a simmer, whisking frequently to prevent clumping. Cook over very low heat, whisking every 10 minutes or so, until the rice resembles a thickened but very runny porridge, about 2 hours. Remove from the heat, and stir in the butter. Transfer to a serving bowl, and let the pudding cool for at least 30 minutes before serving. Top each portion with a few spoonfuls of dried fruits and a bit of the syrup. Garnish with spoonfuls of mascarpone and almonds.

> COOK'S NOTE: *When the pudding stands for any length of time, it forms a skin. The skin can easily be peeled off before serving.*

Set Dressing

Most travelers who have stopped in the northern Italian countryside on a frigid day know what the welcoming interior of a northern Italian country home or inn feels like: less Mediterranean than you'd expect, with a more somber palette, tastefully rustic, a place where you might imagine hooded Cappucine monks huddling around mugs of cappuccino! The notion of "warmth-out-of-the-cold" is a very important element here, and, therefore, anything you can include in your set dressing that implies human defense against the elements is a winner.

Fire leads the list—echoing the fire that glows under your pots of bollito misto. The ideal set piece is a huge, baronial stone fireplace, stoked with cords of wood—not gonna happen for most of us, I'm afraid. But if you do have a fireplace, use it. In addition, any arrangement you can dream up that uses live fire in lanterns or lamps would also be great. The possibility that will definitely work for most of us is candles, but I would want you to choose stubby, off-color ones, not tall, sleek, white, elegant ones.

Carry on with the motif of "warmth." Drape rustic, woolly blankets or afghans over non-rustic furniture. Move coarse-textured carpets or throw rugs into the party space. I'll never forget the pile-up of mud-caked heavy boots near the fire in one Tuscan *albergo* I visited in a snowy January; you might want to approximate that image by placing a few well-chosen boots of your own subtly on view (nothing says winter in the country like the clothes that farmers need to put on to go out and feed the animals).

"Warmth," finally, applies to your attitude. This is a good party for pushing the envelope of your hospitality. Make those people coming in from the cold as instantly warmed as they can be. Fuss over the coats you're removing. Be quick in offering that glass of Prosecco. Point out the bowls of nuts that you've stationed around the room. Make your guests feel the warmth of your welcome throughout the evening.

Table Dressing

Despite the refinement today of the people who choose to serve it, bollito misto is peasant fare, and you should set your table accordingly. Simple dinnerware, humble linens, and table elements inspired by the agrarian origins of the dish (fieldstone or attractive rocks, pots of herbs brought into the house for winter, squatty candles) all add to the bucolic background.

However, just because we're peasants for a day doesn't mean we can't eat and celebrate heartily! The birthplace of bollito misto, Emilia-Romagna, is Italy's "land of plenty"; its capital city, Bologna, is known as *La Grassa* ("The Fat"). A meal like bollito misto has always been viewed as wickedly indulgent, a veritable feast of good things from the earth. So I propose that the table reflect that prosperity.

For specific motifs, I looked to the della Robbia family, artisans of the Italian Renaissance. They perfected an enamel glaze for terra-cotta, and to this day baroque displays of ripe fruits and vegetables, especially in garlands, are referred to collectively as "della Robbia." (The della Robbias' studio was actually in Florence, but hey, they could've gone over the Apennine Mountains, lured by the smell of bollito misto!)

So start with a nice tablecloth in a solid color. Station two or three portly cachepots, either enameled or terra-cotta with cast relief, in a line down the center of the table. Fill with low plants of trailing ivy. Punctuate the spaces between the pots with sumptuous tumbles of winter fruit (pomegranates, persimmons, pears, apples, and any dried fruits you fancy). Arrange the tendrils of ivy attractively over and around the display.

Dinnerware could run the gamut from colorful glazed Italian ceramics found in specialty shops to the generic but attractive solid-color plates found in nearly any store that stocks tableware. Look for sets that have cups for serving the broth. Match napkins to your dinnerware, and tie with a sprig of ivy, if desired. Serve the Prosecco in flutes; but if you go the red-wine route, it's tumblers all the way.

Where to Find It

igourmet.com

877.446.8763 (toll free)
www.igourmet.com
Carries cotechino from Fratelli Beretta, a New Jersey company that produces cotechino to Italian specifications.

A.G. Ferrari Foods

14234 Catalina St.
San Leandro, CA 94577
877.878.2783 (toll free)
510.346.2100 (tel)
510.351.2672 (fax)
www.agferrari.com
Many wonderful Italian gourmet products, including the coteghino of P.G. Molinari.

Todaro Bros.

555 Second Ave.
New York, NY 10016
212.532.0633 (tel)
212.689.1679 (fax)
www.todarobros.com
Great Italian food store, and a mail-order source for the supernal Alps cotechini.

Salumeria Biellese

378 Eighth Ave.
New York, NY 10001
212.736.7376 (tel)
212.736.1093 (fax)
A miraculous place for all kinds of house-made sausages— including zampone!

BendenWilliams

490 Main St.
Glen Ellyn, IL 60137
866.923.6336 (toll free)
630.790.2620 (tel)
630.790.2648 (fax)
www.bendenwilliams.com
Imported dinnerware (casual as well as formal), and unusual Italian flatware designed by the Bugatti family.

Bellezza

129 Newbury St.
Boston, MA 02116
617.266.1183 (tel)
617.424.6724 (fax)
www.bellezzahome.com
Specializes in hand-painted Italian ceramics for home and garden.

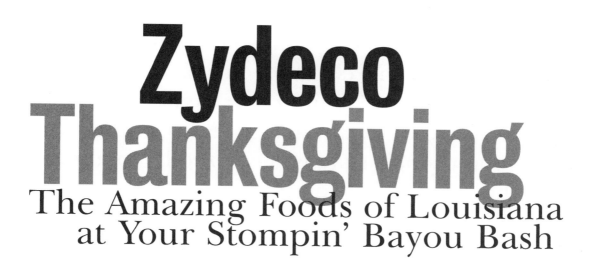

Zydeco Thanksgiving

The Amazing Foods of Louisiana at Your Stompin' Bayou Bash

A Party for 12

The Menu

Cajun Bloody Mary with Pickled Vegetables

Raw Gulf Oysters with Green Tabasco Sauce

Cajun Crab Boil

Soft-Shelled Crawfish "Popcorn"

Dark Gumbo, Country Style, with Spare Ribs and Andouille

Roast Turducken
(A Chicken Inside a Duck Inside a Turkey, with Various Stuffings)

Vanilla Ice Cream with Pecans, Bananas Foster-Cointreau Sauce, and Pralines

Just as the Texans have figured out that there's a big market across the country for mail-order Texas BBQ, so have the Louisianans realized that the great food of their state is: 1) prized by foodies in the other 49, and 2) eminently shippable. So I say, without fear of contradiction—as I say on the subject of Texas BBQ—why not build one hell of a party with the goods you'll receive off the truck? Real Louisiana food (and not just the spicy stuff from Cajun country) has a very particular, old-fashioned taste to it—a taste that is easiest to find when the food's really from Louisiana, and when Louisiana cooks have prepared it. This party—with its combo of Louisiana ingredients, mail-order Louisiana-prepared specialties, and your ingenuity in bringing it all together—will have you and your guests stomping to zydeco music in Louisiana heaven.

When should you stomp? The late fall is the ideal time for this party: crabs are still in season, the oysters are getting good, and the first chill requires a big hearty main course—like the amazing chicken stuffed inside a duck stuffed inside a turkey! In fact, given that last item, why not make this the tastiest Thanksgiving feast you've ever thrown?

Add a little zydeco music—the funky, accordion-based genre hailing from the prairies of south-central and southwest Louisiana—and your good times are all ready to roll.

The
Plan

Because we're all used to sitting down at one big table for the grand Thanksgiving feast, I've set this party up as a sit-down event. If you wish to, converting it into a buffet would be very easy.

As your guests arrive, treat them to a demo at the Bloody Mary station, so they can then make their own at will. While they're still standing, pass trays of oysters on the half shell, on ice, each mollusk punctuated with a dot of Green Tabasco Sauce. Have extra green Tabasco on hand for hardier souls, and have bowls set around the room for easy shell disposal.

For the first course, spread the table with newspaper or brown paper—the perfect background for the mess o' crabs you'll be spilling right onto the table. Only napkins, wooden mallets, and Bloody Marys or beers are needed for this course. Worked-over shells can be scattered right on the paper. When the eatin's over, simply roll up the newspaper or brown paper, capturing all the shells; discard, and you have a clean table.

You've selected all of your china and silverware for the rest of the meal in advance. While you're preparing the crawfish popcorn, have someone set the table with the pieces you've selected (guests may remain seated with their Bloody Marys during this stage!). When the "popcorn" is ready, serve individual plates of it to your guests. Do the same with the next course, the pork and andouille gumbo.

The turducken gets its own spotlight. Carve that big bird on or near the table, so all can see the amazing architecture. Working with a stack of dinner plates, place individual portions on plates, and serve as the plates are ready. If you've made a pan gravy, drizzle a little over each turducken slice, then serve the extra gravy in a sauce boat. This is a big meal already, but if you want, make some collards or stewed okra to serve with the turducken.

Dessert, once again, gets individually plated and passed.

This is a sit-down dinner with multiple plated courses, so you might want to try my "Big Easy" solution to dirty-dish pile ups on kitchen highways. Set up a couple of big, lidded, molded plastic storage containers (mine have an 18-gallon capacity) in a back hallway or utility room convenient to the kitchen. Park dishes and pots and pans there until you have the time to deal with them. Later.

● **The day before the party**

> **Make the Cajun Bloody Mary Mix.**
>
> **Make Pralines (optional).**
>
> **Scoop the ice cream, cover, and freeze.**
>
> **Make the Homemade Cajun Crab Boil Seasoning (optional).**
>
> **Prepare the Dark Gumbo, Country Style, with Spare Ribs and Andouille.**
>
> **Cover the dining table with paper (for the crabs).**
>
> **Organize your tableware for the various courses.**

● **The day of the party**

> **Prep your ingredients for the Bananas Foster–Cointreau Sauce (save peeling the bananas until service so they don't brown).**
>
> **Roast the turducken (4 to 6 hours ahead). Tent with foil and allow to rest at least 20 minutes before carving.**
>
> **Coat the soft-shelled crawfish in the spice blend and refrigerate for at least 2 hours.**
>
> **Set up the beverage station.**
>
> **Shuck the oysters and set them out on ice (close to guests' arrival time).**

● **During dinner**

> **Make white rice.**
>
> **Reheat gumbo gently.**
>
> **Boil the crabs.**
>
> **Fry the Soft-Shelled Crawfish "Popcorn."**
>
> **Carve the turducken.**
>
> **Make the Bananas Foster–Cointreau Sauce and assemble the dessert.**

The Ingredient

Turducken, for sure. What is it about Louisiana and turkeys? Those great and restless cooks down there never seem to be content with the plain old, tried-and-true, traditional roast turkey. And I'm sure glad they're not!

First came the buzz, a few years back, about the Cajun deep-fried turkey—injected with spicy butter, totally immersed in a special, tall and narrow pot of bubbling oil set over a propane burner, cooking for less than an hour, and coming to the table in crispy, juicy glory. I have made it many times, and I love it—but I can tell you, it is a whole lot of trouble. And that much boiling oil does carry some real dangers.

Now we hear of another turkey craze (invented about 20 years ago). It's turducken, the wacky-sounding lineup of three birds sharing the physical space of one. Each bird is stuffed with stuffing, as well as another bird, and if the birds are succulent and the stuffings (you can use three!) are excellent, the turducken excitement level rises way above the excitement of any traditional roast turkey I know.

This new turkey route would be a whole heap of trouble, too, if you made it from scratch; unless you're Jacques Pépin, boning whole birds is no fun. Do you wish to go to the trouble? Well, you don't have to bone all those birds! There is now a huge industry in mail-order turducken from Louisiana. Some of the companies preparing this dish have this thing figured out perfectly, yielding—in your kitchen!—a crisp-skinned, gorgeously seasoned, endlessly varied treasure trove of poultry that will be the hit of your zydeco Thanksgiving party (or any party you choose to throw).

So here's what you do: contact either Hebert's (pronounced AY-bears) Specialty Meats or Gourmet Butcher Block **(see Where to Find It, page 285)**; these are the Louisiana companies that make the finest turduckens I've tasted. Order yourself a big turkey (it'll be boneless inside, with just a little wing and drumstick left on the exterior) that's stuffed with a boneless duck that's stuffed with a boneless chicken. You will have multiple stuffing options, featuring rice, meat, and seafood possibilities. The turducken I love the most is from Hebert's, and it features a pork-and-rice stuffing, a crawfish stuffing, and a shrimp stuffing—delicious beyond belief. The turducken will weigh 16 to 20 pounds, and will easily feed 12 people (20, more likely).

Beverage Time

The Bloody Mary was not invented by Cajuns, but surely, they gave it one of the greatest upgrades of all time! The kinds of spices that usually go into Cajun seasoning powders work wonderfully well with tomato juice and vodka. Moreover, the Cajuns ran with the "vegetable stirrer" idea, replacing the celery stalk with pickled vegetables—and usually more than just one in a glass! If you're in New Orleans and want to see how all of this works on its home turf, hie thee to Liuzza's by the Tracks, which makes one of the world's great Bloody Marys.

You, too, can serve one of the world's great Bloody Marys. It's quite easy to work this into your party; simply set up a do-it-yourself Bloody Mary station at the beginning of the party. You'll need pitchers of the Bloody Mary mixture you've made (page 267), buckets of ice, tongs, 12 squat tumblers that hold about 8 ounces of liquid each, iced vodka bottles (in case the guests want to add more vodka), a bottle of Tabasco sauce (in case the guests want to add more heat), stirrers, and an array of pickled vegetables (which you can place in cut- or pressed-glass bowls, or in a fanciful epergne, or on an old-fashioned 1950s relish tray). At the beginning of the party, get everyone's attention and make one demonstration Bloody Mary. Encourage your guests to add more vodka or Tabasco as they dare. Latecomers to the party? Deputize a guest to fix 'em up—or do it yourself.

Now, I'm inclined to just stick with my Bloody for the duration of the meal; the alcohol content in this Bloody is low enough to do so! However, not everyone, I'm sure, will follow my lead. So you might want to lay in a supply of good beer—preferably on ice in a large washtub. Any good, crisp, lager will do—though, if you can find it, the excellent beer of Abita, brewed in New Orleans, would add a lovely authentic touch. I like the Abita Amber.

The spicy food at this great party does not make it a perfect event for wine connoisseurs. But I'd have on hand some decent, off-dry white (like German Kabinett Riesling or French Vouvray); some decent, off-dry rosé (you know, White Zinfandel wouldn't be out of place here!); and some rollicking bottles of fruity young red (like Beaujolais Nouveau).

The.
Recipes

Cajun Bloody Mary with Pickled Vegetables

· · ● · ·

This recipe is fairly low in vodka content. To my taste, the taste of distilled alcohol, particularly if too much is used, harshens the whole Bloody Mary. Now, if your guests want to add more vodka, they're welcome to doctor their drinks. If you're expecting guests who don't want any alcohol, consider making an extra batch without the vodka. It still tastes great! Then, on the self-service Bloody Mary bar, point out that you've got "rowdy" pitchers of Bloody Marys, and "polite" ones too.

makes at least 3 dozen 4-ounce Bloody Marys

> **4 (28-ounce) cans whole tomatoes in thick tomato purée, chilled**
> **6 cups tomato juice, chilled**
> **2 tablespoons celery salt**
> **2 tablespoons sugar**
> **1 ½ teaspoons garlic powder**
> **1 ½ teaspoons onion powder**
> **1 ½ teaspoons freshly ground black pepper**
> **1 ½ teaspoons cayenne**
> **1 ½ teaspoons Tabasco sauce**
> **1 ½ cups chilled vodka**
> **Kosher salt**
> **Pickled vegetable garnishes (page 268)**

1. Working in batches, purée the canned tomatoes and their thick purée in a food processor until smooth. You should have a rich liquid with no lumps.

2. Combine the purée with the tomato juice in a large bowl, blending well.

3. Add the celery salt, sugar, garlic powder, onion powder, black pepper, cayenne, Tabasco, and vodka. Season with salt; you may need more than you expect to bring up the flavor of the mix (canned tomatoes have less salt than tomato juice). Keep the mixture cold.

4. For each serving, fill an 8-ounce tumbler with ice cubes. Pour about 4 ounces of the Bloody Mary mixture over the ice, which should almost fill the glass. Garnish with pickled vegetables, at least three pieces per drink.

Vegetable Garnishes

Arrange at least four or five different kinds of pickled vegetables on four or five dishes. Generally speaking, "long" vegetables work best as stirrers. But "short" vegetables can work too, as long as you thread several of each on a toothpick or 6-inch bamboo skewer. Here are a few specific ideas:

Pickled Okra. This, of course, is the perfect garnish for a Cajun Bloody Mary. Strive to find it! Luckily, a company called Talk o' Texas makes pickled okra in two varieties (I prefer the "hot"), and distributes the product to supermarkets across the country **(see Where to Find It, page 285)**.

Pickled String Beans. This is another pickled vegetable you often see in Louisiana Bloodies. A Washington State company called Hogue Farms makes a pickled string bean that is widely distributed **(see Where to Find It, page 285)**.

Pickled Asparagus Spears. Hogue Farms makes this as well.

Pepperoncini. Also called "Tuscan peppers," and available in most supermarkets across the U.S.

Pickled Cocktail Onions. Available everywhere. I like to thread three of them on a fancy toothpick, then assemble dozens of these picks on a plate.

Pimiento-Stuffed Olives. Choose smaller olives, and arrange on toothpicks like the cocktail onions.

Raw Gulf Oysters with Green Tabasco Sauce

· • • • • ·

As the weather gets chillier, oysters the world over get better, crisper, saltier, and more intense in flavor; Louisiana oysters from the Gulf of Mexico are no exception! Of course, they will never have the stinging salinity of Eastern Canadian oysters or Brittany oysters; but with their softer, sweeter taste profile, they certainly have their own set of charms. For me—normally an oyster purist, an eschewer of add-ons—raw Louisiana oysters taste best when you supply an enlivening jolt of something to them. I discovered this at the venerable Acme Oyster Bar in New Orleans, where I was encouraged to add a squirt of Green Tabasco Sauce to my bivalves. Bingo! I stopped missing the salt, and started loving the combo of earthy Gulf oysters with earthy green chile-and-vinegar. And the really great news is: anyone in the U.S., with very little trouble, can now enjoy this perfect party-starter at home.

The first task is ingredient acquisition. Don't worry about the Green Tabasco Sauce; any supermarket carries that. You could, of course, buy any kind of oysters at your local seafood shop, open 'em up, and squirt 'em with Green Tabasco Sauce; if your oysters are fresh and full of juice, the party will achieve lift-off no matter where the oysters came from. But tell the truth: wouldn't there be a special thrill in telling your guests that the oysters they're eating were in the Gulf yesterday morning—and on your table tonight?

Recently, I found a terrific source for Gulf oysters. The company is the P&J Oyster Company, in New Orleans, founded in 1876, and supplier of 40,000 oysters a week to U.S. restaurants—and now to you, as well **(see Where to Find It, page 285)**! P&J will send you a "minisack" of raw, live, in-shell Louisiana oysters, weighing approximately 45 pounds, and carrying about 120 3- to 3½-inch oysters.

Serving the oysters, of course, is a snap. Get yourself a few short, pointy oyster knives and deputize a few shuckers. Set up large platters with beds of crushed ice, ready to receive the mollusks on the half shell as you shuck 'em. Just before the guests arrive, get to work. Using gloves or dish towels to protect your hands, hold an oyster with its bulging, curved side down and its flat side up. Insert the pointy tip of the oyster knife into the hinge you'll find at the narrow end of the oyster, where the two shells meet. There's a tiny opening there, a mere crack. Twist your knife, rocking back and forth in that opening, until you've made the top shell "pop" away from the bottom shell. Now run your knife through the oyster, just under the top shell, scraping that top shell with the knife blade as you go. You should now be able to tear that top shell away. Discard it. If everything has gone well, you're looking at the curved bottom shell, filled with an oyster and a few teaspoons of oyster "liquor." Don't tilt that oyster! Do everything you can to preserve the liquor in the shell. Now, take your knife and run it under the oyster, on top of the bottom shell, separating the oyster from the bottom shell, but leaving it in the shell. Place this oyster on the half shell on the crushed ice on the platters.

When you have enough oysters to make a respectable showing in the party room—at least a dozen—give each one a squirt with Green Tabasco Sauce, then walk around the party, offering oysters to your guests, along with small napkins. You should also have the Tabasco at hand for those guests who want more, and bowls or buckets for discarding the shells.

If a guest is really skillful, he or she can hold a Bloody Mary in one hand while slipping an oyster into his or her mouth with the other!

Cajun Crab Boil

. . ● . .

There is an old Cajun practice that involves boiling some type of shellfish—crawfish or shrimp or crab—in a big pot of water seasoned with Cajun spices and herbs, along with corn and potatoes. Traditionally, this "boil" would be the main course. But I don't want it to be the main course of this party! So I've removed the vegetables, reduced the quantities, and focused on crab for this party's first sit-down course. Since this is only one of four pre-main-course courses, there'll be only two crabs per customer.

Once again, the hardest part of this dish is acquisition.

As with the oysters, you don't have to go to the trouble of acquiring Louisiana shellfish. Simply find two dozen large, live crabs at your local seafood market, fill a pot with water that will cover the crabs, season it with a Cajun mix of spices, drop the crabs in, cover, and serve 'em up about 12 minutes later. You could even make your own Cajun mix (Homemade Cajun Crab Boil Seasoning, page 271).

This much would be just fine. But there are improvements you can make! For one thing, you could acquire Louisiana crabs. Lil Kats—a humble seafood store in Metairie, just outside of New Orleans **(see Where to Find It, page 285)**—is a great source that will ship you, in season (roughly July through January), amazingly sweet, staggeringly large jumbo crabs from Louisiana. Order two dozen, and you're ready to rumble.

Now, another option involves the seasoning itself. Yes, I love my recipe, but I also love a product called Crawfish Crab and Shrimp Boil, with a wild clovelike, macelike, pinelike taste. Louisiana Fish Fry Products will ship you a 1-pound package of this powder from Baton Rouge. It is ample seasoning for two dozen crabs **(see Where to Find It, page 285)**.

Lastly, what with all the Thanksgiving festivities going on, you might like to have someone else handle your Cajun Crab Boil for you! Lil Kats can also send you perfectly seasoned cooked crabs. You would order 24 cooked crabs (which cost just a little bit more than the live crabs), and simply resteam them lightly until they're warm.

Whichever you choose, when the crabs are warm all you have to do is drain them and spill them out on the dining table (which you've covered with brown paper or newspaper). Supply your guests with small wooden mallets for breaking open the claws, and let the games begin!

COOK'S NOTE: *Some Cajun chefs like to leave the cooked shellfish in the cooking water, off the heat, for 20 or 30 minutes longer, because the spices penetrate better that way. But the seafood does get overcooked. Your call.*

Homemade Cajun Crab Boil Seasoning

. . ● . . .

makes about 2 cups, enough for 24 crabs

2/3 **cup table salt**

3 **tablespoons crushed black peppercorns**

3 **tablespoons dill seed**

2 **tablespoons crushed coriander seed**

2 **tablespoons brown mustard seed**

2 **tablespoons celery seed**

2 **tablespoons whole cloves**

1 **tablespoon ground allspice**

1 **tablespoon crushed red pepper**

1 **tablespoon cayenne (or more)**

1 **tablespoon garlic powder**

1 **tablespoon onion powder**

12 **bay leaves**

Combine all the ingredients. Add to a large pot that has enough water in it to cover the crabs. Bring the water to a boil before adding the live crabs.

Soft-Shelled Crawfish "Popcorn"

· · ● · · ·

In the first wave of Cajun mania that swept America years ago, Paul Prudhomme popularized a Louisiana treat that he called "Cajun Popcorn." These crawfish tails, coated in a spicy batter and deep-fried, were so good and so addictive, you popped 'em in your mouth like popcorn; hence the name. It wasn't long before something called "Popcorn Shrimp" appeared, too.

It's all good—but recently, I discovered what I consider to be the best variation of all: Cajun Popcorn made with soft-shelled crawfish! This will rock your party, and rock your guests, I *gar-on-TEE!* The crawfish are beautiful to look at; they come to you a glistening purple-black-brown with, as advertised, spongy, edible shells; when you cook them, they transform to bright orange-red. They are very sweet and very deep in crustacean flavor. Best of all: they are available year-round from Marshall Shnider, a fanatic purveyor of quality seafood in upstate New York. The company is called Farm-2-Market; he gets the crawfish from Louisiana and freezes them (because he believes they freeze well). All you have to do is log on to his website to receive these rare jewels **(see Where to Find It, page 285)**.

Before you get started, there's one more ingredient to consider: Cajun seasoning powder. Please go ahead and use any one you like! There are many in the marketplace, with "Chef Paul Prudhomme's Magic Seasoning Blends" being the most visible across the country. My favorite, by far, is Comeaux's Cajun Creole Seasoning **(see Where to Find It, page 285)**. Onions, celery, and "other spices" are thrown into the mix, and the result is a bewitching taste, salty and complex, not super-hot—that seems to suggest something high-toned like mace. Really fabulous on seafood.

3 dozen thawed soft-shelled crawfish (or 2 pounds cooked and shelled crawfish tails)

½ cup Cajun seasoning powder

Vegetable oil for deep-frying

2 cups all-purpose flour

1 cup finely ground cornmeal

½ tablespoon cayenne

1 ½ teaspoons freshly ground black pepper

2 teaspoons garlic powder

2 teaspoons onion powder

2 teaspoons sugar

Kosher salt

1. Place the soft-shelled crawfish in a bowl, and toss well with the seasoning powder. Let rest, covered and refrigerated, for 2 hours.

2. When ready to cook, heat the oil to 365°F in a deep-fryer or a deep, wide vessel (like a wok).

3. Meanwhile, place the flour, cornmeal, cayenne, black pepper—more or less cayenne and black pepper, if you want—garlic powder, onion powder, and sugar in a large paper bag. Shake well. Taste the Cajun seasoning powder you're using; if it's not very salty, add a little salt to the flour mixture in the bag.

4. When the oil is hot, dampen the marinating crawfish with a few tablespoons of water. Add them in batches to the flour in the bag, and shake well. Transfer the crawfish from the bag to the oil. Fry for a minute or so—a little less for the crawfish tails, if you're using them. They should be golden-brown and crunchy. Drain on paper towels. Season with coarse salt, if necessary. Divide the crawfish among 12 plates, and serve immediately.

Dark Gumbo, Country Style, with Spare Ribs and Andouille

• • • • •

Up North, the word "gumbo" usually conjures visions of a tomato-ey soup, reddish, and rife with chunky things like okra. You *can* find this kind of gumbo in Louisiana, but the amazing thing about gumbo there is its variety! Gumbos can have different colors, different textures, and different ingredients.

This is one of my very favorite types: a dark-brown, medium-rich one, with chunks of meat but no okra. What makes it so special? This is one of those amazing Louisiana dishes you hear about that involves the darkening of the roux—for at least an hour—until it's the color of mahogany. This adds not only color but incredible flavor to the gumbo: nutty, toasty, almost coffeelike. I had a gumbo like this at Mr. B's Bistro in New Orleans, made with chicken and andouille sausage, and loved it so much I asked for the recipe. I have transformed the dish to make it easier for the home cook, and have changed it by converting chicken to pork—which I think does nothing but emphasize the wild, back-country character of the dish. Is it hot enough for you? I suggest initially going with my spice ratios below, because the gumbo gets "hotter" as it cooks; you can always adjust with Tabasco sauce or spices at the last minute. Speaking of which, I find that a tiny pinch of ground clove just before serving adds a lovely accent.

serves 12

1 tablespoon vegetable oil

Kosher salt

2 ½ pounds country-style spare ribs

3 quarts chicken stock

1 garlic clove, peeled and smashed

½ pound (2 sticks) unsalted butter

1 ½ cups all-purpose flour

2 medium green bell peppers, seeded and cut into medium-fine dice

2 medium jalapeños, seeded and cut into medium-fine dice

1 medium onion, cut into medium-fine dice

3 scallions, green and white, cut into medium-fine dice, plus extra chopped scallion for garnish

1 stalk celery, cut into medium-fine dice

½ teaspoon dried thyme

½ teaspoon dried oregano

¼ teaspoon garlic powder

¼ teaspoon onion powder

¼ teaspoon cayenne (or more)

¼ teaspoon crushed red pepper (or more)

¼ teaspoon freshly ground black pepper (or more)

⅛ teaspoon ground allspice

1 bay leaf

½ pound andouille sausage, cut into ¼-inch-thick slices
  (see Cook's Note)

Pinch of ground clove

6 cups hot cooked white rice

1. Place the oil in a large, heavy stockpot over high heat. Lightly salt the spare ribs and add them to the pot. Sear the meat on both sides until it's golden brown, about 4 minutes per side.

2. Add the chicken stock to the pot, scraping the bottom with a wooden spoon to loosen any crusty bits. Add the garlic clove. Bring to a boil, remove any scum on top by skimming with a large spoon, then turn the heat down to medium. Cook at a lightly rolling simmer for 2 hours. When done, the pork should be tender and you should have about 8 cups of stock. Remove the spare ribs from the stock with a slotted spoon and reserve. Measure the stock; if there's less than 8 cups, add water to bring it up to 8 cups. Keep the stock hot.

3. Start the roux after the pork has simmered for about 1 hour. Place the butter in a large, heavy pot over medium-low heat. When it's melted, add ½ cup of flour all at once, stirring vigorously into the melted butter with a wooden spoon. When it's incorporated, repeat with another ½ cup of flour. When that's incorporated, gradually add the remaining ½ cup of flour; you will need most of it, but you may not need it all. Stop adding flour as soon as the roux begins to clump up and is on the verge of turning solid; it should remain a very thick, but runny, paste. Continue to cook the roux over medium-low heat, stirring often and monitoring its color, for about an hour. It will darken as it cooks, finally reaching a color like dark mahogany or rich fudge. Don't let the roux get too dark (as dark as black coffee, say), because it can burn.

4. When the roux is cooked, stir the green peppers into the roux and cook for 30 seconds. Immediately add the jalapeños, onion, 3 scallions, and celery. Stir into the roux, and cook for 30 seconds.

5. Add the hot stock all at once to the roux. Turn the heat up to medium-high. Stir vigorously with a wooden spoon until the roux melts entirely and thickens the stock. Reduce the heat to medium.

6. Add the thyme, oregano, garlic powder, onion powder, cayenne, crushed red pepper, black pepper, allspice, and bay leaf. Remove the pork meat from the bones; break it into walnut-sized chunks with your fingers. Discard the bones and add the meat to the gumbo. Simmer for 20 minutes, partially covered.

7. Add the andouille. Cover the pot, and turn the heat to low. Simmer for 15 minutes more. You can make the gumbo to this step a day ahead.

8. When you're ready to serve, add the clove, taste for seasoning, and adjust. Fill a small teacup with hot white rice and invert it into a wide, shallow soup bowl; the rice should sit in a mound in the center of the bowl. Ladle the hot gumbo with chunks of pork and slices of andouille around the rice, garnish with a little chopped scallion, and serve immediately. Keep plating until 12 bowls altogether are served.

COOK'S NOTE: *These days, finding andouille sausage at your local gourmet food store—even your local supermarket!—isn't so difficult. But there's no guarantee of finding great andouille that way. That's why I always take the trouble, when I'm cookin' Cajun, to mail-order one of the best andouilles in Louisiana, the one made by Poche's in Breaux Bridge, the heart of Cajun country (see **Where to Find It, page 285**). This andouille is among the thickest available, measuring almost 2 inches in diameter. It has a very wild, very real look, a brown-orange color—and the biggest flavor by far of any I've tasted, with pepper and paprika playing off deep porkiness. It's not as highly cured as some and not as smoky, but I love its texture, with great chunks of pork and pork fat reposing in a tender, juicy background of ground meat.*

Roast Turducken

· • ● • ·

(A Chicken Inside a Duck Inside a Turkey, with Various Stuffings)

So, you've ordered your turducken (see page 264); cooking it couldn't be simpler. Instructions are enclosed with every turducken, and most recipes say the same thing: roast in the oven at 350°F for 4 to 5 hours, making sure the bird is uncovered for the last 30 minutes. All agree basting is not needed. The one disagreement is over internal temperature; I've seen everything from 165°F to 190°F. Your poultry will be completely safe to eat at 165°F, say I, and a whole lot juicier. Measure the temperature at the center of the roast with a meat thermometer. One other cooking touch: deglaze the pan with water or stock for a fabulous gravy.

And serving? First, make sure to let this baby rest for at least 20 minutes. Then show it to your guests; you might even want to carve it on the dining table in front of everyone. The best way to do this is to cut it in half lengthwise, then cut each half into crosswise slices, revealing all the glorious layers of meat and stuffing.

Vanilla Ice Cream with Pecans, Bananas Foster–Cointreau Sauce, and Pralines

• • ● • •

Much of this dish can be done in advance, but you'll have to bring it all together at the last minute. The pralines can be either bought or made by you hours before (recipe follows). The ice cream can be pre-scooped and kept covered with plastic wrap in a Pyrex dish in the freezer. Stack bowls in the freezer as well. The Bananas Foster–Cointreau sauce should be made at the last minute. It only takes about 5 minutes; just make sure to have the ingredients for it prepped and measured in advance.

Please note: Exercise caution when you add the bourbon and the Cointreau. Stand well back from the pan, and keep the area as clear as possible.

serves 12

12 tablespoons (1 ½ sticks) unsalted butter

1 cup firmly packed dark brown sugar

4 tablespoons chopped pecans

1 teaspoon ground cinnamon

8 ripe bananas sliced in ½-inch diagonal rounds

½ cup bourbon

1 cup Cointreau

1 cup heavy cream

4 teaspoons firmly packed grated orange zest

½ gallon store-bought vanilla ice cream (enough for 12 generous scoops)

3 Pralines, quartered (page 280)

1. Divide the butter, brown sugar, pecans, and cinnamon evenly between two large, heavy skillets over medium-high heat. Stir until the sugar is dissolved and the mixture is brown and bubbling, about 2 minutes.

2. Divide the bananas between the two skillets and continue to cook, turning once or twice, until the bananas just begin to brown, about 2 minutes.

3. Remove the skillets from the heat and divide the bourbon between them. Return the skillets to medium-high heat and tip the pans slightly over the flame to ignite the bourbon (or use a long safety match). Cook until the flames are completely exhausted.

4. Remove the skillets from the heat and divide the Cointreau between them. Return the skillets to medium-high heat and tip the pans slightly over the flame to ignite the Cointreau (or use a long safety match). Cook until the flames are completely exhausted.

5. Remove the skillets from the heat, divide the heavy cream and orange zest between them, and stir the contents of each pan until blended.

6. Divide scoops of vanilla ice cream among 12 bowls. Divide the sauce, ladling it evenly around the ice cream. Garnish each ice cream scoop with a quarter praline stuck into the top. Serve immediately.

Pralines

· · ● · · ·

It's a snap to make these sugar-and-pecan candies, a specialty of New Orleans (where they're pronounced PRAW-leens). But if you'd rather receive them by mail, some awfully good and delicate ones are available from Aunt Sally's Praline Shops; order their "Original Praline" for garnishing your ice cream **(see Where to Find It, page 285)**.

makes 10 to 12 pralines

> **1 cup firmly packed dark brown sugar**
> **1 cup granulated sugar**
> **½ cup half-and-half**
> **2 tablespoons unsalted butter**
> **1 cup coarsely chopped pecans**
> **1 teaspoon vanilla extract**

1. Place the brown sugar, granulated sugar, and half-and-half in a heavy saucepan (with a candy thermometer clipped to the side) over medium heat, stirring constantly. When the temperature reaches 228°F, stir in the butter, pecans, and vanilla and continue to cook, stirring constantly, until the mixture reaches 235°F.

2. Remove from the heat and let the mixture cool for 6 minutes. Then stir the mixture with a wooden spoon until the pecans begin to cling to the spoon, about 1 minute. Stop stirring immediately (if you keep stirring, the mixture will lose its gloss).

3. Drop the mixture, 1 tablespoon at a time, onto a piece of well-greased aluminum foil or well-greased marble, creating rough rounds about 2½ inches in diameter. Allow to cool until set, about 10 to 15 minutes.

> COOK'S NOTE: *If you are making these pralines as a garnish for the dish on page 278, you will need to cut three of them into quarters. The extra pralines can be kept for at least 2 weeks in an airtight container. Or, if you're feeling generous, send them home as* lagniappes *with guests!)*

Set Dressing

The irresistible imagery of New Orleans is a great start for your Louisiana bash. Think dark-colored louvered shutters, peeling paint, porches, palmettos, wrought-iron fences and gates, secret overgrown gardens, and battle-scarred musical instruments. It's almost as if the joie de vivre that tourists find so compelling in New Orleans results from a laissez-faire policy with regard to general upkeep. The effect, of course, is unique and undeniably charming, and invites at least temporary imitation. I would start my search for atmospheric enhancements at an architectural salvage house, or do a survey of firms that specialize in building demolition or remodeling. Old shutters or weathered doors, hinged together to make screens, would go a long way toward setting the scene if placed strategically in the dining area. Lumberyards, of course, carry shutters too. For the walls, try to find a canvas or two of scenes that could be construed as Louisianan—especially canvases that feature cracked and fading paint, whether real or faux (as it's called in the trade). You get the idea: You want your maison to look as if it's aging—gloriously!

Prop a vintage accordion in a conspicuous place. (Hopefully, none of your guests will be spontaneously inspired to play "Lady of Spain" or "Besame Mucho" for the assemblage.) Punctuate the corners with something leafy like potted palms (a salute to palmettos), and disguise the growing medium with an airy blanket of Spanish moss. Or entwine a soulful iron garden chair or bench with tendrils of ivy, and post it in a strategic location. Paint-deprived patio and garden furniture would look great; if you don't own any, check with sympathetic acquaintances. Second-hand shops are a potential source of party props, too, and are sometimes willing to deal, especially if it's the end of the season. While you're there, look for decrepit gilt-edged mirrors to hang, the larger the better, preferably with cloudy glass.

If your modern upholstered furniture is a set-spoiler, disguise it by draping it with sheets. (Don't sew, just tuck.)

If space and logistics permit, clear an area for people to dance, even if it means moving furniture after the meal or, weather permitting, moving the bash outside.

Lastly, I think I have found the ultimate Cajun party prop, though it's only for those really commited to drama. A company in Milwaukee, Wisconsin, sells castings of real alligators—12 feet long with glass eyes!—and, on sale, only $1225.50 (www.buycostumes.com).

Table
Dressing

Gravy spills be damned! Grandma's damasks aren't doing anyone any good locked up in the cedar chest. If ever there was an occasion to bring out the "don't you dare put these through the dishwasher" glasses, the "good" dishes, the mismatched tabletop treasures you've accumulated or inherited over the years, this is the one. You say you don't have 12 of anything? Or even six? Mix and match tableware and chairs with confident impunity, and your table will project verve and personality—and yes, joie de vivre!

Some ideas:

● Fan magnolia leaves out in a flat oval or circle on the center of the table and top them with a flower-filled soup tureen. Camellias, azaleas, and magnolias thrive in Louisiana, but may be seasonally unavailable; check with your florist, and be flexible. You can't go wrong with roses. Or put a small vase with a single stem at each place setting.

● Pile pretty seasonal fruits and vegetables (such as pumpkins, quince, kumquats, miniature pumpkins, osage oranges, pomegranates, or mirlitons) as well as gilded pecans—you spraypaint the pecans—in a large footed bowl, or on stacked glass cake stands; tuck in ivy, magnolia leaves, or tufts of Spanish moss.

● Group Depression glass candlesticks on the table, or employ a collection of glass oil lamps; I love their soft light. Small replicas of iron garden urns make nice holders for squatty candles, and as a plus, won't obstruct your guests' vision.

- Silver napkin rings haven't been in mainstream use since Ike was in the White House, but if you have some languishing in a drawer, polish them up. Or tie up your napkins with velvet ribbon.

- Put several sets of miniature salt and pepper shakers on the table so diners aren't forced to pass.

- Just for fun, tuck Tabasco cinnamon-flavored lollipops in the napkins or hide them under the rim of each dinner plate **(see Where to Find It, page 285)**.

- Vintage French wireware bowls or urns, lined with moss and filled with fruit or flowers, would be spectacular. Reproductions are easy to find.

- As noted above, this is an opportunity to use your best tableware. Charger plates are practical when multiple courses are served.

Entertainment

There are two great Louisiana words that come to mind when planning entertainment for this feast: zydeco and *fais-do-do*.

Zydeco is, of course, a type of popular music now almost emblematic of good old times in Louisiana. Actually, it's a late starter; the music first appeared after World War II when pioneers of the genre like Clifton Chenier and BooZoo Chavis combined more traditional sounds with new rhythm and blues elements. And its roots, contrary to popular belief, are not Cajun. Zydeco is the music of south Louisiana's "Creoles of Color," who, it must be admitted, did borrow many of zydeco's defining elements from their Cajun friends. Zydeco has evolved considerably over the decades, and now draws on pop music sources like soul, disco, rap, and even reggae. It is also increasingly performed in English, instead of in its original Creole dialect.

Your job: find some great zydeco recordings and crank up the CD player. Appropriately, for this party, one of the genre's most popular musicians, Stanley "Buckwheat" Dural (aka Buckwheat Zydeco), recorded one of his most popular CDs to date in his hometown of Lafayette, Louisiana, on Thanksgiving night, 2000! Kismet! The title is "Down Home Live." Also look for recordings by Geno Delafose & French Rockin' Boogie, Steve Riley & the Mamou Players, Nathan & the Zydeco Cha-Chas, Terrance Simien and the Mallet Playboys, Chris Ardoin, and Rockin' Dopsie, Jr.

Want to go whole hog? Call clubs in your area to see if you can get a lead on a live zydeco band!

As for *fais-do-do*: this is a communal dance traditionally held in Louisiana's rural dancehalls, where Cajun men and women gathered for long evenings of dancing and socializing. Adolescent girls attended under chaperones' watchful eyes, while young males—unless they were dancing—were restricted to a holding pen called *une cage aux chiens,* or "dogs' cage." Children were put to bed before the dance started, giving rise to the term *fais-do-do* (meaning "go to sleep" in Cajun French). Popular dances at *fais-do-dos* were the two-step and waltz. Wanna dance? Whether the children are put to bed or not, drawing on the *fais-do-do* tradition might be a great way for your guests (particularly those who love de Bloody Marys) to get up and work off dinner!

Another way to keep things lively at this party might be to tell Cajun jokes, as long as there are no sensitive Cajuns present. A collection of them, totally politically incorrect, has been assembled by a Cajun with a great sense of humor, Larry Boudreaux; you can find his jokes by logging on to www.pages.zdnet.com.

Here's an example, written in Cajun-accented English:

"Boudreaux got on de elevator w'eet a beautiful lady. He pushed de button for de fifteend floor. As de elevator waz going up de lady ripped her clodes off and hollowed for Boudreaux to make her feel like a real lady. Boudreaux ripped off hees clodes too and tole her to wash and iron dose clodes on de floor."

Capture the rollicking crowd on film, then ask for a black-and-white process at your photo lab. As your guests go out the door, invoke one of Louisiana's most charming customs, the *lagniappe,* which means a little something extra given away. Tiny Tabasco Sauce bottles? Oyster shells with the date of the party painted on? Miniature stuffed alligators? Use your imagination!

Where to Find It

P & J Oyster Company
1039 Toulouse St.
New Orleans, LA 70122
888.522.2968 (toll free)
504.522.2968 (tel)
www.oysterlover.com
Amazing source of super-fresh Louisiana oysters.

Lil Kats
8006 West Metairie Ave.
Metairie, LA 70003
504.469.7216 (tel)
Live Louisiana jumbo crabs, or precooked Louisiana jumbo crabs with Cajun spices.

Louisiana Fish Fry Products
5267 Plank Rd.
Baton Rouge, LA 70805
800.356.2905 (toll free)
225.356.2905 (tel)
www.louisianafishfry.com
The best Cajun seasoning mix for shellfish boils.

Farm-2-Market
P.O. Box 124
Trout Town Rd.
Roscoe, NY 12776
800.663.4326 (toll free)
607.498.5275 (fax)
www.farm-2-market.com
Terrific, high-quality seafood.

Comeaux's, Inc.
Retail Store and Restaurant:
2807 Kaliste Saloom Rd.
Lafayette, LA 70508
337.988.0516 (tel)
337.989.0091 (tel)
www.comeaux.com
The best general-use Cajun seasoning mix that I've tasted.

Talk o' Texas Brands, Inc.
1610 Roosevelt
San Angelo, TX 76905
800.749.6572 (toll free)
915.325.7967 (fax)
www.talkotexas.com
This company's pickled okra may be ordered directly from the website.

Far Away Foods
1443 Rollins Ave.
Burlingame, CA 94010
650.334.1013 (tel)
www.farawayfoods.com
Pickled vegetables from Hogue Farms.

Poche's
3015-A Main Hwy.
Breaux Bridge, LA 70517
800.370.2437 (toll free)
337.332.2108 (tel)
337.332.5051 (fax)
www.pochesmarket.com
Great andouille and other Cajun meat specialties.

Hebert's Specialty Meats
8212 Maurice Ave.
Maurice, LA 70555
337.893.5062 (tel)
337.291.6022 (shipping)
www.hebertsmeats.com
Great turducken, as well as lots of other meat specialties.

Gourmet Butcher Block
3215 Edenborn Ave.
Metairie, LA 70002
800.230.5229 (toll free)
504.455.2545 (tel)
504.393.1232 (fax)
www.butcherblockturducken.com
Features a line of turducken and other specialties.

Aunt Sally's Praline Shops, Inc.
(retail store)
810 Decatur St.
New Orleans, LA 70116
800.642.7257 (toll free)
504.524.3336 (fax)
www.auntsallys.com
The best mail-order source for thin, refined pralines.

Cajun-Shop.com
4013 Meadow Ridge Dr.
Baton Rouge, LA 70817
866.813.6816 (toll free)
225.751.8112 (tel)
225.751.3695 (fax)
www.cajun-shop.com
Zydeco music, Cajun groceries, and Tabasco cinnamon-flavored lollipops.

www.tabasco.com
Many Tabasco Sauce products (including Green Tabasco), Tabasco miniatures, zydeco music.

www.amazon.com
Zydeco music, including some early recordings.

Cassoulet
Show Up Chez Moi for Beans and Wienies!

A Party for 12

The Menu

Pousse Rapière

Terrine of Duck Foie Gras with Sauternes Aspic

Leafy Green Salad with Walnuts, Walnut Vinaigrette, and Crumbled Roquefort

Cassoulet with Home-Cured Duck, Home-Cured Pork, and Garlic Sausage

Gascon Prune Tart with Orange Zest, Fresh Thyme, and Armagnac

T he cassoulet is the god of the Occitan cuisine," wrote Prosper Montaigne in *Larousse Gastronomique* more than one hundred years ago. "The cassoulet from Castelnaudary is the father God, the one from Carcassonne is the Son, and the one from Toulouse is the Holy Spirit."

Who other than the French could make such a big occasion out of this pot of franks and beans? Cassoulet takes its name from the earthenware dish it's traditionally cooked in, a *cassole*. In the southwest of France, families, gourmands, and hosts argue endlessly at festive meals about the perfect cassoulet. They argue about which meats to use, how to cook them, which regional style to employ; and they also argue passionately about the beans. Very, very rarely do you see these arguments, or this dish, in a fancy restaurant or at a fancy party.

We Americans tend to think that anything French is fancy, but it ain't so. It is the down-home part of French entertaining that I particularly love—and cassoulet is undoubtedly the ultimate down-home French soul food. The soulful recipe for cassoulet in this chapter takes time to prepare; but the result, the centerpiece of a rip-roaring party, has nothing fussy or pretentious about it. The thing your guests will notice is the deep-down succulence of it all. Surround the cassoulet with other ideas from southwest France—expressed as heroic amounts of hearty food, like foie gras terrine—and more than three of your guests, I guarantee, will begin to believe they're musketeers.

The Plan

First, you don't have to make the spectacular southwest French opener, a terrine of foie gras, for you can purchase it directly from D'Artagnan, a great online purveyor **(see Where to Find It, page 309)**. Or you could, if you wish, even skip the whole foie gras business and begin with the salad! But you will have to prepare the rest of the menu, from the salad on.

The party itself begins at a buffet table. That is where your guests will find the terrine, accompanied by spreading knives and bread; as your guests are happily munching, you will pass glasses of Pousse Rapière. As for the rest of the menu, you have a big serving choice: continue the buffet, or seat everyone for the main event at a large table.

If it remains a buffet throughout the evening, I would recommend serving the salad and the cassoulet at the same time from the buffet table. Guests come by with large dinner plates and help themselves to the two dishes—scooping the hot cassoulet right out of the casserole with a large spoon, taking up their salads right out of a large, decorative salad bowl.

If you prefer to seat your guests—given that you have room for 12 at a table or tables—place several large salad bowls on the dining table, and ask your guests to serve themselves salad from these as a first sit-down course. Then, after clearing the salad plates, arrive at the table with the steaming cassoulet and 12 dinner plates. Break the "crust," and standing at your place at the table, serve massive portions, passing each plate of cassoulet as it's ready to a waiting diner. (Be like the French: encourage people to eat the food as soon as it's served! No waiting for everyone to get served before eating!)

The dessert course can follow whichever pattern you've established: it could be a buffet course or a sit-down course.

●Four days before the party (or up to 10 days before)
Prepare the Terrine of Duck Foie Gras with Sauternes Aspic (optional).

●At least one day before the party, but up to two days
Prepare the home-cured duck and pork.

- ## The day before the party

    Prepare the Cassoulet if desired, or complete through step 8 and finish early the day of the party.

- ## Early in the day of the party

    Make the Gascon Prune Tart.

    Make the vinaigrette; toast the walnuts; wash, dry, and refrigerate the greens for the salad.

    Bring the Cassoulet to room temperature if cooked the day before.

    Reheat, moistening with broth as needed.

- ## Before the party begins

    Set up the beverage center and put out the Terrine of Duck Foie Gras with slices of crusty bread or toasted brioche and coarse salt.

- ## During the party

    Assemble the salad just before serving.

    Finish baking the Cassoulet. Or, if baked ahead, reheat, moistening with hot broth as needed. Brown the crust under the broiler before serving, if desired.

    Reheat the remaining meat broth to serve with the Cassoulet.

The Ingredient

There are many great ingredients in this party, but I would focus on the vastly upscale "beans and franks" that are at the heart of the cassoulet.

Beans first. Most recipes in American cookbooks recommend Great Northern beans because they are widely available. However, though they are good beans, they don't have the size and richness of the beans used in France. Because bean selection is one of the great, ongoing cassoulet debates, there is no one type of large bean that everyone in France uses. But the trick is to find the largest white beans you can. When their meaty insides turn to creamy, duck-and-pork-enriched ooze, you've really got something. A southwest French bean that is now available here in top gourmet stores is the Tarbais bean **(see Where to Find It, page 309)**. Another possibility is the fat Christmas lima (which doesn't taste like a lima bean). And there is also a large Italian bean called Corona that does the job extremely well.

As for the franks: The very best "frank" you can use is the French garlic sausage called *saucisson a l'ail*; the version you want is pink, garlicky, cured, and precooked. Good gourmet stores carry it these days, and D'Artagnan **(see Where to Find It, page 309)** will ship you a fine version. If you can't find it, however, you're still in luck—because top-quality, precooked kielbasa also does the job very well! Try to find a brand that looks as un-commercial as possible; you'll be amazed at how a simple supermarket product gets ennobled by the Gascon context.

Beverage Time

Nothing will lift this party off the ground more effectively than a special southwestern French cocktail that few Americans have ever tasted; it's delicious, and it's a great conversation starter! It is called Pousse Rapière, and in France they make it with an orange-flavored liqueur of Armagnac and a sparkling wine of the Southwest. Those ingredients are hard to find here—but, luckily, when you make the drink with Cointreau and Champagne, it's also very delicious.

When main-course time rolls around, nothing could be more classic—or more satisfying—than a thick, stout, winter-weight red wine to go with the cassoulet. If you want to stick to southwestern French tradition, wines from either Cahors or Madiran would be absolutely dead-on (I like 'em on the young side for cassoulet, just a few years old). Young red Bordeaux would also work nicely, as would a young Coteaux de Languedoc. You could, of course, substitute hearty young red wines from other places: Zinfandel from California, Shiraz from Australia, Priorat or Toro from Spain, or, returning to France, a good northern Rhône red, like Côte Rôtie.

After the meal, of course, a grand round of the great Gascon brandy, Armagnac, is absolutely de rigueur.

The Recipes

Pousse Rapière

· · • · ·

The Gascons call this drink Pousse Rapière, or "rapier thrust," because the derring-do of the musketeers, who were Gascon, is never far from anyone's mind in that part of the country. The cocktail supposedly has the same quick and deadly effect on you as the thrust of a rapier. Frankly, it seems much more benign and simply delicious to me. And it'll be an excellent partner for your foie gras!

makes 1 drink

1 (3 x ½-inch) piece orange zest
6 ounces Champagne (or other good sparkling wine)
1 tablespoon Cointreau

Place the orange peel in a Champagne flute. Pour the Champagne into the flute, then the Cointreau. Using a long spoon, whip the drink into a foamy froth and serve immediately. Repeat as often as there are thirsty guests.

Terrine of Duck Foie Gras with Sauternes Aspic

· · • ● • · ·

Believe it or not, foie gras has its down-home side, too! A cold terrine of duck liver is often served as an opener in France at funky bistros and at unfussy family gatherings. It is not chi-chi food to the French—it is real food! The only daunting aspect of it all is the trouble it takes to prepare a terrine. Despair not! You can serve this treat from southwest France simply by picking up the phone and calling the great New Jersey purveyor D'Artagnan **(see Where to Find It, page 309)**. Should you wish to prepare the terrine yourself, however, you should also call D'Artagnan, who will send you the whole, raw, fattened duck livers that you'll need to make it. It's actually not as difficult as it sounds; just follow my instructions, and your guests will be as impressed with your skill as they are delighted by the velvety terrine.

Serve the terrine on the buffet with crusty bread or toasted slices of brioche. Guests will help themselves to the terrine—cutting away a chunk, placing it on bread, topping it with diced aspic (if desired) and coarse salt.

If you do make the terrine yourself, you can make it as many as 10 days in advance of the party! Begin at least 4 days ahead.

serves 12

2 fresh duck foie gras, about 3 pounds total (see sidebar, page 297)

2 tablespoons kosher salt

1/2 teaspoon crushed white peppercorns

1 cup Sauternes (sweet white wine from southwest France)

Sauternes Aspic (page 296)

Coarse sea salt for topping

1. Remove the veins from the foie gras (page 297).

2. Pour enough ice water into a bowl to cover the 2 foie gras. Stir in 1 tablespoon of salt. Immerse the foie gras, cover with plastic wrap, and let soak, refrigerated, for 4 hours.

3. Combine all but 1/8 teaspoon each of the remaining tablespoon of salt and the pepper. Remove the foie gras from the water, sprinkle evenly with the salt mixture, and put in a bowl with the Sauternes. Cover with plastic wrap and refrigerate for 2 more hours.

4. Heat the oven to 230°F. Bring a large pot of water to a bare simmer.

5. Remove the foie gras from the Sauternes and sprinkle with the remaining 1/8 teaspoon each of salt and pepper. You should have a combination of larger pieces and smaller pieces.

6. Place half of the large pieces of foie gras into a heavy terrine, 12 1/2 x 4 x 3 inches, pushing them into the bottom of the pan. Put the smaller broken pieces in the middle and top with the rest of the large pieces, pressing to make a compact mass. The terrine should be nearly filled, but not level with the top. (Since foie gras varies in size, you may have some left over. Reserve it for another use.)

7. Place a folded dish towel in the bottom of a deep roasting pan and set the terrine of foie gras on it. Pour in enough hot water (just below a simmer) to come halfway up the sides of the terrine, and carefully place the pan in the center of the oven. Bake for 50 to 60 minutes, or until the internal temperature in the center reaches 116°F on a meat thermometer.

8. Remove the terrine from the oven. Pour off any excess fat from the terrine, and reserve the fat. Allow the terrine to cool completely.

9. Pour the reserved fat on top of the terrine and down the sides until the terrine is full. Cover tightly and refrigerate overnight.

10. The next day, cut a piece of cardboard to just fit the inside dimensions of the terrine, and cover it with plastic wrap. Place the cardboard on top of the foie gras in the terrine. Place a heavy, well-distributed weight on the cardboard to compress the foie gras (cans will do), and refrigerate. The terrine will be ready to serve in 3 to 4 days, and will keep in the refrigerator for up to 10 days.

11. When ready to serve, remove the cans and cardboard, and run a thin-bladed knife around the inside of the terrine. Unmold the foie gras onto a platter; if it sticks in the terrine, immerse the terrine briefly in hot water and try again. Surround the foie gras on the platter with diced aspic. Provide a bowl of coarse salt for guests to sprinkle on the foie gras.

Sauternes Aspic

. . . ● . .

makes 2 cups

1 ½ cups intensely flavored, degreased chicken stock
1 large egg white
2 ½ teaspoons powdered gelatin
1 cup good quality Sauternes

1. Bring 1 cup of stock to a boil in a saucepan.

2. Clarify the stock. Whisk the egg white into the remaining ½ cup stock until frothy. Gradually pour the boiling stock in a stream into the egg-white stock. Pour all the stock back into the saucepan and set over medium heat.

3. Whisk the stock gently for 1 to 2 minutes. When the egg coagulates and comes to the surface, move the saucepan to one side of the burner so only half is simmering. After 3 minutes, pull the saucepan to the opposite side and repeat the simmering for 3 minutes more. Then place the pan squarely over the heat and simmer another 3 minutes.

4. Line a fine strainer with a doubled piece of damp cheesecloth.

5. Use a slotted spoon to gently remove the coagulated egg whites and discard. Pour the stock into the cheesecloth-lined strainer set over a bowl. The clear stock will drain through. Cool the clarified stock.

6. When the clarified stock is cool, place ½ cup of it in a bowl. Sprinkle the gelatin evenly over the surface of the stock; let it sit for 3 minutes.

7. Heat another ½ cup clarified stock and the Sauternes together in a saucepan over medium-low heat until just below simmering.

8. Pour the gelatin mixture into the hot stock mixture. If any gelatin clings to the bowl, pour in some hot stock to melt it and return the mixture to the saucepan. Stir for 3 to 4 minutes until the gelatin has completely dissolved.

9. Pour this mixture into a pan that's 6 x 12 inches and at least 1 inch deep. The mixture should be ½ inch deep. Refrigerate on a level surface until firm, about ½ hour.

10. When the aspic is firm, run a thin-bladed knife around the sides. Turn the pan upside down over a rectangle of plastic wrap. Cut in ¼-inch cubes. Refrigerate, covered.

To Remove Veins from a Raw Foie Gras

The deveining that's called for in the accompanying recipe creates a terrine with fewer red spots; the soaking in ice water, a technique recommended by the great French chef Joël Robuchon, also evens out the color (some terrines can be positively motley).

To devein: Separate the two lobes of the liver by gently pulling them apart. Scrape off any traces of green bile and let the foie gras warm up a little so it is more flexible. Don't let it get too warm, or the warmth of your hands will melt it. Using a small knife, carefully dig into the middle of each lobe along each vein and, using the tip of the knife or your fingertips, pull the vein out. Remove any other veins that you can. In the process, the liver will inevitably break into chunks. Don't worry. Just try to keep the chunks as large as possible—at least as large as golf balls; when the terrine is cooked, the chunks will meld together into a smooth, even block.

Purchasing Foie Gras Terrines or Raw Foie Gras

If you wish to purchase a ready-made, ready-to-eat terrine of foie gras, you can very easily do so by contacting D'Artagnan in New Jersey **(see Where to Find It, page 309)**. Order a terrine without Sauternes aspic, or even better, a terrine with Sauternes aspic. One terrine will give 12 guests satisfying portions.

If you're feeling ambitious and want to make your own foie gras terrine, D'Artagnan sells whole, raw, vacuum-packed, refrigerated duck livers. But you have to decide which grade of fattened duck liver you want.

"A" quality livers, which weigh about 1 ½ pounds each, are the best. They are relatively free of veins, and have the proper texture; if you push your thumb into the liver, the depression will linger for a few seconds before the foie gras springs back. This resiliency indicates that the foie gras has the right amount of fat; too much fat, and foie gras isn't resilient, which indicates that it won't cook properly.

"B" quality livers are smaller than "A" livers, and have many more veins.

"C" livers, the smallest, least attractive, and least expensive, are sold only to restaurants; they are not available to the public. Chefs purée them for use in sauces and stuffings.

If you've never worked with foie gras before, you might be surprised when you unpack your first liver. It looks nothing like raw liver you've seen before; it is neither red, nor bloody, nor soft. It has a firmness to it as well as a fleshy-pink color. In fact, it looks already cooked—but it's not.

Vacuum-packed raw foie gras, if unopened and kept refrigerated, will remain fresh for about 10 days.

Leafy Green Salad with Walnuts, Walnut Vinaigrette, and Crumbled Roquefort

serves 12

for the vinaigrette:

4 tablespoons finely minced shallot

2 ½ tablespoons kosher salt, more or less

8 to 12 generous grindings of black pepper

½ cup good white wine vinegar

1 cup best quality walnut oil (see Cook's Note #1)

for the salad:

2 cups shelled walnuts

2 tablespoons best quality walnut oil

24 cups loosely packed assorted salad greens, washed, dried, and torn into large bite–sized pieces (see Cook's Note #2)

1 pound Roquefort, crumbled

1. Heat the oven to 375°F.

2. Make the vinaigrette: Whisk the shallot, salt, pepper, and vinegar together in a mixing bowl until the salt has dissolved. Very gradually whisk in the 1 cup of walnut oil to make an emulsified dressing. Reserve.

3. Make the salad: Toss the walnuts with 2 tablespoons of walnut oil, spread them on a baking sheet, and place in the oven until fragrant, about 8 to 10 minutes. Allow them to cool, and coarsely chop them into big pieces.

4. When you're ready to serve the salad, combine the walnuts, greens, and Roquefort in a very large mixing bowl (or divide the mixture and do it in two batches). Whisk the vinaigrette again, and drizzle most, but not all, of it over the greens. Be sure to spoon in most of the shallots that may have sunk to the bottom of the vinaigrette. Using your hands, toss the greens to thoroughly coat them with the vinaigrette. Taste and add more of the vinaigrette as needed, tossing again with each addition. Serve immediately, making sure all diners get some Roquefort and walnuts on their plates.

*COOK'S NOTE #1: There is generally a huge difference between walnut oils commercially produced in this country and those that are hand-pressed by a few small, top-quality producers in France. I used the top-quality walnut oil of J. LeBlanc, produced in Iguerande, in southwest France (**see Where to Find It, page 309**). You can also order good artisan oil from California made in the French manner; contact The French Press (**see Where to Find It, page 309**). Of course, after you've selected the best, there still may be a problem: poor storage conditions or long storage can make a walnut oil taste rancid. If you get a fresh, healthy oil, make sure to store it in a cool, dark place after opening; the refrigerator works just fine.*

COOK'S NOTE #2: A mix that includes 2/3 mild, tender lettuces like Boston or red leaf combined with 1/3 firm, bitter greens such as frisée or other chicories, works nicely. If you can find it, use mâche (lamb's lettuce) as one of the mild lettuces; it has a real affinity for the walnut oil vinaigrette.

Cassoulet with Home-Cured Duck, Home-Cured Pork, and Garlic Sausage

· · · ● · · ·

This amazing recipe yields the rustic, oozy essence of cassoulet. But getting there
takes many steps. So open a good bottle of red wine on a winter's day, as many as 2 days before
the party, and slowly savor the prep. Oh, you can take short cuts if you like; for example, the
curing of the duck and pork in Step 1 could be simplified by salting the meats for an hour while you
prepare the other ingredients—but the result won't be quite as spectacular. Other little steps—like
puréeing the duck skin, and squeezing the melted garlic out of the garlic peels—all add up to
a pot that has the same rich, almost sticky savor you find in France's best cassoulets.

Start the day before.

serves 12

for the home-cured duck and pork:

4 cloves garlic

6 tablespoons kosher salt

2 tablespoons fresh thyme leaves, chopped

1 ½ pounds country-style spare ribs, bone-in, cut ¾ inch thick

2 whole duck legs (including thighs), with skin

for the cassoulet:

2 tablespoons duck fat (see Where to Find It, page 309) or vegetable oil

6 ounces salt pork (fatback), blanched and rinsed, cut in half

7 cups unsalted chicken stock

2 cups water

1 (4-ounce) piece of prosciutto, preferably with some fat attached, cut in half

2 medium onions, halved

1 carrot, peeled and halved

1 stalk celery, halved

1 (15-ounce) can whole tomatoes, drained and halved

2 bouquet garni (see Cook's Note #2)

2 large heads of garlic

4 cups large dried white beans (see The Ingredient, page 290)

Kosher salt

for assembly:

1 ½ pounds saucisson a l'ail, cut on the bias into ½-inch slices (see The Ingredient, page 290)

Nutmeg for grating

¾ cup dry unseasoned bread crumbs

Duck fat (see Where to Find It, page 309) or vegetable oil for drizzling

1. Cure the duck and pork: The night before making the cassoulet, crush the 4 garlic cloves with 1 tablespoon kosher salt until reduced to a paste. Crush the thyme into the paste. Transfer to a small bowl and add the remaining 5 tablespoons of salt, stirring to combine. Rub the seasoned salt firmly and evenly over all the surfaces of the pork and duck. Wrap tightly in plastic and place in the refrigerator overnight.

2. The next day, make the cassoulet: Brush off most of the salt from the meats and heat the duck fat in a large, heavy stockpot over medium-high heat. Sear the pork, duck, and salt pork (in batches if necessary) until golden brown on all sides, adjusting the heat if the meats threaten to burn. Transfer the meats to a platter and set aside.

3. Add the stock and water to the pot, scraping the bottom to loosen any browned bits. Reserve one piece of salt pork to cook with the beans. Return the meat and any juices on the plate to the pot. Add half each of the prosciutto, onions, carrot, celery, and tomatoes. Add 1 bouquet garni. Separate 1 head of garlic into unpeeled cloves, and add them to the pot. Bring gradually to a simmer over medium-high heat, skimming off any impurities that rise to the top. Let the meats braise at a bare simmer until the pork is very tender and almost falling from the bone, about 2 hours. Check regularly to make sure the simmer is gentle and the meats are submerged. Turn off the heat and allow the stew to rest for at least 30 minutes before proceeding.

4. Meanwhile, place the beans in a large, heavy stockpot and cover with cold water by 1 inch. Bring to a simmer over medium heat, stirring occasionally. Turn off the heat and let the beans stand for 5 minutes. Drain the beans, return them to the pot, and cover again with cold water by 1 inch. Bring the beans to a simmer, skimming any impurities that rise to the top. Add the remaining salt pork, prosciutto, onion, carrot, celery, tomatoes, bouquet garni, and head of garlic (separated into unpeeled cloves). Simmer the beans very gently, stirring occasionally, until just tender but still whole. Taste often. If you see more than a few of the beans have burst, remove from the heat. Depending on the type and age of your beans, this could take as little as 30 minutes and as long as a few hours. Just as the beans begin to soften but are not yet done—about two-thirds of the way—salt generously. When they are cooked, remove from the heat and allow to rest at least 30 minutes before proceeding.

5. When you're ready to assemble the cassoulet, drain the beans in a colander. Discard the cooking liquid. Pick out the garlic cloves and reserve. Discard the remaining vegetables and return the beans to their pot.

6. Line a colander with cheesecloth, set it over a large bowl, and strain the meats. Return the broth to the pot and place over low heat to keep warm. Remove the skin from the duck legs and reserve. Discard the salt pork. Working over a bowl, shred the duck and pork with your fingers into small bite-sized pieces, discarding any bones or cartilage. Cover the meats and set aside. From the colander, pick out as much of the tomato and onion as possible and put them in a blender jar. Remove all the garlic and, along with the garlic reserved from the beans, squeeze the paste of each clove into the blender, discarding the peels. Add the duck skin and blend the mixture with enough reserved meat broth to produce a smooth, thick, pourable purée. Thoroughly combine the purée with the beans. Cover and refrigerate overnight.

7. When ready to cook, heat the oven to 325°F.

8. Evenly spread one-third of the bean mixture into a large, deep ovenproof casserole (see Cook's Note #3). Evenly distribute half the shredded meat mixture and half the saucisson on top of the beans. Top with a second layer of beans, a second layer of the meats, and a last layer of beans—five layers in all. Pour enough of the reserved meat broth into the casserole to come just above the level of the beans. Keep the remaining meat broth warm.

9. Place in the oven and cook for a total of 2 to 2 ½ hours. After the first 30 minutes, check to see that the cassoulet is gently bubbling at the edges—if not, adjust the oven temperature as necessary. After another 30 minutes, ladle in more of the reserved hot meat broth to come, again, just above the surface of the beans, coaxing it to filter down to the bottom of the cassoulet. Repeat these additions of hot broth as needed during the cooking to keep the beans moist.

10. After about 2 hours, top the cassoulet with a generous addition of hot broth and 6 to 8 gratings of nutmeg, and top with the bread crumbs, spreading them out evenly. Drizzle duck fat or vegetable oil over the crumbs.

11. Increase the oven temperature to 400°F and bake until golden brown, 15 to 20 minutes more. If desired, very carefully brown the crumbs under a broiler. They could brown in less than a minute. Serve piping hot, with the remaining hot meat broth on the side so that diners may moisten their portions, if desired.

COOK'S NOTE #1: *In the finished stew, the meats and beans should be sur-rounded by—but not quite drowning in—the thickened broth in the casserole. Because the beans will continue to absorb a lot of liquid once they're removed from the oven, peek down into the casserole before serving and add more hot broth if you feel the dish needs it, especially if you plan on holding it for any time.*

The cassoulet does reheat extremely well, which means that you can make it through Step 8 the day before your party. If you choose this option, cool the cassoulet, cover, and refrigerate. The next day, remove the cassoulet from the refrigerator and bring it to room temperature. Heat the oven to 325°F and reheat the cassoulet, moistening with hot broth as needed. Allow at least an hour. Proceed with Step 9.

COOK'S NOTE #2: *A bouquet garni is an ingenious way of submerging loose herbs and spices in a stew without "muddying" the stew with lots of floating herb and spice fragments. The trick is wrapping the herbs and spices in cheesecloth (this is the "bouquet garni"), placing the cheesecloth bundle in the stew, then removing the bundle late in the cooking. This recipe requires 2 bouquets garni. To make 1, cut a 4-inch-square piece of cheesecloth. Place 2 sprigs of thyme, 2 sprigs of parsley, 2 bay leaves, 2 whole cloves, and 8 pep-percorns in the center of the square. Fold the sides inward, covering the herbs, and tie it off into a bundle; you should have enough excess cheesecloth to make a knot. Repeat for the second bouquet garni.*

COOK'S NOTE #3: *I make my cassoulet in an oval 5-quart Dutch oven from Le Creuset (made of enameled cast iron); it's very sturdy, and the shape holds the liquid in suspension very well. But feel free to use any oven-ready pot or casserole dish with high sides that has roughly a 5-quart capacity.*

Gascon Prune Tart with Orange Zest, Fresh Thyme, and Armagnac

· · ● · ·

makes 12 servings

for the pastry:

1 ½ cups all-purpose flour

1 ½ tablespoons sugar

⅛ teaspoon kosher salt

Grated zest of ½ large orange

8 tablespoons (1 stick) cold unsalted butter, cut into 8 pieces

4 tablespoons vegetable shortening

2 tablespoons cold water

½ teaspoon vanilla extract

for the filling:

1 ½ cups pitted prunes

½ cup Armagnac (or Cognac)

1 tablespoon fresh lemon juice

2 ½ tablespoons sugar

2 large egg yolks

1 cup heavy cream

2 teaspoons minced fresh thyme leaves

Grated zest of ½ large orange

1. Make the pastry shell: Mix the flour, 1 1/2 tablespoons sugar, salt, and orange zest in a large bowl. Add the butter and the shortening and use your fingers to work the butter into the flour mixture, pinching until it resembles coarse cornmeal, with some of the butter still visible in small, separate lumps. Add the water and the vanilla extract and continue to gently work the mixture until the dough just holds together with light pressure—this should take no more than 30 seconds. Form the dough into a loose ball, wrap it in plastic wrap, and chill in the refrigerator for at least 30 minutes.

2. Roll out the dough on a lightly floured surface with a floured rolling pin to a 14-inch circle and an even 1/8-inch thickness. As you work, gently patch any cracks that form with bits of dough taken from the outer edges. Roll the dough up on your rolling pin and carefully transfer the dough to a buttered 11-inch tart pan with a removable bottom. Gently press the dough into the corners and against the sides of the pan. Trim the excess dough and lightly prick the tart bottom a few times with a fork. Wrap the tart shell in foil and place in the freezer for at least 30 minutes.

3. Heat the oven to 375°F.

4. Unwrap the chilled tart shell, place it in the oven, and bake until it is light golden in color, about 25 minutes. Remove from the oven and cool on a rack. Leave the oven on.

5. Meanwhile, prepare the filling: Put the prunes, Armagnac, lemon juice, and 1 1/2 tablespoons sugar in a medium saucepan. Add enough water to barely cover the prunes and bring to a boil over high heat. Reduce the heat and simmer for 5 minutes. Remove from the heat, cover the pot, and let rest for 30 minutes, turning the prunes in the liquid once or twice during that time.

6. Drain the prunes, discarding the liquid, and carefully cut each one open so it spreads out like a book. Distribute them evenly, opened like a book, cut sides down, in the tart shell.

7. Whisk together the egg yolks, cream, thyme, orange zest, and 1 tablespoon of sugar. Pour this mixture into the tart shell, distributing it evenly over and around the prunes. Return the tart to the oven and bake until the filling just barely sets in the center of the tart, 20 to 25 minutes. Place on a rack to cool completely, cut into wedges, and serve.

You've Got
Options

This party would be magnificently enhanced by crusty loaves of artisanal bread and great French butter to spread on them! One real show-stopper French butter comes from Quimper, in Brittany; it's creamy, flavorful, and vastly enhanced by crunchy bits of the best sea salt, fleur de sel, embedded in it. It's called Beurre de Baratte, Fleur de Sel au Sel de Guerande, from a French company called Le Gall. The owner of Galluci's, a great food shop in Cleveland that sells the butter, says that he takes it to dinner parties instead of wine, and people love it! He'll be happy to ship some to you if you contact him **(see Where to Find It, page 309)**.

Set
Dressing

The menu's origins are unapologetically rustic, suggesting a humble French farmhouse. Take your cues from the Country Mouse, not the City Mouse of Aesop's famous fable. The "French Country" genre is familiar to anyone who's opened a decorating magazine in the last two decades. We're talking about pine and provincial prints, about red and blue and yellow. To emphasize the "country" still further, consider staging this feast as a homey, familial, Sunday Night Supper. If your kitchen is commodious, you might serve your guests dinner there, rather than in the dining room. If you've ever succumbed to a desire for a wormy pine farmhouse table with attendant benches—preferably 10 feet long!—then you are ahead of the game where this party is concerned. Étagères would help define the space and could double as staging areas for the bar, or for dinnerware, or for food. Of course, a working fireplace would be a plus! But if it's not possible, just be sure to light lots of candles and keep things simple.

Table Dressing

Warmth and conviviality are the goals here, and you can accomplish them on any table. So, if you have the pine table of choice, use no cloth; if you don't, find a rustic beige-cream cloth—homespun linen, perhaps. Put a bold swath of chicken wire down the center of the table (all sharp ends defused with needle-nosed pliers, thank you), complemented by a few well-placed tufts of straw, small pots of French herbs, ceramic fowl, and at center stage, the cassoulet.

Set the table with rough, antique-looking napkins (newness altered by a bath in strongly brewed tea, if need be). Tableware (remember I said "Country Mouse") should be provincial-looking. Glazed earthenware plates are preferred, but solid colors—even mismatched!—are true to the theme, too. Chipped? *Pas probleme.* Set out little dishes of sea salt and cracked pepper, and bring out the chunky goblets for the wine. Remember, restaurant supply houses are terrific sources of inexpensive tableware and utensils.

Entertainment

I think the meal and the conviviality should be the focus here, a cozy winter evening with friends. A little Edith Piaf, with that fabulously smoky voice, would not be a bad choice for background music.

If you'd like a little more drama, however, it might be fun to ask one of the guests to administer the loosely translated medieval oath of the "Grande Confrerie du Cassoulet de Castelnaudary" to the host/chef, just before the cassoulet is served. Bring the lights down, and have the inducting guest utter these words (to be repeated by the inductee chef) over the hot *cassole* of steaming beans:

"I swear to defend all my life, and further the quality and the glory, of this so large Cassoulet; if I fail, may my head fall into the cassole."

Then the guest playing the role of Grand Cassoulet Pooh-Bah says:

"Guard your life, we do want you. I, Grand Master, wish you long life and I make you dignitary of our brotherhood of the Cassoulet of Castelnaudary. The Cassoulet Lives!"

Bring the lights back up, turn up the music, and break into that crust with gusto.

Now, if you really want to play this kind of thing up, you could issue little documents to every guest, attesting to the fact that they have enjoyed an authentic Cassoulet, witnessed the induction of a new Cassoulet dignitary, and are themselves bound to uphold the dignity of the Cassoulet throughout the course of their natural lives, or until their LDL gets a little too high.

Where to Find It

D'Artagnan
280 Wilson Ave.
Newark, NJ 07105
800.327.8246 (toll free)
973.465.1870 (fax)
www.dartagnan.com
Known among gourmands as one of the top sources in the country for poultry, foie gras, duck fat, and charcuterie.

Joie de Vivre
P.O. Box 875
Modesto, CA 95353
209.869.0788 (tel)
209.869.2704 (fax)
www.frenchselections.com
An online catalog specializing in French food, including Tarbais beans—but also offering books, clothing, kitchenware, home decor, paper goods, and toiletries.

Crossings
800.209.6461 (toll free, call for nearest stores)
www.crossingsfrenchfood.com
Importers of specialty French foods.

Rosenthal Wine Merchants
P.O. Box 658
Pine Plains, NY 12567
518.398.1800 (tel)
Importers of J. LeBlanc walnut oil.

The French Press
5120 North Arena Way
Atwater, CA 95301
209.394.2944 (tel)
Producers of artisanal walnut oil.

Gallucci's
6610 Euclid Ave.
Cleveland, OH 44103
888.425.5822 (toll free)
216.881.0045 (tel)
216.881.4838 (fax)
www.gusgallucci.com
Retail source of Beurre de Barette (sold as "French Basket Butter").

Pierre Deux
French Country
40 Enterprise Ave.
Secaucus, NJ 07094
888.743.7732 (toll free)
www.pierredeux.com
A well-known source of French Country housewares, furniture, and antiques.

Lucullus
610 Chartres St.
New Orleans, LA 70130
504.528.9620 (tel)
A large collection of antique tableware with a French emphasis.

Sur La Table
1765 6th Ave. S.
Seattle, WA 98134
800.243.0852 (toll free)
206.682.1026 (fax)
www.surlatable.com
A source of cookware and specialty kitchen items (including Dutch ovens for cassoulet), long respected by professional chefs and home cooks.

Zorba the Grill

A Dionysian Cook-Out in the Ecstatic Greek Manner

A Party for 12

The Menu

Ouzo

Simple Mezedes:
Olives, Feta, and Pita

Grilled Octopus with Red Peppers, Purple Onions, Parsley, Lemon, and Capers

Potato Purée with Garlic and Almonds
(Skordalia)

Yogurt with Cucumbers and Garlic
(Tzatziki)

The Real Greek Salad

Grilled Chicken Kebabs with Cinnamon, Fresh Oregano, and Cherry Tomatoes

Tiny Grilled Lamb Chops with Marjoram

Galaktoboureko Triangles

In its elemental simplicity,

In its elemental simplicity, Greek cuisine is, to me, one of the most exciting cuisines on earth—providing, of course, that you find top-notch Greek ingredients. When you do find them, you have on your hands the makings of a spectacular grill party.

The reason Greek food gets passed over sometimes in culinary reckonings must be because Greece's best ingredients are normally not sought out. It can't be that Greek food hasn't been around long enough to get noticed! When you read what folks in Athens were eating in 500 B.C.—not so different from what their descendents eat today—your mouth starts to water. Though there is controversy, we have evidence that the traditional chef's toque had its origins in food-crazed Greece. And of course, the very word "epicurean" is derived from the name "Epicurus," a Greek philosopher.

Ah, philosophers. Could, perhaps, the relegation of Greek food to the lower culinary tiers stem from that widely held image of Greece as a land of grim-visaged intellectuals? Would you want to get down at a grill party with stern Plato? In fact, you might—because alongside all of that Apollonian order inherent in Greek culture, there is also the whole underworld of Dionysian revel. Greek party? Are you kidding? What could get rowdier and more sensuous than that? These people have smashed countless plates at untold parties through the ages (though the custom is now on the wane). And it is at a Greek party that you would never feel self-conscious about shouting *opa!*—which means, roughly, "Begin the night!" I especially love it when they shout *opa!* at about midnight—for the four-hundredth time.

The Plan

This is a big party, but an easy one in its mechanics—especially if you go the outdoor-grill and buffet-table route that I've envisioned.

The party starts simply with mezedes, and bottles of Greek olive oil set around the party venue as well as on the buffet table. You'll pass ouzo, the great Greek anise-flavored aperitif.

Things get more serious as you light up the grill. Sear the octopus, then toss it into a salad. Place that salad on the buffet table, along with the olives, feta, and pita, then bring out the skordalia, tzatziki, and Greek salad. Leave all these items on the buffet for the duration of the party, and refresh them as necessary.

This is the perfect moment for you to start cooking the chicken kebabs on the grill. When they are ready, they make a grand mid-party appearance on the buffet table.

A few minutes later, it's time to start preparing the climactic savory, the lamb chops. Intensify the fire, then place the chops over it. Make a big presentation of the chops, festively plattered, on the buffet table.

At some point you will clear that table. All that is left is to sprinkle the cinnamon sugar over the waiting Galaktoboureko Triangles and to circulate them around the room on a platter.

The Ingredient

Despite the wonderful array of foods that precedes it, the climactic event in this party is the presentation of small, succulent lamb chops cooked quickly on the grill. Most Americans are not used to eating small chops—and the combination of the novel size, the savory Mediterranean marinade, and the flash-grilling will make this a memorable bite for all. Naturally, however, one other factor will make the memory even stronger: spectacular quality of lamb.

For starters, it's not easy to find smaller lamb chops at all. But I have a strategy. First, I look for the smallest racks of lamb I can find in the supermarket butcher case; I've been finding 8-rib racks that weigh approximately 1 ½ pounds a rack (you wouldn't want heavier ones). Next is the cutting: I cut the racks into chops myself, at home, and I try to cut 12 "chops" out of each 8-rib rack. Obviously, what you want to do is to carve off very thin "chops," some of them cut without a bone at all. One thing I always do is carve off 2 boneless outside "chops" from meat that extends beyond the bones on the ends of the rack. Inside the rack, I cheat and cut out an extra "chop" here and there when the meat is thicker between bones. It sounds harder than it is. Simply take a good, sharp boning knife to an 8-rib rack, and be armed with the understanding that you're trying to get "12" out of "8"—and you should be able to improvise your way to great little chops (even if some of them have no bone). This is the best way I know of to reproduce the size of small European lamb chops.

I've got a slightly different idea for the quality-obsessed: mail order! If you go this route, you won't get the very smallest chops—but you *will* get the best.

The great Pennsylvania lamb producer, Jamison Farm **(see Where to Find It, page 333)**, offers a product called Jamison Farm Single Rib Chops. These are fairly small, fairly thin, almost European-style chops with long, curving, frenched bones. When you order, make sure to tell them what you're up to, and to ask for chops that are cut as thinly as possible (certainly no more than ½ inch thick). The meat is mild, but has a lovely texture.

There is, however, one higher level—for which even I would gladly sacrifice a little thinness. I'm talking about the unbelievable Prime Rib Lamb Chops from a butcher called Ceriello, a company that owns five shops in the New York City area **(see Where to Find It, page 333)**. The chops are thinner than most American ones (again: tell them what you want!), but a little fatter and fleshier than the Jamison chops and the ideal European miniatures. And they are crazily pricey. However, if it's quality you seek, you will not believe the juicy, tender, buttery succulence of the eyes of these chops. Bigger than European, yes—but very European in the quality of the meat.

Beverage Time

You have no dearth of choices here; Greece was one of the first wine-producing regions in the world, and is still at that noble pursuit with furious energy. And Greece doesn't have a johnny-come-lately drinking reputation, either; the "symposium" alluded to by Plato was originally a males-only "shots" party. But let's not wallow in the past. I say: let the gals in!

The starter for the party is ouzo, the clear, anise-heavy, sweet distillate that, for me, sounds all the right Pavlovian notes for a Greek celebration. As soon as ouzo's alcohol-rich body touches my lips, I automatically go into high *opa* mode.

Now, not everyone likes ouzo. But I think that's because not everyone has been drinking it correctly. At your party, stand a few ouzo bottles up on the bar—preferably the ouzo of Barbayanni, my favorite ouzo producer, whose distillery is on the island of Lésvos. Prepare trays with six squat tumblers and six long spoons, as well as a pitcher of water on each tray; fill each glass with ice, then fill each tumbler no more than a quarter of the way with ouzo. Work your way among the crowd, offering ouzo to your guests. When a guest accepts, tell him or her that not only is it cool to watch the ouzo turn cloudy when you add water, but the dilution actually makes the ouzo taste a whole lot better! If you get approval, pour water from the pitcher into one of the ouzo glasses, bringing the level of liquid in the glass up to about halfway. Stir with one of the spoons. Offer a taste, and ask if the guest would like more water still. Put the spoon in a discard pile, and move on to the next guest. Don't let those ouzo-carrying guests go far without tasting a Kalamata olive.

Some guests, undoubtedly, will be deaf to your blandishments. Ouzo can be a hard sell. Have some wine on hand for these people. You'll want to have some wine on hand anyway, for you can't sell even me on ouzo with the rest of the dinner.

The wine I'd choose above all others—unfortunately for the eager host!—is also a hard sell. Say "Retsina" to a wine snob and watch the cringing begin. The only thing about Retsina that makes me cringe is the thought of *not* having it with a Greek meal! I find Retsina absolutely essential to Greek dining. Greek food without Retsina to me, is like French food without butter, Chinese food without soy sauce, Mexican food without chiles. Sure, Retsina has a flavor that's a little different from the international white wines of the world—the flavor of pine resin—but once you get used to that flavor, particularly the way that flavor blends with other Greek flavors, you become a Retsina addict.

I would, without question, keep lots of Retsina on ice throughout the party (prices are deliciously low). Find a crisp, lively, youthful example of Retsina; some bottles in the market can taste heavy or washed-out. My favorite is called Malamatina; it comes in a 500ml bottle that looks a lot like a soda bottle. Great for informal dining—but it is not widely available **(see Where to Find It, page 333)**. A Retsina I love that's in wider distribution is Kourtaki, imported by Nestor Imports in New York City **(see Where to Find It, page 333)**. Despite my fierce traditionalism, I recently found a new-fangled Retsina that blew my sandals off. I hesitate to confess this, since it's a modernist, experimental Retsina I'm talking about that even uses some new oak (horrors!) in the aging—but it is one of the most delicious white-wine glasses of *anything* that I've tasted in recent years. It is the Ritinitis Nobilis, produced by the Greek winery Gaia, and imported by Athenee Importers & Distributors **(see Where to Find It, page 333)**. It is staggeringly wonderful.

So, for those guests who refuse to drink either ouzo *or* Retsina, whatcha gonna do? No problem. The Greek wine industry is in full renaissance, and some of the world's most delicious wines are being made today in that ancient wine-producing country. For crisp white wine (my favorite kind of white), seek out wines made from the Assyrtiko grape on Santorini, wines made from the Moschofilero grape in Mantinia, and wines made from the Robóla grape on the island of Cephalonia. Make sure they're young and fresh! For red wines, I'm loving the wines made from a blend of Krassato, Xinomavro, and Stavroto grapes in Rapsani; the wines made from the Agiorgitiko grape in Nemea; and the amazing wines made from the Kotsifali grape on Crete. Keep in mind that many Greek producers today are making terrific red wines from French grape varieties like Cabernet and Merlot. Some wineries that excel at this practice are Gaia, Hatzimichalis, Nico Lazaridi, Chateau Harlaftis, Tsantali, and the astonishing Antonopoulos Vineyards in the northern Peloponnese.
Opa!

The
Recipes

Simple Mezedes

· · ● · ·

In accord with Greek tradition, you will offer the simplest of cocktail foods at the start of the party, to accompany those glasses of iced ouzo: just olives, feta, and pita bread.

But which olives, feta, and pita?

No olive says "Greek party" more than Greece's own Kalamatas from the Peloponnese. These purple-black, fantastically meaty olives have lots of flavor, but not too much bitterness. I buy them with pits still inside, which seems to preserve their firm texture. You can find good ones these days at specialty grocers, even at supermarkets, but my favorite of all in the U.S. are put in jars by a great company called Divina **(see Where to Find It, page 333)** under FoodMatch); their Kalamatas are fresh-looking, not too dark, crunchier than others, with fabulous secondary flavors suggesting cheese and butter. Simply place the olives in bowls around the room or patio with smaller bowls nearby to catch the pits. Bus the pit bowls frequently.

Now cheese. The market is glutted with feta from all over the map. For me, the very best feta of all is made in Bulgaria, a country also fabulously adept at yogurt. Bulgaria is a land once called Thrace, which was part of Greece, so it makes sense that great Greek traditions exist here. A fairly new product in the U.S. market, Tangra Feta from Bulgaria **(see Where to Find It, page 333)** is the best one I've tasted: wonderfully creamy and velvety, yet crumbly at the same time, quite salty, tangy, and loaded with sheepy flavor. Another worthwhile feta is a Greek one that is imported by a superb company for Greek cheeses: Mt. Vikos, in Massachusetts **(see Where to Find It, page 333)**. The Barrel-Aged Feta I tasted from them had sexy, buttery notes, and an almost smoky undertone. Place platters of sliced feta all around the venue with bottles of Greek olive oil in case your guests want to drizzle. Also arrange baskets of warm pita bread nearby to facilitate the spontaneous preparation of open-faced, oil-drizzled feta sandwiches!

Which pita to choose? Well, I would strongly advise you to eschew those dry, cardboard-y packages of pocket pita that you find in the supermarket. There's much better pita out there. First, lose the notion that pita needs to have a pocket at all! The pita that's consumed in Greece is usually just a warm, soft, circular flat bread without a pocket. You can now find pita like this in specialty stores, even supermarkets. Other breads to look for as substitutes are packaged Indian naans and packaged Afghan rectangular breads. For any of these, a quick warming in the oven or a brief visit to the outdoor grill will restore the doughy tenderness.

Grilled Octopus with Red Peppers, Purple Onions, Parsley, Lemon, and Capers

· · · ● · · ·

Please don't be intimidated by octopus! It is one of the most delicious things you can cook. Despite its reputation for spongy toughness, you'll find this cephalopod is actually quite easy to tenderize. Simmering the octopus in a flavored broth does the trick nicely. Feel free to throw a few wine corks into the pot, which is a legendary Mediterranean way to guarantee tenderness (some people swear by it, others think its efficacy is a myth). After the octopus cools in its poaching liquid, it is ready for a quick turn on your grill—which adds wonderful charred flavor to the white meat.

You can poach the octopus up to 2 days before the party, but the best time to actually grill the octopus is just a few minutes before you plan to serve it. I love the salad dressed with lemon juice only. Some may prefer a drizzle or two of excellent olive oil, preferably Greek, over the octopus at the very last minute. You'll have bottles available, of course.

The best capers are the salted ones from the island of Pantelleria. Rinse them well.

serves 12

2 to 4 octopuses, totaling 6 pounds, cleaned (see Cook's Note)

3 large yellow onions, quartered

10 bay leaves

Kosher salt

4 wine corks (optional)

3 medium red bell peppers

1 medium purple onion, halved lengthwise and sliced paper-thin

Plain olive oil for brushing the octopus

1 cup loosely packed flat-leaf parsley leaves

3 tablespoons capers, rinsed and drained if salted, crushed lightly with the flat side of a knife

6 tablespoons fresh lemon juice

Best-quality extra-virgin olive oil for drizzling (optional)

1. Divide the octopuses, onions, and bay leaves between two large pots and cover with water to within a few inches of the rims. Remove the octopuses for the moment. Bring the pots of water to a boil over high heat and reduce to a simmer. Stir in enough salt so the water tastes lightly, but distinctly, salty. Divide the corks, if using, between the pots. Return the octopuses to the pots and bring to a very gentle simmer. Maintain a gentle simmer until the octopuses are tender, usually 1 to 1 1/2 hours. When tender, the purplish skin will rub off somewhat easily between your fingertips. Turn off the heat and let the octopuses cool to room temperature in the liquid. Cut off the head of each octopus where it meets the tentacles and discard the heads. Return the tentacles to the cooking liquid until ready to grill. The octopuses can be cooked up to 2 days ahead and stored, refrigerated, in the cooking liquid. Bring to room temperature in the liquid before grilling.

2. Roast the peppers by setting them directly over a gas flame (resting on the grates) or under a broiler, until the skins are blackened and blistered all over, turning as necessary. Enclose the peppers in a plastic or paper bag and let cool for about 20 minutes. Peel the peppers, removing most of the bits of blackened skin with your fingers. Do not rinse the peppers. Slice them in half and discard the stems and seeds. Cut the peppers into diamonds, 1/2 inch per side, and reserve.

3. Soak the purple onion slices in a bowl of cold water for 5 minutes. Drain, blot dry, and reserve.

4. Prepare a medium-hot charcoal or gas fire and heat the grate.

5. When you're ready to grill the octopuses, remove them from the cooking liquid and blot them dry. When the coals are covered in a light gray ash, or when the gas fire is medium-hot, lightly brush the tentacles all over with the plain olive oil. Grill on both sides until lightly charred—even a bit crispy in places—but still moist, about 5 minutes per side. Remove to a cutting board. Though they taste best within a few minutes of grilling, the octopuses can be grilled a few hours ahead and held at room temperature until ready to finish the dish.

6. When you're ready to serve, cut each octopus into individual tentacles. Then cut each tentacle on the bias into 3/4-inch pieces. Combine the octopus pieces in a large bowl with the peppers, onions, parsley, and capers. Add the lemon juice and toss well. Serve warm or at room temperature on a platter. Drizzle with extra-virgin olive oil, if you like.

> COOK'S NOTE: *Try to buy octopuses of the same weight. Two 3-pound octopuses would be just fine for this dish, as would four 1 1/2 -pound octopuses.*
>
> *Now, if you'd rather not deal at all with the initial poaching of the octopus, and are willing to spend more money, I've got a deal for you. Sotirios Karamouzis, owner of New York City's International Grocery* **(see Where to Find It, page 333)**, *will sell you the tenderest, tastiest, poached octopuses ever, all ready to be placed on your grill. You can buy them at his store, near the Port Authority Terminal in Manhattan. Or you can have them shipped.*

Preparing a Fire

I must confess. I am a charcoal guy all the way, despite the fuss, muss, and clean-up. I think a charcoal fire makes Mediterranean grilled food taste even better.

Gas advocates sometimes avoid the charcoal option simply because they don't like the uncertainty of lighting a charcoal fire. If that describes you, and if you've never used a chimney starter, please give this inexpensive device a try. It is a tall metal cylinder with a wire base and a handle. To start a fire easily, stuff a sheet of newspaper just under the wire base, then top the wire base with as much charcoal (I like lump hardwood charcoal) as you can fit into the cylinder. Put a match to the newspaper, place the chimney on your grill or the stone floor of a patio, and, after about 10 minutes, the chimney starter will contain a roaring inferno. Dump the coals into the bed of your grill, and you're ready to glow.

One of the best aspects of the chimney starter system is that they're inexpensive; I own three. You can prepare multiple starters, like premade cocktails. Typically, I will stuff all three with newspaper and charcoal, then get things started by lighting two. I begin cooking with the coals from the first two starters. If, later on in the meal, I need a fire that's hotter still, I light the third chimney starter about 15 minutes before I need the extra heat.

For this Greek grill party, commence with two chimney starter loads of charcoal for the octopus and the chicken. Later, when you're getting ready to fire up the lamb chops—which require a really hot, fresh fire—stoke up starter number three.

Gas grill owners, despair not! This party will taste great when cooked on your beloved, fuss-free contraptions. You know what to do.

Potato Purée with Garlic and Almonds

· · ● · ·

(Skordalia)

Skordalia—a room-temperature potato purée served as a dip—is a real crowd pleaser, particularly if your crowd loves garlic!

I've suggested a hefty amount of garlic in this recipe, but there are people out there, like me, who would want even more. Adjust as you see fit. Skordalia goes beautifully with pita bread—but there is also a tradition of serving it with beet slices. If you wish, simply boil some fresh beets, peel them, slice them, and use them to garnish your skordalia platter.

makes enough for 12

2 pounds waxy potatoes, peeled and cut into equal chunks

Kosher salt

5 large cloves garlic (or more), coarsely chopped

½ cup shelled roasted almonds (unsalted)

2 slices white sandwich bread, crusts removed, and torn into large pieces

⅓ cup extra-virgin olive oil

2 tablespoons white wine vinegar

1 ¼ cups hot chicken broth, or more as needed

1. Cover the potatoes by a few inches with salted water in a medium saucepan, and bring to a boil. Reduce the heat to a simmer, and cook until the potatoes are very tender when pierced with the tip of a knife, 20 to 30 minutes. Drain them. Pass them through a potato ricer or food mill (outfitted with the smallest disc) into a large mixing bowl.

2. Meanwhile, process the garlic, almonds, and bread in a food processor, pausing occasionally to scrape the sides and bottom, until the mixture resembles coarse meal, 1 to 2 minutes. Reserve.

3. With a sturdy rubber spatula or wooden spoon, mix the reserved garlic mixture into the potatoes. Then add the oil and the vinegar, beating well to lighten the texture of the purée. Gradually add the hot chicken broth, beating as you go; use only enough stock so that the texture of the skordalia resembles very loose mashed potatoes. Reserve any remaining stock for another use. Taste, and add more garlic (mashed to a paste with the flat side of a knife), salt, or vinegar. Serve as a dip surrounded by warm pita bread. Skordalia tastes best when freshly made, but can be held in the refrigerator for up to a week.

Yogurt with Cucumbers and Garlic

· · · ● · ·

(Tzatziki)

This classic Greek/Turkish dish is often served as a dip for bread, in which case it's brought to the table quite firm and thick. For this party, I'm recommending a thinner tzatziki, more like a sauce, which goes insanely well with the chicken kebabs to follow. And you can still dip it.

serves 12

2 medium cucumbers, peeled, halved lengthwise, and seeded
4 cups whole milk yogurt (see Cook's Note)
2 teaspoons kosher salt
4 teaspoons minced garlic
2 cups half-and-half, or as needed

Grate the cucumber through the large holes of a grater, working over a large mixing bowl to catch all the pulp. Stir in the yogurt, salt, and garlic. Thin the mixture with the half-and-half, adding as much as necessary until the mixture is fluid but still thick, like a very dense soup. Taste for salt. Serve as a sauce for meats.

> COOK'S NOTE: *Really tart, tangy, un-sweet yogurt works best in this great Greek sauce and is most authentic. My favorite yogurt in the country for tzatziki is a new one from Vermont: the Star Hill Dairy Water Buffalo Yogurt, Plain* **(see Where to Finid It, page 333)**. *Their water buffalo are the only herd in the U.S. used to produce milk for yogurt—and water buffalo are the very animal preferred by the Bulgarians, who are yogurt masters.*

The Real Greek Salad

· · • · ·

Forget those horrors called "Greek Salad" that you see in deli cases; often they are not freshly made, they're dripping with liquid, and they contain all kinds of inappropriate ingredients. They are not "Greek" at all! In Greece and Turkey, a very fresh salad, sometimes called "Shepherd's Salad," is often served. It is made with basic elements. Here's a great version.

serves 12

6 tablespoons fresh lemon juice

1 teaspoon kosher salt

Freshly ground black pepper

1 cup extra-virgin olive oil

1 large purple onion, halved, and cut into ½-inch pieces

8 medium tomatoes, stemmed, cored, and cut into ¾-inch chunks (about 6 cups)

5 medium cucumbers, peeled, sliced lengthwise, seeded, and cut into ½-inch pieces (about 5 ½ cups)

2 medium green bell peppers, seeded and cut into ½-inch pieces

3 cups loosely packed whole flat-leaf parsley leaves

6 tablespoons finely chopped mint leaves

1 cup Kalamata olives, pitted and halved

⅔ pound feta cheese, coarsely crumbled

1. Whisk the lemon juice, salt, and a few generous grindings of black pepper in a small bowl. Add the oil in a thin stream, whisking constantly to form an emulsion. Set the dressing aside.

2. Soak the onion in a bowl of cold water for 5 minutes. Drain, blot dry, and reserve. Meanwhile, drain the tomatoes in a colander for a few minutes to rid them of excess liquid.

3. When you're ready to serve, combine the onion, tomatoes, cucumbers, green peppers, parsley, mint, olives, and half of the feta cheese in a large mixing bowl, tossing to combine. Whisk the dressing again for a few moments and add it to the vegetables, tossing thoroughly. Taste for salt. Immediately transfer the salad to a large serving bowl, leaving any excess liquid behind in the mixing bowl. Top with the remaining feta cheese and serve at once.

Grilled Chicken Kebabs with Cinnamon, Fresh Oregano, and Cherry Tomatoes

. . . ● . .

Here's the middle section of your Greek grill party. Start cooking the kebabs just after you've placed the octopus and all the other dishes on the buffet. When the kebabs are done, simply place them on a platter, and bring them to the buffet table. Have warm pita nearby in case your guests fancy kebab sandwiches.

If you've just grilled the octopus, your fire should be hot enough for the chicken. Otherwise, see Preparing a Fire (page 321).

makes 12 kebabs

1 medium yellow onion

2 tablespoons kosher salt

3 large cloves garlic, minced

Finely grated zest of 1 ½ lemons

1 ½ tablespoons finely minced fresh oregano (or 1 ½ teaspoons dried oregano)

¾ teaspoon sweet paprika

¾ teaspoon ground cinnamon

¾ teaspoon ground allspice

Generous ⅛ teaspoon cayenne

3 cups plain whole-milk yogurt

3 to 3 ½ pounds boneless, skinless chicken breasts or thighs, cut into 36 equal chunks

36 bay leaves

12 (12-inch) wooden skewers

1 large Vidalia onion, halved lengthwise, cut into ½-inch-wide wedges

24 large cherry tomatoes

Olive oil for basting

1. Grate the yellow onion through the large holes of a grater, working over a large mixing bowl to catch all the pulp and juices. Stir in the salt until dissolved. Add the garlic, lemon zest, oregano, paprika, cinnamon, allspice, cayenne, and yogurt, stirring well to combine. Add the chicken and coat thoroughly. Cover with plastic wrap and refrigerate for 4 hours.

2. While the chicken marinates, soak the bay leaves and skewers in cold water for at least an hour.

3. To assemble the kebabs, thread each of the 12 skewers in the following order: First, slide a bay leaf about two-thirds of the way down the skewer. Follow with a piece of chicken, nestling it up next to the bay leaf. Next, slide on three large single-layer pieces from a wedge of Vidalia onion. Follow with a tomato. Repeat this order on the same skewer, nestling each item comfortably against the next one. Complete each skewer with a third and final piece of chicken, topped with a third and final bay leaf. Transfer the kebabs to a tray or baking dish, cover with foil or plastic wrap, and refrigerate. Discard the yogurt marinade and reserve any remaining Vidalia onion for another use.

4. When you're ready to grill, bring the kebabs to room temperature. Grill the kebabs on two sides until the chicken is cooked through, but still moist, about 7 to 8 minutes per side. Rearrange the kebabs as needed to avoid excessive charring (but expect the bay leaves to burn a bit, which smells great!) and keep the longer, exposed skewer ends away from direct flame. Baste with olive oil after turning the kebabs, and again after removing them from the fire. Serve at once.

Tiny Grilled Lamb Chops with Marjoram

· · • • • · ·

No knife or fork is needed for these lamb "lollipops;" you just pick them up in your fingers, and you down the eye of the chop in one magnificent bite. This will be the ultimate bite at your grill party—so start to prepare for cooking the chops soon after you've served the chicken kebabs. You can easily attain the higher heat you need to cook these small chops either by turning up your gas grill or by adding another chimney starter's worth of charcoal to the fire (see Preparing a Fire, page 321).

serves 12

6 large cloves garlic, finely minced

2 tablespoons dried marjoram leaves

¾ cup extra-virgin olive oil

3 (8-rib) racks of lamb, 1 ½ to 2 pounds each (see The Ingredient, page 314), cut into 36 chops (or buy 36 thin rib chops)

Kosher salt

1. Combine the garlic, marjoram, and oil in a small bowl and let stand for at least 5 minutes. Transfer the marinade to a flat baking dish. One by one, dip each lamb chop into the marinade, massaging the chops with the mixture and making sure that each chop is coated with at least a few bits of garlic. Transfer the chops to another dish or container, toss with any remaining marinade, cover, and let marinate in the refrigerator for 6 to 8 hours. Bring to room temperature before grilling.

2. Prepare a hot charcoal or gas fire, and heat the grate. When the coals are glowing red and starting to turn to ash, or when the gas fire is hot, place the lamb chops on the grill (in batches, if necessary). Sprinkle each side of the chops with kosher salt. Cook about 3 minutes per side for medium doneness. The exterior of the chops should be crunchy-brown. Serve immediately.

Galaktoboureko Triangles

· ● ● ● ● ● ·

Galaktoboureko—a pie of crispy, flaky filo pastry, stuffed with custard, drizzled with syrup, cut into squares, and served at room temperature—is one of my favorite Greek desserts. I've adapted the classic recipe to make the dessert much easier to serve: the custard is now baked into individual filo triangles, enabling you to simply pass them out to your guests (who may eat them out of hand, standing up, if desired). I've eliminated the sticky syrup that traditionally goes on top of the galaktoboureko, and replaced it with a light and easy sprinkle of cinnamon-scented sugar.

You can make the custard for this dish the day before the party, but you should make the triangles themselves on the day they'll be served.

makes 12 triangles

3 cups whole milk

½ cup sugar

6 tablespoons quick-cooking farina (cream of wheat)

4 large egg yolks

Pinch of salt

1 teaspoon vanilla extract

1 (1-pound) package filo dough, thawed if frozen

About ¾ cup (1 ½ sticks) unsalted butter, melted

1 ½ teaspoons ground cinnamon

¼ cup confectioners' sugar, sieved

1. Scald the milk in a 2-quart saucepan over medium heat. Do not let it come to a boil.

2. While the milk is heating, combine the sugar, farina, egg yolks, and salt in a medium bowl. Add the heated milk in a thin stream, slowly at first, whisking rapidly to blend well.

3. Return the custard to the saucepan. Bring to a boil over medium-high heat. Reduce heat to low, and continue cooking for 3 minutes, stirring constantly.

4. Remove the custard from the heat and stir in the vanilla extract. Scrape the custard into a bowl, cover the surface with plastic wrap to prevent a skin from forming, and cool at room temperature. The custard can be made a day ahead up to this point; store in the refrigerator overnight.

5. Heat the oven to 375°F.

6. Unwrap the filo and cover it with a damp towel.

7. Place one sheet of filo on the countertop, a long side in front of you. Brush the filo with melted butter. Top that sheet with another sheet, and brush the second sheet with butter. Repeat until you have a stack of 6 buttered sheets. Cut the stack, from the long side in front of you to the long side farthest from you, four times, creating four long rectangles that are 4 inches wide and 12 inches long.

8. Working quickly, place ¼ cup of the custard at the bottom of one rectangle. Fold the bottom right-hand corner toward the left edge diagonally over the filling to form a triangle. Now fold the triangle over to the right, against the right edge, maintaining the shape of the triangle. Continue folding left, then right—as in folding a flag—until you've reached the top of the filo strip. When you're finished, you should have a triangle that perfectly encases the filling. Repeat with the remaining filo rectangles until 4 galaktoboureko triangles are complete. Place the triangles on a buttered baking sheet, transfer to a rack, and brush the tops with melted butter.

9. Repeat steps 7 and 8 twice more, finishing with a total of 12 galaktoboureko triangles on a baking sheet. Bake until golden, about 15 to 20 minutes. Remove from the baking sheet, and let cool to room temperature.

10. Before serving, mix the cinnamon into the sieved confectioners' sugar, and sprinkle the tops of the triangles with the cinnamon-sugar mixture.

You've Got Options

I've already given you a great deal to play with in this party, but if you want to offer even more variety to your guests, it wouldn't be hard.

There are, for example, many more Greek spreads and dips that could go on the buffet table, ready for pita duty. These days, most specialty food shops and many supermarkets can offer you an array of chickpea spreads, eggplant spreads, feta spreads with flavorings (like red pepper), that will provide visual and gustatory excitement. If you have plans to order from the International Grocery in New York City **(see Where to Find It, page 333)**, you might want to include a pound or two of their amazing taramosalata, the classic mousse of fish eggs (usually mullet or carp), whipped up with olive oil, potatoes (or bread), and lemon juice. Sotirios Karamouzis makes his taramosalata from Minnesota carp roe, and he adds club soda for lightness; it is the best taramosalata I've ever tasted, and would be a great addition to your buffet table.

Another item from the International Grocery that I also love is the loukanika, or fresh Greek sausage; you can find good examples of it in other specialty stores as well. What distinguishes loukanika from its cousin, fresh Italian sausage, is the more liberal use of spices and flavorings in the Greek version; the lamb-and-pork one from the International Grocery has cinnamon, orange peel, lemon, leeks, parsley, and cayenne. If you're so inclined, you might grill it, along with the lamb chops.

Lastly, there's halloumi, a wonderful grill-ready, goat-and-sheep's-milk cheese from Cyprus. There are terrific examples available. My favorite is Christis Halloumi, Traditional (or Village) Style, imported by a New York company called Trans Mid-East **(see Where to Find It, page 333)**. Cut any halloumi into ⅜-inch slices, soak the slices in cold water for 2 hours or so, then dry the slices thoroughly and toss them on a grate over a medium-hot fire. Cook about 4 minutes per side, until golden brown on both sides. Fantastic! This would be a great party addition when you serve the octopus, or when you serve the chicken.

Set Dressing

I recently came across an evocative geographical statistic: you can't be in Greece and not be within 85 miles of the sea. The emotional force of that number got me thinking about my ideal fantasy spot for a Greek party. It would be outdoors, of course, on a rocky promontory jutting into the Aegean Sea or the Ionian Sea. There would be ancient olive trees on the site, as well as the ruins of an old Greek temple. The bright blue sky would feature the occasional puffy cloud, sped on its journey by the sailor-friendly Mediterranean breeze. Long flats with blazing charcoal would be grilling the simple food, the meaty smoke trailing off into the cerulean blue, against the backdrop of wine barrels from the local vineyard.

The year of this ideal party? Frankly, it could fall into any century from the 6th B.C. to the 21st A.D.

Such wonderful dreams. For the real Greek grill party at my house, timelessness would be a key element. If tastefully done, references to the glorious history of Greece could set a mystical and elegiac tone. Columns, of course. Pedestals. Billowing drapery. Plaster busts, preferably chipped. Large Grecian urns with ivy and flowers, or with profuse bunches of dried herbs. Gnarled trunks of olive trees (or any trees). Above all, the liberating feeling of openness and light.

And order up, if you can, a perfect summer day.

Table
Dressing

Create outdoor tables (buffet or dining) with con-
crete blocks or sawhorses (as supports) topped with plywood. Completely cover the
tables with azure-colored or bright yellow tablecloths. (Fishing weights, which have a
convenient loop on their leaden ends, can be attached to the extreme corners of the
tablecloths, and will calm the cloths in case a zephyr threatens!) Think primary, complementary colors. If you're using a blue cloth, for example, punctuate it with yellow
napkins. And vice versa.

If you want to, get a little fussier. I love the thought of a narrow, visually exciting
diorama running the length of the table—a replica of the Parthenon, perhaps. Cover
it with miniature busts, Grecian statues, masks, drifts of sea glass **(see Where to Find It,
page 333)**, lots of lemons, and at intervals, fragrant pots of mint and oregano inter-
spersed with bottles of Greek olive oil. Thoughtfully provide a few pairs of gardener's
scissors for snipping the fresh herbs into saucers of the olive oil, of course. Fill in any
blanks on the table with long tendrils of trailing ivy. Check wholesale floral supply
houses, craft stores, and even cake decorating suppliers (think of all the supporting
Ionic columns you've seen on wedding cakes!) for spontaneous inspiration.

Keep flowers simple. Anchor sturdy blooms like gerbera daisies to sea-tumbled
rocks with small-gauge copper or brass wire (available at craft or hardware stores),
keeping the stems short. Submerse them in squatty, straight-sided, clear-glass containers. Consider putting one at each place setting.

Line up bottles of mineral water for quenching thirst or diluting ouzo, preferably
a brand that comes in sensational-looking cobalt-blue bottles, along with sliced lemons.
Serve wine in small, heavy tumblers or juice glasses. Also fill up a few wineskins with
wine, and have your guests try their skill.

This is an "over-the-top" idea—but what the halloumi! Marble plates and platters
would be outstanding, and they *are* available. But any sedate white or cream-colored
chargers and/or platters would work beautifully; they'll be like blank canvases for the
colorful food.

Lastly, cinch napkins at each place setting with an "evil eye" bracelet **(see Where to
Find It, page 333)**!

Where to Find It

Jamison Farm
171 Jamison Lane
Latrobe, PA 15650
800.237.5262 (toll free)
724.837.2287 (fax)
www.jamisonfarm.com
Wonderful lamb chops.

Ceriello Fine Foods
541 Willis Ave.
Williston Park, NY 11569
516.747.0277 (tel)
www.ceriellofinefoods.com
Miraculous lamb chops.

Nestor Imports, Inc.
225 Broadway, Suite 2911
New York, NY 10007
800.775.8857 (outside New
York)
212.267.1133 (tel)
www.nestorimports.com
Call this importer for availability of Kourtaki Retsina.

Fantis Foods, Inc
60 Triangle Blvd.
Rutherford, NY 07070
201.933.6200 (tel)
www.fantisfoods.com
Importer of Malamatina Retsina; call for availability.

Athenee Importers & Distributors
515 Peninsula Blvd.
Hempstead, NY 11550
516.505.4800 (tel)
Ask to speak to Andrea Englisis; she can tell you if Ritinitis Nobilis is being sold in your area. It is delicious!

Star Hill Dairy, LLC
P.O Box 295
South Woodstock, VT 05701
802.457.4540 (tel)
www.woodstockwaterbuffalo.com
My preferred yogurt for tzatziki.

Trans Mid-East Shipping and Trading Agency, Inc.
5101 Second Ave.
Brooklyn, NY 11232
718.492.8500 (tel)
This importer represents Christis Halloumi, a Cyprus dairy, and can steer you to a retail source. Ask for Rami Joudeh.

FoodMatch
180 Duane St.
New York, NY 10013
800.350.3411 (toll free)
This terrific importer of olives and many other treats carries the whole Divina line.

Tangra Group, LLC
11 East 84th St.
New York, NY 10028
800.249.0272 (toll free)
917.498.8889 (cell phone)
www.tangragroup.com
If you can't find it, you can order wonderful Bulgarian feta directly from Tangra.

Mt. Vikos
4 Calypso Lane
Marshfield, MA 02050
781.834.0828 (tel)
781.837.8403 (fax)
Importers of great Greek products.

International Grocery
543 Ninth Ave. (between 40th and 41st Sts.)
New York, NY 10018
212.279.5514 (tel)
This is your one-stop Greek shop.

GreekShops.com
2665 30th St., Suite 206
Santa Monica, CA 90405
310.581.5059 (tel)
310.581.4290 (fax)
www.greekshops.com
An internet retailer of a broad range of Greek products, Evil Eye jewelry, clothing, etc.

Columns.com
277 North Front St.
Historic Wilmington, NC 28401
800.265.8667 (toll free)
910.763.3191 (fax)
www.columns.com
Premade columns in various styles, heights, and price ranges.

KPTiles.com
1832 Star Batt
Rochester Hills, MI 48309
248.853.0418 (tel)
www.kptiles.com
Sells sea glass by the pound, and carries a large selection of decorative tiles.

The Hell with Fidel, Let's Party!

Roast Suckling Pig, in the Cuban Style

A Party for 12

The Menu

Jade Mojitos for a Crowd

Red Snapper Ceviche with
Plantain Chips

Cuban Roast Suckling Pig with
Crispy Achiote Skin

Variations on Black Beans
with White Rice
(*Moros y Cristianos*)

Boiled Yuca with Mojo

Ripe Plantains Sautéed in Butter
(*Plátanos Maduros*)

Tangled Salad of Purple Onions, Light
Green Peppers, Oranges, and Cilantro
with Creamy Avocado Dressing

Golden Flan with Caramel

Cuban-Style Coffee

There are, of course, all kinds of Cuban eating options for a party. But to me, the one that most deeply touches the party-happy nerve of Cuba is roast suckling pig, so beloved by the Cubans on Christmas Eve *(Noche Buena)*. Drinks could also go in many directions, but Mojitos by the pitcherful is my choice, guaranteed fuel for a wild ride of a night.

Lastly, though the food and drink are enough to create a special and specific ambience, party planners who wish to indulge in atmosphere-building can go nuts when working in the Cuban idiom. We Americans are bewitched by Cuba. It lies just 90 miles away from Florida, and its proximity always makes us think of party lights in Havana twinkling just beyond the horizon, of rum smuggling, of indulgent Floridian nights ending in dangerous, devil-may-care speedboat rides to sin.

Cuba also happens to be the repository of many knick-knacks, large and small, from the old pre-Castro, Batista days—making a modern snapshot of Cuban culture a veritable glimpse of a caught-in-time 1950s, a decade in which it was vogue-ish for Cubans to emulate American style. Fantastic for party-makers! Old cars, old shirts, old posters, old sensibilities—these can make for a deliriously tongue-in-chic gathering at your *casa*.

The
Plan

This party works just as well outside, on a steamy summer night, as it does inside, by the warmth of the fire. The choice is yours: roast suckling pig in a covered Weber on the patio, or roast suckling pig in your kitchen oven. The recipe accommodates both options, enabling you to throw this great party on any night of the year.

This is a buffet, all the way. You'll need a Mojito Master to step behind the buffet counter; he'll start the party, as ceviche on plantain chips is being passed around, and return to his post as needed. After cocktails, you'll bring the pig and all the side dishes out to the buffet table. You, or an appointee, should stand ready to carve the pig into individual portions. When the main course is cleared, the buffet will hold the flan; Cuban coffee can be served with dessert or after dessert.

Plan ahead. You need to start preparing for this party the day before: marinate the pig and soak the beans.

The
Ingredient

Nothing at this party will dazzle guests and family more than a high-quality pig, ready to emerge from the oven or Weber with crunchy skin and meltingly tender meat. Happily, such a high-impact item is extremely easy to acquire: you simply contact the folks at D'Artagnan **(see Where to Find It, page 360)**. Within 24 hours, a gorgeous suckling pig will be delivered to your door.

Now, if for some reason you prefer the idea of a neater pork roast to a messier pig roast, there's no reason why you shouldn't follow through with this amazing Cuban party anyway! Simply substitute a large, bone-in rack of pork, soak it with the achiote marinade (in the suckling pig recipe) overnight, then roast it in your oven at 375°F until the meat reaches 138°F on a meat thermometer. Keep everything else in the party exactly as is.

Here's an idea if you want your pork roast to be extra special. Lobel's, the great Manhattan butcher shop, has recently begun carrying a type of pork known as "Kurobuta"—named by the Japanese after the British government gave Japan a gift of purebred Berkshire pigs in the 19th century. Today, pork from these pigs is a delicacy in Japan, where it is considered to be the porcine equivalent of Kobe beef. The meat is well marbled, a little darker, richer, juicier, and porkier than most pork that's available. Lobel's gets its Kurobuta pork, which is unusual in the U.S., from purebred Berkshire pigs raised on small family farms in the Midwest. Three of their five-bone bone-in rack roasts would be ideal for this party; everyone gets a chop with a bone, with a few chops to spare **(see Where to Find It, page 360)**.

Beverage Time

All kinds of libations work well with this perfectly porky

party: icy beer, off-dry white wine, and slightly chilled fruity red wine are some second-tier candidates that come to mind. But the one drink that is an *absolute must* in setting the mirthful Caribbean tone is the Mojito, so beloved of Cuba-lover Ernest Hemingway. At the very least, offer Mojitos at the start of this party, along with the ceviche on plantain chips. But consider keeping the Big Mo going throughout the party until the last morsel of suckling pig has been devoured. The Mojito is a great cocktail, *sí*, but it's a food-loving beverage as well.

The Mojito is a blend of fresh mint, rum, sugar, lime juice, and usually, a little sparkling water. Typically, the drink is made one by one, Mojito by Mojito. The bartender muddles the mint and sugar in each glass, then mixes in the rest of the ingredients. Muddling takes a few moments, though, and individual muddling can cause problems for the host of a 12-person gathering. Therefore, I have devised a system for making Mojitos for a crowd. It takes seconds to whip up six of them, and seconds to whip up six more. In the process of development, I hit upon a new kind of Mojito—one with a gorgeous jade color throughout, and no floating bits of swampy muddled mint. I love it. It does take more fresh mint than usual to pull it off, but that's not a problem at all if you have a good supply.

In advance of the party, spend some time with your mint: tear the leaves off the stems and place them in a 2-cup measuring cup, packing them firmly. Two cups of mint leaves are sufficient for six Mojitos; keep them together, possibly in a plastic bag. Continue measuring out leaves until you have at least two premeasured batches ready to go. Remember, every time you want six more Mojitos, you will need another 2-cup batch of mint leaves, so you may want to prep more.

A few other items are necessary. Juice your limes: you'll need 1 cup of juice for 12 Mojitos. Make sure you have lots of shaved or crushed ice in a nearby freezer; you'll need 8 cups for 12 Mojitos. It would be wise to select someone to be the Designated Mojito Master. Set up a blender or a food processor, wherever the action will take place. Set out a big bowl of granulated sugar near the blender or food processor and stand a few bottles of white rum nearby. Basic Bacardi works for me; this is not an instance in which rum connoisseurship yields extra rewards. You'll also need measuring cups, a big pitcher, a fine mesh strainer, a wooden spoon, mint sprigs for garnish, raw sugar cane sticks as stirrers (if desired), and glasses. The type of glass you choose is up to you: I like my Mojitos in a wide, squat tumbler.

The Mojito is traditionally made with a splash of club soda. However, my Jade Mojitos for a Crowd are so well balanced without bubbly water that no additional liquid is necessary. If your guests miss the effervescence—or if they find the Mojitos too sweet, or too rummy, or too *whatever*—they can make their own adjustments if you've lined up bottles of club soda and Seven-Up (an idea from New York Chef Douglas Rodriguez) in the vicinity of the Designated Mojito Master.

The.
Recipes

Jade Mojitos for a Crowd

· · · ● · · ·

This will be the deepest, wildest, mintiest Mojito you've
ever tasted, as well as the simplest to make.

makes 6 Mojitos in under 2 minutes

**2 cups of firmly packed fresh, unblemished mint leaves, no stems,
plus extra leaves for garnish (you will probably need 2 to 3 large
bunches of mint)**

¼ cup sugar

½ cup fresh lime juice

2 cups white rum

4 cups shaved or crushed ice

6 pieces of raw sugar cane, optional (see Cook's Note)

Club soda or Seven-Up, optional

1. Place the mint, sugar, lime juice, and rum in a blender jar or a food processor. Blend or process
for a minute or so, until only tiny pieces of mint are floating in a green liquid.

2. Place ice in a large pitcher, one that holds at least 1 ½ quarts. Set a fine mesh strainer over the
mouth of the pitcher, and pour the contents of the blender or food processor through the strainer
into the pitcher. Stir once with a wooden spoon and serve immediately, dividing the mixture among
six cocktail glasses. Garnish with mint leaves and, if using, sugar-cane stirrers. Have the club soda
or Seven-Up available for guests who want to add a splash.

> COOK'S NOTE: *Raw sugar cane sticks make wonderful stirrers. An additional
> benefit is that you can chew on them after they've absorbed some of the Mojito
> flavors. They are hard to find in local stores in most parts of the country, but
> they are available from Melissa's/World Variety Produce, Inc., in Los Angeles
> (see Where to Find It, page 360).*

Red Snapper Ceviche with Plantain Chips

. . ● . . .

Plantain chips, available in bags at Hispanic groceries, are smaller than most potato chips, a little more brittle, and a little sweeter. They are the perfect base for the following light and lovely, grapefruit-scented ceviche. If you can't find plantain chips, you might try one of the many "root" chips in wide distribution from the Terra company **(see Where to Find It, page 360)**.

makes 48 canapes

> **1 pound red bell peppers**
> **1 pound skinless red snapper filets**
> **¾ cup fresh grapefruit juice**
> **1 teaspoon grated grapefruit zest**
> **3 tablespoons finely minced scallion**
> **48 plantain chips**
> **Sea salt**

1. Place the red peppers directly over a gas flame (resting on the grates) or under a broiler. Roast, occasionally turning with tongs, until the skins are evenly blackened. Place the peppers in a paper bag. Close tightly and let the peppers rest for 15 to 20 minutes.

2. Cut the red snapper filets into strips about ¼ inch wide and 2 inches long. Keep them refrigerated in a bowl.

3. When you're ready to serve, pour the grapefruit juice over the snapper and mix well. Add the grapefruit zest, distributing the zest well with your fingers.

4. Remove the peppers from the bag, and rub off the blackened skins with your fingers. (Whatever you do, don't run the peppers under water! A little blackened skin remaining on a pepper is OK.) Remove the stems, seeds, and thick inner ribs from the peppers. Cut the peppers into strips the same size as the red snapper.

5. Toss the red pepper strips and the minced scallion together with the red snapper ceviche, distributing evenly. Mound a bit of the ceviche on 24 of the plantain chips, using half the ceviche mixture and distributing it evenly. Sprinkle sea salt over all. Pass the ceviche on a plate or platter. After your guests have finished the first 24 ceviche chips, mound and serve the last 24.

Boiled Yuca with Mojo

· · · ● · · ·

Nothing makes me feel I'm eating "Cuban" as much as yuca (YOO-ka)—a starchy white tuber with an ineffably delicious taste; my best shot at description is "mineral-y," but yuca actually just tastes like yuca. It is always served alongside roast suckling pig, and under a mantle of "Mojo"—a downpour of blended citrus juice, oil, and garlic. The yuca can be held in its cooking water for an hour or two before serving, though it loses a noticeable amount of freshness and life. I recommend cooking it during the 30 minutes that the suckling pig is off the heat and resting. The Mojo can be made ahead of time.

serves 12

6 pounds medium-sized yuca, peeled, halved lengthwise, and cut into 1 ½-inch-long pieces (see Cook's Note)

2 cups cold water

Kosher salt

Approximately 2 ½ cups Mojo (page 352)

1. Place the yuca in a large pot and cover with cold water by a least 1 inch, leaving at least another inch to the top of the pot. Bring to a boil over medium-high heat. Pour in the cold water. Return to a simmer and cook, stirring occasionally, until the yuca is tender when pierced with a knife, 15 to 25 minutes. Remove from the heat and stir in enough salt so that the liquid tastes nearly as salty as seawater. Allow the yuca to rest for 5 minutes.

2. Drain the yuca well and place it in a warmed serving dish. Pour the Mojo over the yuca so that all the pieces are smothered in the sauce. Serve immediately.

Cook's Note: Yuca is a little difficult to peel; the brown skin is almost like bark. If you can find frozen yuca—peeled, raw, ready for cooking—you will save a good deal of trouble. And yuca does freeze well. Fresh yuca is available in Hispanic markets.

If you can't find frozen yuca, Melissa's/World Variety Produce, Inc., recommends scrubbing the yuca before cutting it into 2-inch sections. Score each section lengthwise with a paring knife, cutting through the tough bark like skin and the underlying membrane. Carefully pry the two layers away from the root, starting at the slit. Rinse well, and place in cold water.

Cuban Roast Suckling Pig with Crispy Achiote Skin

· · • · ·

You have the option of cooking this pig in the oven or on a covered grill outside. Now, once you get past that choice, I'm giving you one further set of options: you can cook the pig whole in the classic fashion, or you can cook it in pieces. The former method has the great advantage of yielding a gorgeous gastronomic sight: a whole roast pig on a large platter. But there are two problems with this. First, your oven or outdoor grill might not be large enough to accommodate a whole pig. Second, some guests may not appreciate the sight of a whole animal on a platter (other than a chicken or turkey). If you have a small oven, and suspect your guests have a small tolerance for plated beasts, you may want to consider plan number two, cooking the pig in pieces. The whole pig and the pig-in-parts follow the same routine: each gets an overnight marinade, and each gets a long, slow roast. The differences between the finished products of the two methods, in flavor and texture, are practically nonexistent. For my parties, I go with the pieces.

2 tablespoon achiote seeds (annatto)

1 cup inexpensive olive oil

1 large head of garlic, cloves thinly sliced

2 teaspoons dried oregano

1 tablespoon dried thyme

1 ½ tablespoons ground cumin

1 tablespoon freshly ground black pepper

10 bay leaves, finely ground in a spice grinder or a mortar

Finely grated zest of 2 oranges

Finely grated zest of 2 limes

2 tablespoons kosher salt, plus additional as needed

**1 (13– to 15-pound) suckling pig, whole or in parts
(see Special Instructions for Pig Options, page 346)**

1. For the marinade: Combine the achiote seeds and the olive oil in a small saucepan, bring to a very gentle simmer, and cook for 5 minutes. Remove the pan from the heat and let it rest for 10 minutes, allowing the achiote to flavor and color the oil. Meanwhile, combine the remaining ingredients (except the pig) in a mixing bowl. Strain the warm oil into the spice mix, stirring to combine the dry ingredients with the oil. Discard the achiote seeds in the strainer. Let the flavors of the marinade develop for at least 30 minutes.

2. Using a sharp knife, score the pig skin diagonally at 2-inch intervals, taking care not to penetrate the flesh. Rub the marinade all over the pig, inside and out. Place the pig on a tray large enough to hold it and cover with foil. Let the pig marinate in the refrigerator overnight.

3. If cooking the pig in the oven: Heat the oven to 325°F. Bring the pig or pig pieces to room temperature before roasting. Salt them well. Place the pig or pig pieces in a roasting pan (or pans); arrange pig pieces skin-side up. Reserve any leftover marinade. Roast for 1 ½ hours, basting once or twice with any remaining marinade. Increase the oven temperature to 450°F, and continue roasting for another 1 to 1 ½ hours, or until the internal temperature registers 170°F to 180°F on a meat thermometer and the skin is reddish-brown and crispy. Carefully transfer the pig from the oven onto a large cutting board and let it rest for 30 minutes. Cut into portions (preferably at the buffet table), making sure that each guest gets a taste of leg meat, rib/loin meat, and crispy skin. Accompany with Mojo (page 352). If you're cooking the pig whole in the oven, see Special Instructions for Pig Options (page 346).

4. If cooking the pig on a grill: Bring the pig or pig pieces to room temperature before roasting. Salt them well. Build a charcoal fire, preferably in a chimney starter; when the coals are covered with light gray ash, spill them into the grill, along one side of the wall only, covering no more than ⅓ of the circumference of the kettle wall. Place the grate over the coals. Arrange the meat, skin side up, not directly over the coals themselves; if cooking the pig in pieces, try not to crowd the pieces. Cover the grill and open the vents just a crack. Cook for 3 to 3 ½ hours, adding more coals as necessary (see Special Instructions for Pig Options). Cook until the skin is a rich reddish-brown and the internal temperature reaches 170°F to 180°F. Occasionally, either a) rearrange the pieces so that those closest to the heat source get to spend some time farther away from it, or b) turn and rotate the whole pig. Baste the pig with any remaining marinade once or twice during the cooking. If, after 3 ½ hours (or 180°F on a meat thermometer), the skin has not achieved a crisp-crackling texture, remove the grate and spread medium-hot coals evenly across the bottom of the kettle. Return the grate to position and grill the pig, uncovered, until crispy—no more than a few minutes. (If cooking pieces, cook them skin-side down; if cooking a whole pig, turn it once during the crisping.) Take care that the skin doesn't burn. Remove the meat to a cutting board and let it rest for 30 minutes. Cut into portions and serve, making sure that each guest gets a taste of leg meat, rib/loin meat, and crispy skin. Accompany with Mojo (page 352).

Special Instructions for Pig Options

Cutting the Pig into Parts

Cooking the pig in parts is my preferred method for cooking a suckling pig at home. The easiest way of all to get your pig into parts is to ask your butcher to do it for you! Even if you didn't buy the pig from him, he'll be able to dress it for you (likely, for a charge). Just let him know that you want six parts altogether: two rear legs, two front legs, one entire central rib/loin section, and the head. Well, maybe five parts. There is some great meat in the head, but not everyone likes looking at it.

Roasting the Pig Whole in the Oven

You will want to be sure that your pig fits into your roasting pan and oven prior to the day of the party. Depending on the size of your pig, it may require a bit of jerry-rigging, but nothing too complicated. A 13- to 15-pound pig will usually just fit within the walls of a 36-inch oven. Typically, the pig is placed in a very large, heavy-duty roasting pan, though two large nested disposable aluminum roasting pans would work, too. The pig is usually placed at an angle in the roasting pan to more readily fit in the oven. Rear legs can usually be folded beneath the animal and held in place by pushing the pig's hindquarters into one corner of the roasting pan. At the other end of the animal, you may find that the pig's snout seems a bit too long to fit in the oven. Unless your oven is much smaller than 36 inches, this shouldn't be a problem. You can pick up a couple of inches of clearance by turning the head upward before sliding the pig in the oven and resting the chin against the oven wall. The cooking of the pig and its finished appearance won't be affected at all. But if, in the end, you can't get it to fit, just follow the directions for roasting your pig in pieces. It's less dramatic, but equally delicious.

Roasting on a Covered Grill

I use a round 22½-inch diameter, kettle-type grill by Weber, with a cover outfitted with an adjustable air vent. For most of the roasting, I adjust the vents to let a tiny amount of air in. (You could also use a gas grill with a cover. Heat adjustment will be easier, but you'll lose that whiff of charcoal in the finished product.)

Through the duration of the 3- to 3½-hour roasting time, keep a charcoal chimney-starter of hot coals ready to be added to the covered grill when the internal temperature drops too low. The proper temperature (325°F to 350°F) can be monitored by thermometer. I check the old-fashioned way—by completely opening the air vent on the cover and holding the palm of my hand 1 inch above the holes of the vent. The goal is to hold my palm in position for 1 to 2 seconds before the heat becomes too great to continue. If I can hold my hand over the holes for longer than 2 seconds, the heat is too low and the fire needs replenishing. Conversely, if I can't keep my hand in position for at least a second, the fire is too hot.

When coal is needed, I remove the kettle cover and add glowing coals through a side opening in the grate, which is a feature of many Weber units. The openings are placed in front of each of the grate handles and are wide enough to let preheated coals pass into the kettle below, which means that I don't have to lift up a hot grate (and 13 pounds of pork!) each time I want to add charcoal.

Remember that one of the characteristics of roasting within a covered grill is that the meat is cooked by indirect heat over a fairly long period of time. If the coals are sitting directly beneath the meat, the pig will certainly burn before it has finished cooking. This is why it's important to pile your charcoal on one side of the kettle basin.

Indirect heat means that you're basically reproducing the environment of your kitchen oven. For the heat to do its job, it has to be contained. So, think of your grill cover as you would an oven door: open it only when necessary, and close it as soon as possible after tending the meat or the charcoal. On the other hand, suckling pig is a very forgiving animal to cook. So even if the temperature of your fire seems to be all over the place, just remember three things: let the meat reach an internal temperature of 170°F to 180°F, get the skin crispy, and let it rest for 30 minutes before serving; it will definitely be delicious.

Variations on Black Beans with White Rice

· ◦ ● ◦◦ ·

(Moros y Cristianos)

This dish was supposedly invented by early Spanish explorers who came to Cuba. I love the quaint title: the "Moors" are black beans, and the "Christians" are white rice. The name commemorates the fact that the two were "mixing it up" in 15th-century Spain. I prefer the "Moors" and "Christians" to be mixed up in a bowl, as they often are at mealtime in Cuba. Ah, but how to mix? Some people prefer them cooked together, which gives the rice a brownish-purplish cast, but a deeper taste. Others prefer the black beans and rice to be cooked separately; the chief advantages here are whiter rice, and more sauce surrounding the beans. I can't decide which one I like better. So for this Cuban party, you have your choice: recipes for both methods are printed below.

White Rice with Black Beans I

· ◦ ● ◦◦ ·

The time-saving cook's advantage in this cooked-together version is that you can start with canned black beans.

serves 12

⅓ cup olive oil

1 medium onion, finely chopped

8 medium scallions, thinly sliced into rounds

8 large cloves garlic, minced

½ green bell pepper, seeded and chopped

1 ½ teaspoons ground cumin

1 (4-ounce) jar pimientos, drained and chopped

1 ½ cups cooked black beans, or 1 (15.5-ounce) can, drained and rinsed

1 tablespoon kosher salt

4 cups long grain white rice, rinsed thoroughly (see Cook's Note)
3 cups chicken stock
3 cups water

1. Warm the olive oil in a large pot with a tight-fitting lid over medium-low heat. Add the onion and cook 3 minutes. Add the scallions, garlic, green pepper, and cumin, and cook gently for 5 minutes, stirring occasionally. Do not let the mixture brown.

2. Stir in the pimientos, black beans, salt, and the rice, stirring well. Add the stock and the water, increase the heat to high, and bring to a boil.

3. Reduce the heat to medium-high, stir the mixture, and cover the pot. Let the rice and beans cook, undisturbed, for 12 minutes. (There will be rapid bubbling and hissing steam.) Turn off the heat, wrap the pot lid in a clean kitchen towel, and place it back over the rice and beans, making a tight seal. Let the rice and beans steam this way for 20 minutes. Fluff the rice with a fork and serve. You can hold this dish with the lid on for another 20 minutes or so.

> COOK'S NOTE: *If you like your long grain white rice to be fluffy—its grains separate and without stickiness—here are some tips:*
>
> ● *Wash the rice well. Rinse it in successive changes of water (usually eight or more), using a big bowl and a strainer to help the process along. Agitate the rice under water with your hands; drain and repeat until the water is no longer cloudy.*
>
> ● *Use a pot that's appropriately sized for the amount of rice and liquid you are using. There's no exact rule, but if your pot is too wide, the liquid will evaporate too fast. If it's too tall and narrow, the rice on the bottom will turn mushy before the rice on top has finished cooking.*
>
> ● *As in the recipe, allow the rice to steam (when the heat has been turned off) in a tightly covered pot, it's lid lined with a clean dish towel. The towel traps moisture that would otherwise fall back on the rice, making it wet and heavy.*

White Rice with Black Beans II

. . ● . .

This version gives you a separate bowl of rice and a separate bowl of beans; ultimately, I may prefer it because it allows me to have things both ways. I can use the greater soupiness of the beans to spoon up a kind of sauce for my pieces of roast suckling pig. Then, I can mix some of the black beans with some of the rice right on my plate for a perfect pile of rice and beans. By the way, I would urge you to go for the lard option in the beans and the rice recipes below; its chemical structure (in case you're worried) is quite like the structure of olive oil! And the taste is pure Cubano.

serves 12

for the beans:

⅓ cup lard or olive oil

2 medium onions, finely chopped

12 large cloves garlic, thinly sliced

1 ½ teaspoons ground cumin

2 pounds dried black beans, soaked overnight

2 bay leaves

4 ½ cups chicken broth

4 ½ cups water

2 ½ tablespoons kosher salt

for the rice:

½ cup lard or olive oil

4 cups long grain white rice, washed (see Cook's Note, page 349)

1 tablespoon plus 1 teaspoon kosher salt

6 cups water

1. Warm the lard in a large pot over medium heat and add the onions, garlic, and cumin. Cook gently, stirring occasionally, until the onions soften, about 5 minutes.

2. Drain the beans. Add them to the pot and stir. Add the bay leaves, broth, and water. Bring just to a simmer over medium-high heat. Reduce the heat and cook at a bare simmer until the beans are tender. Depending on the age of the beans, this could take as little as 30 minutes or over 1 hour. The goal is beans that are very tender but still whole, surrounded by a goodly amount of slightly thickened, black cooking liquid. Thoroughly stir in the salt and allow the beans to sit for at least 30 minutes before reheating and serving.

3. Cook the rice: Warm the lard in a large pot with a tight-fitting lid over medium heat. Add the rice and the salt, stirring to coat all the grains. Add the water, increase the heat to high, and bring to a boil.

4. Reduce the heat to medium-high, stir, and cover the pot. Let the rice cook, undisturbed, for 12 minutes. (There will be rapid bubbling and hissing steam.) Turn off the heat, wrap the pot lid in a clean kitchen towel, and place it back on the pot, making a tight seal. Let the rice steam this way for 20 minutes. Fluff with a fork and serve.

Mojo

• • ● • •

This recipe yields so much sauce, it must be where Austin Powers lost his.
But I'm asking you to make this much Mojo so that you may: 1) drown the yuca in it, and 2)
use the leftover Mojo as a moistening at the table for your roast pig.

makes 5 cups

1 cup extra-virgin olive oil

2 large heads of garlic, cloves thinly sliced

$\frac{1}{2}$ teaspoon dried oregano

5 bay leaves

$\frac{3}{4}$ teaspoon ground cumin

$\frac{1}{2}$ teaspoon freshly ground black pepper

2 teaspoons kosher salt

3 cups fresh orange juice (about 12 to 15 oranges)

1 $\frac{1}{2}$ cups fresh lime juice (about 12 to 15 limes)

Combine the oil and garlic in a medium saucepan and cook gently over medium heat, stirring occasionally, until the garlic turns pale golden at its edges. Remove from the heat and whisk in the remaining ingredients. Let the mixture cool before serving.

Ripe Plantains Sautéed in Butter

· · ● ● · ·

(Plátanos Maduros)

Ripe plantains, their skins nearly black in color, are sautéed in butter and sweetened to make a great accompaniment for suckling pig.

serves 12

About ¼ cup olive oil, or more as needed

About ½ pound (2 sticks) unsalted butter, or more as needed

8 large, sweet, very ripe plantains, peeled and cut on a sharp bias into ¾-inch-thick slices (see Cook's Note)

Kosher salt

About 2 tablespoons fresh lemon juice

2 tablespoons sugar

1. Heat the oven to 350°F.

2. Heat 2 tablespoons of the oil and 4 tablespoons of the butter in a large frying pan over medium heat. Working in batches, fry the plantain slices until golden brown, 3 to 4 minutes per side. As each batch finishes browning, sprinkle the plantains with a few pinches of salt and 2 teaspoons of lemon juice. Toss well. Place in a large buttered baking dish or casserole, and proceed with the next batch, adding more oil and butter as needed. Try to keep the browned slices in one layer as you add them to the baking dish; overlap slightly if necessary.

3. When all the plantains are browned and assembled, sprinkle the sugar over the plantains. Cover with foil and bake until warmed through and tender, about 15 minutes. Serve from the baking dish.

COOK'S NOTE: *To peel plantains, cut off the top and bottom; using a sharp paring knife, score the skin, making four lengthwise cuts from top to bottom, trying not to cut into the fruit beneath. Peel each section of skin like a banana.*

Tangled Salad of Purple Onions, Light Green Peppers, Oranges, and Cilantro with Creamy Avocado Dressing

. . • • • . .

This lovely salad requires some gentle handling. To get the freshest, liveliest effect, slice the onions and peppers as close to serving time as possible. The most important thing is tossing the salad at the last minute. You serve it undressed on a platter; your guests will top their own salads with a few dabs of the avocado dressing that you've strategically placed nearby.

makes 12 servings

for the dressing:

2 ripe Haas avocados, peeled and seeded

2 tablespoons fresh lime juice

1/4 firmly packed cup coarsely chopped cilantro leaves

3 tablespoons finely chopped scallion

3/4 cup water

1/2 teaspoon salt

for the tangled salad:

16 navel oranges, peeled and cut into skinless segments

1 teaspoon kosher salt, plus additional

4 long, thin-skinned, light green sweet peppers (see Cook's Note), seeds removed, cut into extremely thin rings

2 medium purple onions, sliced very thin, to yield 4 cups

2 cups cilantro leaves

1 teaspoon ground cumin

Freshly ground black pepper

1. Make the dressing: Chop the avocados into coarse chunks and place them in a food processor. Drizzle evenly with the lime juice. Add the chopped cilantro, scallion, water, and ½ teaspoon of salt. Purée until a smooth sauce is formed. Place in a bowl, cover tightly, and refrigerate for up to 4 hours.

2. About an hour before serving the salad, place the orange segments in a sieve and sprinkle with 1 teaspoon of salt. Toss gently, and let sit over a drain.

3. Make the salad: When you're ready to serve the salad, gently toss together the orange segments, pepper rings, onions, cilantro leaves, and cumin. Season well with salt and freshly ground black pepper. Place the tangled salad on a serving dish and serve immediately, alongside a bowl of the avocado dressing.

> COOK'S NOTE: *The type of sweet pepper you need for this salad is long (roughly 4 to 6 inches), tapered, thin-skinned, and with no heat whatsoever. I've called for light green peppers in the recipe, which is what I most often see. But the color doesn't really matter; it could range from yellow to light green, to darker green, to red. You will see peppers like this at the market designated as "Italian frying peppers," or as other things. The variety I like best, which is sometimes identified by name, is the "Cubanelle."*

Cuban-Style Coffee

· ▫ ● ▪ ● ▫ ·

If you've ever stopped for a coffee at a Cuban place in Miami, you know how potent and delicious it can be. Cubans stop in frequently—all day long, in fact—but also like to throw back a small cup after dinner. Serve Cuban coffee to your guests in espresso cups. But you don't actually have to make espresso. Start with a bag of Cuban coffee, like Café Bustelo, which is ground even finer than espresso-destined coffee is. Latin markets sell cone-shaped strainers lined with cotton flannel that are ideal.

serves 12

5 cups water

⅓ cup Cuban coffee

2 tablespoons sugar (optional)

1. Bring the water to a boil in a saucepan. Stir in the coffee and boil for 3 minutes. Stir in the sugar.

2. Strain the coffee into small cups and serve with the flan, or after.

Golden Flan with Caramel

· · • · · ·

Nothing demonstrates Cuba's rich Spanish heritage as much as flan. I particularly love it when the rich heritage results in a rich flan, like the one below. It must be made hours in advance of the party.

serves 12

for the custard:

12 large egg yolks

1 (14–ounce) can sweetened condensed milk

¼ cup sugar

1 teaspoon vanilla extract

¼ teaspoon ground cinnamon

¼ teaspoon ground nutmeg

¼ teaspoon kosher salt

1 teaspoon cornstarch

1 cup milk

for the caramel:

⅔ cup sugar

2 tablespoons water

1. Heat the oven to 325°F, and arrange an oven rack in the middle of the oven.

2. Make the custard: Lightly beat the egg yolks in a large bowl. Add the sweetened condensed milk, 1/4 cup sugar, vanilla, cinnamon, nutmeg, and salt, whisking lightly to combine. Avoid beating the mixture aggressively to discourage the formation of air bubbles.

3. Dissolve the cornstarch in a few tablespoons of milk, then combine it with the remaining milk. Gently whisk this mixture into the bowl with the custard, and set the mixture aside.

4. Make the caramel: Have ready a round, ovenproof baking dish (mine is 7½ inches in diameter and 3 inches deep). Combine the ⅔ cup sugar and the water in a small pan and place the pan over medium heat. Allow the sugar to dissolve into a syrup, brushing the sides of the pan with a moistened pastry brush if you see sugar crystals forming along its walls. Allow the sugar to bubble gently and to caramelize to an amber color, swirling the pan regularly to help it color evenly. Don't let the mixture burn.

5. When the syrup is uniformly amber, pour it into the baking dish and tilt the dish to coat it evenly with the caramel. Allow the caramel to cool slightly and set. Pour in the reserved custard mixture.

6. Set the custard dish into a larger baking dish, and pour warm water to come two-thirds up the sides of the custard dish. Place the entire assembly on the middle rack in the oven. Bake until the custard is just set but still jiggles slightly in the center, about 1¼ to 1½ hours. Remove from the oven, cool, then refrigerate at least 3 hours.

7. Unmold the flan by running a thin-bladed knife around the inside edge of the custard dish, topping it with a large flat serving plate, and turning the dish over, releasing the flan with its caramel. Reheat any caramel remaining in the custard dish and pour it over the custard before serving. This simple method usually works. If you'd like a fussier but more foolproof method, see Cook's Note.

> COOK'S NOTE: *The following method takes a little more trouble, and may involve re-chilling the flan—but your flan is guaranteed to come out of the custard dish. Place the custard dish in a pan and fill it with water to come just short of halfway up the sides of the dish. Bring the water just to a simmer, then carefully remove the custard dish from the water. Top the dish with a serving plate, and, using a towel so that you don't burn yourself, invert the dish to release the flan onto the plate. Serve immediately if you like, or chill the custard again if desired.*

Set Dressing

Wacky possibilities abound. As a result of the embargo on trade, Cuba has become one of the largest repositories of classic (pre-1961) American cars on the planet—it's estimated between 50,000 and 100,000. A well-placed phone call to a vintage auto club might turn up a few "props." Alternatively, you could set up "Hot Wheels" all around the venue—little matchbox cars for decoration. Wrought iron, sun-faded pastels, crumbling stucco, mossy fountains, and tropical plants hint at the gentility of old Havana without denying the realities of its current condition. Replicas of old posters are available online **(see Where to Find It, page 360)**, and could add to the fun. Scatter a few vintage Hemingway books around. Lighting should be subdued—accomplished mostly with candles, if practical. And if your neighbors have barking dogs, all the better! They'll add to the cacophony of festive food, good friends, and animated conversation.

Table Dressing

The buffet table should look as festive and bounteous as possible (roast suckling pig was a tradition in old Cuba on Christmas Eve and New Year's Eve). I would drape the table with a cloth in a solid, muted color—dusty pink, perhaps—and would mix and match colored napkins in compatible but similarly muted colors. Then I would top the table with one or two kinds of palm leaves (ordered from the florist in advance).

For more color, place a few tall, footed compotes on the buffet, and fill them with tropical fruits and leaves; you can also tuck in exotic flowers such as orchids or hibiscus (in water vials) for emphasis. Glazed tiles in appropriate colors (muted turquoise or azure, pink, yellow), bought piecemeal from a tile supplier, could serve as pads for hot dishes.

Two more irresistible touches: purchase old Havana cigar boxes (with beautiful graphics, and words like "Antonio y Cleopatra: All Havana Leaf") to use as holders for forks, knives, spoons, and napkins on the buffet line. (There are 41 vintage boxes for sale on e-bay at this moment, most under $10!) Additionally, I discovered a website **(see Where to Find It, page 360)** that sells playing cards emblazoned with Cuban "banditos"; these cards could be scattered on the buffet table, and function as drink coasters all around the room.

Entertainment

Cubans are passionate about dominoes; set up one or two games on tables along with explanations of Cuban rules. You can also offer card games with the aforementioned decks. Of course, there must be music; CDs by the late great Celia Cruz, Cuba's Queen of Rhythm, as well as the venerable Buena Vista Social Club, are widely available in mainstream music stores, and online sources expand the options considerably. Really wanna go for it? Have someone teach salsa, rumba, bolero. Of course, an occasional rendition of "Guantanamero" wouldn't be inappropriate—though the meaning has changed considerably, of late.

Where to Find It

D'Artagnan
280 Wilson Ave.
Newark, NJ 07105
800.327.8246 (toll free)
973.465.1870 (fax)
www.dartagnan.com
A great source for suckling pigs, uncooked.

Lobel's
1096 Madison Ave.
New York, NY 10028
877.783.4512 (toll free)
www.lobels.com
One of the country's greatest butchers, and with a huge mail-order business. Good source for pork.

Melissa's/World Variety Produce, Inc.
P.O. Box 21127
Los Angeles, CA 90021
800.588.0151 (toll free)
www.melissas.com
A major supplier of specialty produce to markets throughout the U.S. Contact them for information on the availability of sugar cane swizzle sticks and of yuca root in your area.

Terra Chips
The Hain Celestial Group
58 S. Service Rd. Suite 250
Melville, NY 11747
631.730.2200 (tel)
www.terrachips.com
Terra Chips are widely distributed to supermarkets, but if you can't find them, you can order them online.

www.mycubanstore.com
Large selection of music, guayaberas (Cuban shirts), and posters.

www.cubanfood market.com
This is the equivalent of a Cuban department store! In addition to groceries and produce, it carries cookware, playing cards, music, books, videos, clothing (including a large selection of cigar label T-shirts and guayaberas), gifts, posters, and a host of other products.

The Devon Cream Tea

An Idyllic Afternoon in the English Countryside

A Party for 12

The Menu

English Tea Service

English Tea Sandwiches:

Cucumber and Cream Cheese Sandwiches with Fresh Mint

Egg and Watercress Sandwiches

Rolled Smoked Salmon Sandwiches with Dill

Open-Faced Potted Ham Sandwiches on Rye Melba Toast

Miniature Scones with Clotted Cream and Strawberry Jam

English Tea Cake with Dates, Walnuts, and Apricots

There are few hours in life more agreeable," wrote Henry James, America's great Anglophilic novelist, "than the hour dedicated to the ceremony known as afternoon tea." I am in complete agreement! And you will be too, after you stage one of these delectable events.

Of what do they consist?

Let's look to Devonshire, in the southwest of England, for our model; here the Devon Cream Tea reigns supreme. You'll find tea sandwiches at these gatherings (those light, surprisingly delicious sandwich creations daintily served without crust); an English tea cake (sort of like a fruitcake that went to a good baking school); and warm, fresh-baked scones, slathered with strawberry jam and, of course, rich country cream. Served alongside these munchables is the crowning glory: a steaming pot of perfectly brewed tea.

Just when do they serve this collation? As Rupert Brooke wrote:

"Stands the Church clock at ten to three?
And is there honey for the tea?"

Therein lies perhaps the most significant factor in an English Afternoon Tea: it really is served in the afternoon, neither as lunch nor as dinner. We often hear of "High Tea," but High Tea is a light dinner, served perhaps around 6 PM. The Afternoon Tea is not nearly as practical. Brillat-Savarin, the great French gastronome, wrote that the Afternoon Tea is "an extraordinary meal in that, being offered to persons that have already dined well, it supposes neither appetite nor thirst, and has no object but distraction, no basis but delicate enjoyment." Indeed! Afternoon Tea is a complete indulgence—a wonderful basis for any party!

Why not really indulge yourself and your guests? Turn your Devon Cream Tea into something truly special by offering tea from a terrific set of china, by building layered presentations of sandwich platters, by breaking out the antique silver. Oh, you could just serve tea. But as A.A. Milne once wrote, "*a Proper Tea is much nicer than a Very Nearly Tea, which is one you forget about afterwards.*" Use a little pomp and circumstance, and make your Tea unforgettable.

The Plan

A wag once wrote that an English tea is really an indoor picnic. But the exact venue is up to you: your Tea could indeed be a picnic indoors, or, running the risk of redundancy, a picnic outdoors. Either choice brings the same set of strategies.

I like to offer the tea first, giving my guests an opportunity to taste it undistracted, to consider its subtleties (see The Ingredient). The tea may also serve to stimulate appetites. Seat the guests at a large table, or several smaller ones, set with tea cups and saucers, spoons, forks, knives, sandwich plates, scone plates, and napkins. You—or the "butler"—pour the tea into the individual cups, walking around the table or tables. Guests help themselves to nearby milk and sugar or honey, if desired. That's their first cup; leave teapots on the table, replenishing them as necessary, for additional cups of tea. Tea cozies, or warmers, slipped over the teapots, will keep the tea warm *and* evoke England at the same time.

Next come platters of English tea sandwiches, all four types served simultaneously. Arrangement of the sandwiches is up to you. They may, for example, appear on four separate platters, each platter dedicated to one type of sandwich only. Or you may serve several platters that carry a mix of sandwiches. The platters may be free-standing, or they may hover above each other, secured to a central post (you can find these kinds of "stacked" platter arrangements at fancy houseware stores). Carry the sandwich platters around the table or tables, so each guest can transfer a few sandwiches onto his or her plate, preferably with small silver tongs! Then place the platters on the table or tables, should the guests require more sandwiches.

After the sandwiches have been enjoyed, it's time to start the "main" course: warm scones with clotted cream and jam. Strategically place the copious bowls of cream and jam, with serving spoons, around the table or tables. Use a large basket, covered with an English country towel, to hold the warm scones. Once again, carry the food around so that guests may serve themselves. Each guest will split the scone with a knife, and begin the joyful slathering of cream and jam.

With the last cups of tea, it is time to serve the English Tea Cake with Dates,

Walnuts, and Apricots. I like to bring it in its entirety to the head of the table, along with a stack of plates and a cake slicer. Then I cut it into thin slices, which I plate and pass. Plan ahead. The cake should be made two days in advance.

The Ingredient

Your guests will certainly enjoy all of the lovely foodstuffs at this party. However, if you can make them say, "Wow! That tea is extraordinary," then you've staged a truly successful tea party.

There are literally thousands of teas to choose from. My advice: make your party special by choosing something not available at the supermarket, and not in a tea bag. You can acquire fabulous and exotic teas these days from specialty food shops as well as online **(see Where to Find It, page 382)**. The variety, in fact, will likely blow your mind. So the first thing you must do is organize that mind before you make a selection.

I find that a great way to begin to understand tea is to learn what I call the Basic Continuum of Tea Handling and Oxidation. At one end, tea is processed very little and is not very oxidized. The less a tea is oxidized, meaning the less it's been exposed to the withering effects of oxygen, the more it's likely to be herbaceous, vegetal. It will probably be thinner than oxidized tea, and lighter in color. At the other end of this continuum, tea is processed a lot, and is very oxidized. The more a tea is oxidized, the more likely it is to be fruity, malty. And the more likely it is to be thicker on the palate and darker in color. It is the oxidized type of tea that is preferred by the English for their tea parties.

Here are the way stations on the Basic Continuum of Tea Handling and Oxidation.

White Tea (least handling). White tea can be made anywhere, though most come from China. The leaves are picked, steamed, and dried. That's as simple as it gets. The resultant taste of white tea is very light, clean, un-oxidized. Keep in mind that this is very fresh, unprocessed tea: you want it to smell like leaves before you brew it. The leaves are usually large, and therefore need more steeping time.

Green Tea (a little more handling). White tea and green tea are often referred to as "unfermented teas," which means "un-oxidized teas." Basically, green tea is the second least processed, second least oxidized tea. Leaves are picked, withered (exposed to air and/or sunlight); then their water content is evaporated by various means. That's it. The tea made from green tea often has a vegetal, grassy, fresh taste. I've always been a big fan of green tea at the sushi bar; the lightly nutty, seaweed-y brew goes so well with fish and rice. But green tea is not normally served at an English tea.

Oolong Tea (more handling still). Now we enter the realm of oxidation—though many books call it "fermentation" rather than "oxidation." Oolong teas are picked, withered, then rolled by hand or machine to break down the cells and release some of the internal oils; this makes the leaves a little sticky. The mass of tea just sits there at the processing plant after that, oxidizing, until the process is arrested at a fairly early stage—after the leaves have acquired distinctive fragrances. Because it's only semi-oxidized, the tea is just a little darker, a little stronger, a little more oxidized in flavor than white tea or green tea. But you can already begin to taste that classic, oxidized, breakfast-tea kind of character. Oolong tea strikes me as the one that offers the most diverse and fascinating array of aromas and flavors. The intellectual down side is that oolong is very hard to pin down; there is no "typical" oolong taste. However, you can count on oolong to be a little lighter in color than black teas, sort of a medium copper, and to be smooth, relatively free from bitterness (unless you over-steep.) Some oolongs have a floral quality, and some have a peachy, or peach-pit, kind of taste. Oolong was always a specialty of the Fujian province of China (Fukien), which is not too far from the island of Formosa (or Taiwan). Some years ago, tea plants and tea techniques were shipped to Formosa, and today it is the center of oolong production. Please do not be shocked by the insane prices that oolong tea commands—and gets—from tea connoisseurs. At an English tea, you may see an oolong—and it would be just fine with the food—but it is not traditional.

Black Tea (the most handling). We come to the classic English style of tea. Think of black tea as an oolong that goes all the way. More rolling, to release more inner oils. More oxidation, to get a darker, richer, more oxidized taste. If you have an image of a dark-copper, malty-tasting kind of breakfast tea, it is likely black tea that you're thinking of. That said, there are many types of black tea, each with a distinct character. Here are some of the leading names likely to be on the English table.

Darjeeling Tea

This tea, grown in the foothills of the Himalayas in India, has the most prestigious origin in all of teadom; tea from Darjeeling is often referred to as the "Champagne" of tea, the highest summit, the ultimate. Considerable body, plus lots of tannin and astringency. I'm a renegade on this one; I often find Darjeeling overhyped and overpriced.

Assam Tea

Not only is this classic from northern India a black tea, but I would say this is the black tea of the world. I noticed Assam a long time ago—how it makes a pot of dark, rich, morning tea that tastes exactly like the great tea you remember from your bed-and-breakfast stay in England. Makes sense: English Breakfast Tea blends, and especially Irish Breakfast Tea blends, use a large proportion of Assam. The taste of a good cup of Assam is said to be malty, and I agree; in fact, I think sometimes that it smells a bit like honey even before I put any honey in it! Though tea purists usually eschew additions to tea, many connoisseurs do add things to Assam, because it's so rich to begin with. I sometimes add a little honey, and many like to add a little milk to Assam—which some say actually brings out the tea's malty flavor. A good Assam would be just the thing for your tea party.

Ceylon Black

Ceylon, the island off the southern tip of India, is now called Sri Lanka. But in the English Colonial old-fashionedness of the tea world, tea from Sri Lanka is still called Ceylon tea! Frankly, I don't care what they call it; I love Ceylon tea. It can be something like a blend of Assam and Darjeeling—meaning the rich maltiness of Assam blended with the astringency of Darjeeling. But there are flavor notes here that rise above the typical flavors of both Assam and Darjeeling; "citrusy" and "cedarlike" are common descriptors for the best Ceylon teas. You do, of course, have to acquire the best Ceylon teas because there are huge variations on this island; the ones grown at low altitudes don't have the finesse and complexity of the ones grown up in the mountains. Ceylon teas—less famous than Assam and Darjeeling, but extremely well-respected in tea circles—generally represent excellent value.

You will also find, out there in tea world, many flavored teas. Purists reject most of them; but one flavor—from the oil of bergamot (a citrus fruit something like an orange)—has become a standard at the English tea table. This tea is called Earl Grey, and many people do like to drink it at Afternoon Teatime—a time of day when, it is thought, the palate can use the liveliness of a good Earl Grey.

So now the question recurs: which tea to choose? But there's an even larger question: should you choose just one?

If you wish to turn this Tea Party into a Tea Tasting, be my guest. Or rather, be my host—because I'm not about to do that myself. The scrutiny that tea gets at a tasting—or a "cupping," as they say—seems to me to be at odds with the air of peace and tranquility that I have tried to build into this relaxed Tea Party. Save the tasting, say I, for another time.

So, for my party—much as I love oolong teas, and much as I love Ceylon teas and other "black" variations—I usually go Assam all the way. My favorite is sold by Upton Tea Imports in Hopkinton, Massachusetts **(see Where to Find It, page 382)**; it's the Shyamguri Estate Assam, FTGFOP1 (which just happens to mean Finest Tippy Golden Flowery Orange Pekoe, Grade 1). You will have malt, body, yumminess, and gobs of tradition.

How do you brew tea?

Brewing is about the most important thing of all in getting a great cup of tea. Yes, the specific tea you use matters a lot, but if you brew that tea ten different ways, it will taste like ten different teas.

Brewing is really an easy thing—you simply pour hot water over tea leaves, let them steep, then pour the water (now tea) into a cup. But by paying attention to a few subtle details, you can brew up a big difference!

First of all, here's the big news: no one can tell you exactly how to brew your cup of tea. There is no standard recipe. Every tea has its own brewing requirements, and everyone has his or her own tea tastes. The most important thing for you to know is this: you should experiment with every tea you buy, discovering which combination of elements makes the brewed cup perfect for you.

Here are the factors to consider.

1. Amount of Tea. The standard tea advice is that 1 teaspoon of tea leaves makes one 6-ounce cup of brewed tea. Use that guideline at your tea party, especially if you're using Assam tea. But you should always take into account what type of tea you're using before you start measuring.

If your tea has very fine pieces of leaves, you will need less to make a 6-ounce cup; 1/2 teaspoon to a teaspoon is advisable. I also like to use this lesser measure when I'm brewing Darjeeling tea, lest it become too astringent.

If your tea leaves are larger than normal, it makes sense to use a little more of them to brew a 6-ounce cup—say, a rounded teaspoon.

If your tea leaves are decidedly large, as in many oolongs, you might want to go up to 2 teaspoons per 6-ounce cup.

If you're brewing white tea—which usually has very large leaves and is usually very subtle in flavor—you should probably use 3 teaspoons of leaves (1 tablespoon) per 6-ounce cup of tea.

2. Water and Water Temperature. All tea experts agree on one thing: you should use bottled spring water to brew your cup of tea (not mineral water). There is less agreement on the best temperature for brewing tea. Everyone concedes, however, that letting your water boil away for minutes in a kettle before pouring it over tea leaves is a bad idea; the boiling releases oxygen from the water, and with lower oxygen levels, the resultant tea tastes flat. But exactly how close to boiling should you get? Standard tea advice is to use water that has just come to a boil (212°F). You won't go too far wrong with that. But many tea drinkers have discovered that delicate teas, like white tea, do better with temperatures far below the boiling point—like 175°F. I wouldn't go too much higher than that for green teas either, certainly not above 200°F. And in my kitchen these days, even for heartier oolong teas and heartiest black teas, I like to pull that kettle off the heat just before the whistling begins. Boiling water "cooks" the tea more, I find, and gives it a different, less vibrant taste.

3. Steeping Time. For years, I had a pretty strong opinion about steeping time: I believed that all of the tea books had it terribly wrong when they'd recommend 3 to 6 minutes for steeping tea. My empirical evidence showed that after 2 1/2 minutes, tea starts getting bitter and tannic. Then I read a scientific report claiming that all the flavor there is in tea leaves comes out after 2 $\frac{1}{2}$ minutes; after that, you just get more color and more astringency. Bingo! I was completely sold! I was definitely the 2 $\frac{1}{2}$ minute man!

Well, things have changed lately. Instinctively, I still set my timer for 2 $\frac{1}{2}$ minutes. I still always taste the tea after 2 $\frac{1}{2}$ minutes to see if it's extracted enough. And I still often stop the steeping at 2 $\frac{1}{2}$ minutes. For me, 2 $\frac{1}{2}$ minutes is Assam heaven. But I have learned that different teas do have different ideal steeping times.

One rule is clear: the smaller the leaves or leaf particles, the shorter the brewing time. Another rule of thumb for me: the more delicate and unoxidized the tea, the longer it can steep. Lastly, the more robust the tea—like Darjeeling, or Assam—the shorter the time I like it to steep.

Here are a few permutations based on these principles:

Large-leaf white tea: 5 to 6 minutes of steeping

Large-leaf green tea: 3 to 4 minutes of steeping

Small-leaf (or particle) green tea: 2 to 3 minutes of steeping

Oolongs: these can generally take moderately long steeping times, especially if the leaves are large. I've had some that took 4 to 6 minutes to really open up. Happily, astringency usually remains fairly low.

Black teas: I always check at 2 1/2 minutes. You should, too, then decide if you want more astringency. I still contend that most Assams, Darjeelings, Breakfast Tea blends, China Blacks, and the like won't pick up more flavor after 2 1/2 minutes, only more bitterness.

Remember: over-steeping must be avoided at all costs!

Here is one of the most important secrets in brewing tea: when the tea is ready, make sure to remove the leaves from the water immediately! Many people leave the spent leaves in the pot, and by the time the second cup is poured the tea is bitter and lousy! Now, there are many ways to accomplish that removal: mesh balls that contain tea leaves and can be removed from the pot, mesh strainers that sit over the cup and strain out leaves, etc.

But by far, the easiest and best way is to use a Chatsford Teapot (an English design), sold in the U.S. by Upton Tea Imports **(see Where to Find It, page 382)**. Each teapot has a fine, nylon mesh strainer basket that fits inside the pot. You place the tea leaves in the basket, insert the basket in the pot, add the hot water, and place the perfectly fitted lid over the basket and pot. When the tea is ready, you remove the basket and discard the leaves. Your pot of tea is at, and will stay at, the peak of perfection! It makes the whole tea ritual a snap. The Chatsford pots come in different sizes and are not expensive. If you had, say, six of the four-cup versions of the pots, you could serve one pot to every pair of guests, and each guest would have his or her first two cups ready to go. Slip tea cozies, or warmers, over the pots to keep the tea hot. If your guests want more tea when those pots are drained, it's back to the kitchen with you to replenish the pots!

The Recipes

English Tea Sandwiches

The first three sandwich recipes below taste best when made with extremely thin slices of white or whole wheat bread. Perfect slices are readily available in the grocery stores: Pepperidge Farm white bread and whole wheat bread contain 30 slices to the pound, each slice about $1/8$ inch thick. If you can't find the Pepperidge Farm brand, or would prefer to use another bread, remember that thin slices are best.

Many shops in England that sell sandwiches with tea prepare the sandwiches a few hours in advance of the tea rush. You can do the same with the first three recipes below, if you wish. Place the finished sandwiches on a plate (or plates)—you may stack sandwiches on top of each other—loosely drape damp paper towels over the sandwiches, then cover completely with plastic wrap. Avoid placing anything else on top of the wrapped sandwich plates.

Cucumber and Cream Cheese Sandwiches with Fresh Mint

· · • · ·

Garnish the platter with fresh mint, if desired.

makes 24 triangular half-sandwiches

> **2 large English cucumbers, unpeeled**
> **$1/2$ cup rice wine vinegar**
> **2 cups loosely packed mint leaves**
> **3 cups cream cheese, softened**
> **24 thin slices of white bread**
> **Kosher salt**

1. Cut the cucumber, peel-on, into $1/16$-inch slices. Marinate the cucumber slices in the vinegar for 1 hour.

2. Chop the mint finely and mix it well with the cream cheese.

3. Spread each slice of bread with minted cream cheese, dividing the cream cheese evenly. Drain the cucumber, and arrange the cucumber slices on 12 of the bread slices, spreading the cucumbers out evenly. Salt lightly. Top with the remaining slices of bread.

4. Working with a bread knife or a knife with a serrated edge, remove the crusts from the sandwiches on all 4 sides. Cut the sandwiches on the diagonal; serve immediately, or hold as described above.

Egg and Watercress Sandwiches

· ◦ ● ◦ ·

Garnish the platter with watercress, if desired.

makes 24 triangular half-sandwiches

12 large eggs, hard–cooked
½ cup mayonnaise
¼ cup white wine vinegar
½ cup minced chives
Kosher salt
Freshly ground black pepper
½ pound (2 sticks) unsalted butter, softened
24 thin slices of whole wheat bread
2 medium bunches watercress, leaves only

1. Peel the eggs and mash well with a fork. Add the mayonnaise, vinegar, and chives, blending well. Season with salt and pepper.

2. Divide the butter among the slices of bread, spreading evenly. Top 12 slices of buttered bread with a layer of watercress leaves and the egg salad, both evenly divided. Place the remaining 12 slices of bread on top.

3. Working with a bread knife, or a knife with a serrated edge, remove crusts from the sandwiches on all 4 sides. Cut sandwiches on the diagonal; serve immediately, or hold as described above.

Rolled Smoked Salmon Sandwiches with Dill

· · • · · ·

If you like, garnish this platter with fresh dill and lemon.

makes 24 rolled sandwiches

8 thin slices of whole wheat bread
8 ounces cream cheese, softened
¼ cup finely chopped fresh dill
12 ounces thinly sliced smoked salmon
3 tablespoons fresh lemon juice
Kosher salt
Freshly ground black pepper

1. Place 1 slice of bread in front of you, with the bottom edge facing you. Using a rolling pin, roll the bread away from you until it's about ⅛ inch thick. Trim off the crusts. Repeat until all 8 slices are rolled out with their crusts removed.

2. Mix the cream cheese with the dill and spread evenly over each slice of bread.

3. Sprinkle the salmon with the lemon juice. Arrange the smoked salmon on the cream cheese, trying to cover the whole surface without overlapping salmon slices, and dividing them evenly among the 8 sandwiches. Season with salt and pepper.

4. Working with your fingers, tightly roll the bread slices away from you, as if you were making jelly rolls. Press down on the seams. You will now have 8 cylinders. Cut each cylinder into 3 pinwheel slices, like a sushi roll, yielding 24 pieces.

5. Serve immediately, or hold as described above.

Open-Faced Potted Ham Sandwiches on Rye Melba Toast

· ∘ • ● • ∘ ·

It's an old English tradition to "seal" a spread in a crock with a top layer of fat. Then the whole concoction becomes known as "potted" this or that. I love the combo of mustard, horseradish, and gherkins in the following recipe for "potted" ham, and the way the whole spread tastes on crunchy Rye Melba Toast! For maximum flavor, make the "pot" a few days in advance, and keep refrigerated.

makes 24 open-faced sandwiches

½ cup (1 stick) unsalted butter

½ pound ham, cut into 1–inch cubes

2 tablespoons mayonnaise

1 tablespoon Dijon mustard

2 teaspoons prepared horseradish

Kosher salt

Freshly ground black pepper

6 sweet gherkins

24 triangles of Rye Melba Toast (page 376)

1. Place the butter in a Pyrex container (a 1-cup measuring cup is ideal). Melt the butter in a microwave, then place it in the refrigerator. Chill until a milky residue forms a layer on top. Spoon off this layer, and remelt the remaining butter.

2. Place the ham, mayonnaise, mustard, and horseradish in the work bowl of a food processor. Process until smooth. Season with salt and pepper.

3. Cut the gherkins into ⅛-inch dice. Stir the gherkins into the ham mixture, blending well. Place the mixture in a ramekin (the mixture should come about three-fourths of the way up the sides of the ramekin), and pour the melted butter over the top to seal. Refrigerate at least 3 hours.

4. When ready to serve, spread on Rye Melba Toast triangles (page 376).

Rye Melba Toast

· · ● · ·

makes 24 triangles

6 slices rye bread, each about ⅜ inch thick

1. Heat the oven to 350°F.

2. Trim the crusts from the bread, and if the slices are not square, cut each one into the largest square shape you can. Cut each slice into 2 triangles, then cut each triangle into 2 more triangles. You will end up with 24 triangles.

3. Place the triangles on an ungreased cookie sheet and bake until crisp, about 10 to 15 minutes. Check frequently, turning, to make sure they're not burning; the result should be dark brown, but not too dark, and nicely crunchy. The toasts may be held, exposed to the air, for a few hours before serving.

Miniature Scones with Clotted Cream and Strawberry Jam

· · • • • · ·

Scones come alive when you top them, warm, with rich clotted cream and with strawberry preserves. Sometimes, in fact, the Devon Cream Tea party is called a Strawberry Tea—with reference to both the fresh berries and preserved strawberries out of a jar. This recipe for miniature scones yields my favorite scones of all. And they can be formed early—even the night before—and refrigerated on their cookie sheet, covered.

makes 24 scones

> **2 cups all-purpose flour, plus extra flour for rolling**
> **2 tablespoons sugar**
> **2 teaspoons baking powder**
> **1/2 teaspoon kosher salt**
> **4 tablespoons cold unsalted butter, cut into 4 pieces**
> **1/2 cup whole milk**
> **Clotted cream (page 378)**
> **Strawberry jam**

1. Heat the oven to 400°F.

2. Sift together the 2 cups of flour, sugar, baking powder, and salt into a medium bowl. Working quickly so the butter doesn't melt, rub the butter into the flour with your fingertips until the mixture looks like fine bread crumbs.

3. Gradually pour in the milk while mixing with a fork, until the mixture forms a big clump. You may need a little less milk, or you may need a little more.

4. Turn the mixture out onto a lightly floured counter. Handling it as little as possible, roll the mixture out to a rough rectangle that's 1/2 inch thick. Cut into rounds with a 1 1/2-inch-round cutter.

5. Transfer the scones to an ungreased cookie sheet and bake until the tops are golden and the scones are firm, about 10 minutes. Remove the scones from the oven to cool slightly.

6. After 10 minutes, and while the scones are still warm, place the scones in a basket. Cover with a tea towel or napkin, and serve to your guests. Let your guests split the scones, helping themselves to the clotted cream and strawberry jam on the table.

Clotted Cream

· · · • · · ·

If you can find Clotted Cream in your local supermarket or fancy grocery, by all means, buy it! I even have a mail-order source for you, one that carries a very thick and buttery English Clotted Cream (see igourmet, in **Where to Find It, page 382**).

However, you can also make a pretty good substitute at home. The following recipe yields enough to top 24 miniature scones. It can be made several hours ahead, or even the day before.

makes 1 1/2 cups

1 cup mascarpone
1/2 cup crème fraîche
1 tablespoon heavy cream

Combine the mascarpone, crème fraîche, and heavy cream. Mix well and store in the refrigerator until needed.

English Tea Cake with Dates, Walnuts, and Apricots

· · ● · ·

Wow! Here's a cake that's something like the dreaded fruitcake—but ever so much lighter and more delicious. It is exactly the type of cake they like to serve with tea in England, where it's often made a week in advance and stored in a covered cake tin. You don't have to do the same, but please make it at least 2 days in advance so the flavors can come together. If you don't have a covered cake tin, wrap the cake well in aluminum foil, and refrigerate. Bring to room temperature before serving.

makes one 8-inch cake, enough for 24 thin slices

- 1 cup chopped (¼-inch dice) dried dates
- 1 cup chopped (¼-inch dice) dried apricots
- 1 Earl Grey tea bag
- 1 cup boiling water
- 1 teaspoon baking soda
- ½ teaspoon kosher salt
- ½ cup (1 stick) unsalted butter
- 1 cup sugar
- 2 large eggs
- 2 cups all-purpose flour
- 1 cup coarsely chopped walnuts

1. Heat the oven to 350°F.

2. Film an 8-inch high-sided round cake pan with nonstick spray. Line the bottom of the pan with a circle of parchment paper, and spray that as well.

3. Place the dates, apricots, and tea bag in a medium heatproof bowl. Pour in the boiling water. Add the baking soda and salt, stir, and let the mixture sit until cool, about 15 minutes.

4. Meanwhile, combine the butter, sugar, and eggs in the bowl of an electric stand mixer. Using the paddle attachment, beat on medium speed until the mixture is light in color, about 2 minutes. Reduce the speed to low and gradually add the flour. Mix until just incorporated.

5. Remove the tea bag from the bowl with the dried fruits and discard it. Add the dried fruits and the soaking water to the flour mixture.

6. Mix on low speed until just combined. Add the walnuts, and turn off the mixer as soon as the walnuts are blended in, about 3 seconds.

7. Scrape the batter into the pan and bake until a tester comes out clean from the center of the cake, about 1 hour and 10 minutes. Cool on a rack for 10 minutes, then turn the cake out and carefully remove the parchment paper. Return the cake to the rack, and cool completely. Store, covered, in the refrigerator. Bring to room temperature before serving.

Set Dressing

As I've indicated, the "set" for this party could be outside or inside. In fact, the loveliest option of all might be something in between: a screened-in sun room or a shaded porch. But whichever way you set it up, it'd be lovely to include design motifs that suggest an English garden, preferably at the height of its blooming splendor. This, of course, would involve flowers in all their guises—real ones, needlepointed ones, printed ones, framed botanicals. If the party's inside, mix up your flower holders: pots and vases, yes, but antique English watering cans would also make perfect containers for fresh flowers.

As for other motifs—well, anything you can muster up (furniture, throw pillows, rugs, paintings) that looks Victorian or Edwardian would be spot-on. One idea I like a lot is unmatched vintage teacups (at least a dozen), filled with diminutive African violets or other dwarf plants, displayed on a triple-tiered sweets tray. Send one cup home with each guest as a party favor.

Table Dressing

Whether you set one table or several, bring out your prettiest linens. Or, employ something unexpected, like a shawl, quilt, or matelassé bedcover as a tablecloth; you could also use a lovely toile or silk cloth, and top it with a second lacy cloth. Lay a square tablecloth on a round table; lay a second one on top, alternating the corners (so you have eight points encircling the table). I would choose solid colors to avoid clashes with multiple china patterns on the cups themselves. Scatter edible flowers—such as untreated rose petals, pansies, or johnny-jump-ups—all over your tables. Other table accoutrements could be pairs of vintage ladies' gloves, such as the ones made of kidskin or lace, or vintage hats placed on the table for decorative and conversational interest.

Entertainment

Here are three thematic, very viable ideas if you want to create some "entertainment" at your tea party.

Invite a local antiques expert, and give your guests the option of bringing an item to the party for appraisal.

Ask guests to bring along a favorite English poem, preferably from the Victorian/Edwardian eras. Set aside some time for a poetry reading.

Hire a knowledgeable person to deliver a short lecture on tea; provide visual aids, such as several different teas, and pass them around so people can sniff.

Where to Find It

Upton Tea Imports
231 South St.
Hopkinton, MA 01748
800.234.8327 (toll free)
508.435.9922 (tel)
508.435.9955 (fax)
www.uptontea.com
Great source for mail-order; great catalog that's also a terrific teaching document.

In Pursuit of Tea
P.O. Box 1284
Cooper Station
New York, NY 10003
718.302.0780 (tel)
718.388.3988 (fax)
www.truetea.com
An excellent online tea source.

The Republic of Tea
8 Digital Dr.
Suite 100
Novato, CA 94949
800.298.4TEA (toll free)
415.382.3400 (tel)
415.382.3401 (fax)
www.therepublicoftea.com
Some of my favorite oolong teas have come from this great online source.

Harney & Sons
Village Green
P.O. Box 665
Salisbury, CT 06068
888.427.6398 (toll free)
www.harney.com
Excellent tea purveyor with a long reputation. Terrific source for Assam, in the form of Irish Breakfast Tea.

Stash Tea
P.O. Box 910
7204 SW Durham Rd.
Suite 200
Tigard, OR 97224
800.800.8327 (toll free)
503.684.9275 (tel)
www.stashtea.com
A comprehensive source of tea and tea-related products, as well as information.

Design in Mind, Inc.
375 Brooks Ave. West
Roseville, MN 55113
888.832.6505 (toll free)
651.483.2070 (tel)
651.787.9956 (fax)
www.devotea.com
Your one-stop shop for tea, and everything to service it. Trays, cozies, linens, teapots in classic English designs (including Haviland)—and tea, too!

igourmet.com
877.446.8763 (toll free)
www.igourmet.com
Source for English Clotted Cream.

Englishteastore.com
dba/US-Flag.com
3 Wesco Drive
Export, PA 15632
877.734.2458 (toll free)
www.englishteastore.com
Tons of teapots and tea service sets, including traditional, contemporary, and seasonal possibilities.

www.ebay.com
And lest we forget the cyber-auction possibilities, as of this writing there are on e-bay 217 antique teapots and 7 complete sets of antique teacups.

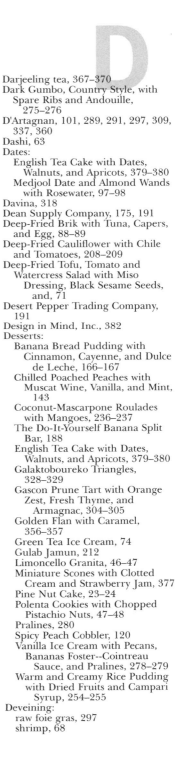